Blood Passion

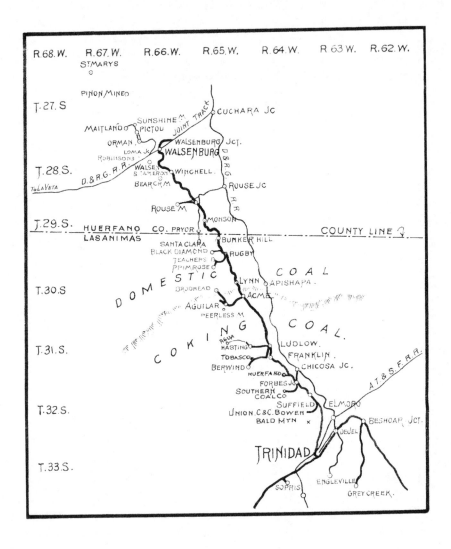

Blood Passion

THE LUDLOW MASSACRE AND CLASS WAR
IN THE AMERICAN WEST

Scott Martelle

Rutgers University Press
NEW BRUNSWICK, NEW JERSEY,
AND LONDON

Frontispiece: The southern Colorado coalfield, as depicted on a 1903 Colorado & Southern Railway map. *Credit: Robert W. Richardson Railroad Library, Colorado Railroad Museum, Golden, Colo.*

ISBN-13: 978–0–8135–4062–7

Printed in the United States of America

Book Club Edition

Contents

Acknowledgements

In a work such as this there are many interconnections with people in many places, and I would be remiss in not thanking the staffs of various archives and libraries visited during the research phase. The Denver Public Library's Western History Collection holds many treasures from which this story was drawn, and its staff was uniformly welcoming and helpful, particularly Bruce Hanson and Joan Harms. Erwin Levold offered valuable navigational aid through the voluminous holdings at the Rockefeller Archive Center, as did Tab Lewis at the National Archives in College Park, Maryland, including referring me to fresh and unexpected sources.

Other researchers and librarians extended professional and courteous assistance at the State University of New York at Binghamton's Bartle Library, which holds the Bowers archives; the Colorado State Historical Society's Hart Library, keeper of many of that state's old newspapers and other critical resources; the Colorado State Archives; and the Los Angeles and New York public libraries, each an irreplaceable gem in its own way. Dean Saitta, professor of anthropology at the University of Denver and co-director of the Colorado Coal Field War Archaeological Project at the Ludlow tent colony, and Denver labor activist Richard Myers also are due thanks for sharing their time and passion for the subject.

Outside the research, my thanks to Jane Dystel and Miriam Goderich, the literary agents who recognized this book's potential; Melanie Halkias, the Rutgers University Press editor who signed the project, and her successor, Kendra Boileau, who guided it into print; Reed Johnson, an old friend and fellow journalist who turned his sharp eye on the manuscript; my

Acknowledgments

parents, Walter and Dorothy Martelle, for raising our family in a house of books; my friends and colleagues from the 1995 Detroit newspaper strike, for understanding the difference between abstract belief and concrete action; and, especially, my wife, Margaret, and our sons, Michael and Andrew, from whom this project stole so much time.

Blood Passion

Introduction

"What experience and history teach is this—that people
and governments never have learned anything from history,
or acted on principles deduced from it."
—Georg Wilhelm Friedrich Hegel, from the introduction
to *Philosophy of History,* 1832

LUDLOW, COLORADO. Hot summer winds whisk across the Colorado
prairie with a distracting persistence, kicking up small dust devils and
swirls of debris that whisper eastward over Interstate 25 and on into the
vast flatness of the Great Plains. A freeway sign at Exit 27 says this spot is
the town of Ludlow, but there's no town here, just a chain-link fence with
an unlocked gate surrounding a white-walled meeting hall, a gazebo with
picnic tables, and a monument that looks like an oversized Victorian grave
marker. A half-dozen isolated ranchettes, some with metal-bar horse cor-
rals, dot the sweeping countryside, giving the place a forgotten feel, like a
Grange Hall amid farms gone fallow. A rusty railroad runs north and
south like a seam stitching the prairie to the Sangre de Cristo—Blood of
Christ—Mountains. In one direction lies Colorado Springs and, farther
north, Denver; the opposite direction takes you to Trinidad and on across
the old Santa Fe Trail into New Mexico. On the west side of the tracks a
washboard road curls into a canyon leading to the ghost towns of Hastings
and Delagua. A little to the south another dirt road trails into another
canyon to more ghost towns—Berwind and Tabasco, reduced now to tan

clusters of crumbling stones along a gurgling creek, the only sound save for the occasional chirp of a bird or the rustle of dry leaves and grasses. Coal once was king here, but emptiness now reigns, and it doesn't take much of a romantic flight to hear the footfalls of the dead.

Less than a century ago this quiet and mostly empty stretch of southern Colorado was the scene of great strife, and great agony. More than seventy-five people died,[1] most of them shot to death in the first eight months of a coal strike that lasted fifteen months and that the miners lost. The United States had endured violent labor battles before, and there have been many since. None, though, reached the level of pitched warfare that erupted here in Colorado's southern coalfields, where East Coast money and power collided with immigrant poverty and need.

The nadir came on a sunny Monday morning in April 1914, when a detachment from the Colorado National Guard engaged in a ten-hour gun battle with union men at Ludlow, where a tent colony housing some eleven hundred strikers and their families had been erected. Seven men and a boy were killed in the shooting, at least three of the men—all striking coal miners, one a leader—apparently executed in cold blood by Colorado National Guardsmen who had taken them captive. As the sun set, the militia moved into the camp itself and an inferno lit up the darkening sky, reducing most of the makeshift village to ashes. It wasn't until the next morning that the bodies of two mothers and eleven children were discovered where they had taken shelter in a dirt bunker beneath one of the tents. The raging fire had sucked the oxygen from the air below, suffocating the families as they hid from the gun battle.

The deaths of the women and children quickly became known as the Ludlow Massacre, and the backlash was vicious and bloody. Over the next ten days striking miners and their supporters poured out their rage in attacks across the coalfields in "an armed and open rebellion against the authority of the state as represented by the militia. This rebellion constituted perhaps one of the nearest approaches to civil war and revolution ever known in this country in connection with an industrial conflict."[2] And it was a guerrilla war that stretched along more than two hundred miles of the eastern slope of the Colorado Rockies. Union men—mostly Greek and Italian immigrants—swept in from the hillsides and burned mine works to the ground before disappearing. Guards and strikebreakers were killed. At one point several dozen mine officials, guards, scabs, and their families were holed up in a mine shaft, the entry partially sealed by dynamite blasts, with rampaging miners ready to kill if they came out. It took the U.S. Army to bring the bloodshed to an end ten days later, after another thirty people were killed and dozens of mine buildings leveled.

Ultimately, the Ludlow Massacre was a single act in a lengthy drama that gripped a nation already riven by the blood politics of capitalism versus socialism, oligarchy versus democracy, big money versus the little guy. It was a battle between two conflicting ideals of America: as a place where the ambitious could build an empire, and as a place where an individual could control his own destiny. Those ideals coexist in the abstract but conflict in the real world, where one person's ambitions can drown another's dreams. Such was the case between the mine owners and the miners, who saw each other as impediments to their own successes. Thus in some ways the collision here in the foothills of the Sangre de Cristo Mountains was inevitable.

This book, a blend of journalism and historic inquiry, aims to peel back time for a look at what transpired in Ludlow and the southern Colorado coalfields and at the lives of some of the key people involved. The goal is to come up with something close to an objective rendering of events, as well as to draw fresh attention to a forgotten moment in American history that sharply defines some of the conflicting perceptions of what it means to be an American—no small issue in the challenging times in which we live. While the killings in southern Colorado came amid a strike, this is more than a labor story. In key ways, it is the saga of hubris and ego, courage and sacrifice, and life and death. A labor dispute was the flashpoint, but the fuel for the fire that followed came from many sources, and the aftereffects reverberated in disparate places. The strike marked the beginning of the modern era of labor disputes, with each side using the media to turn public opinion its way. The mine operators were dominated by John D. Rockefeller Sr.—both reviled and admired as one of the nation's richest barons—and his son and their agents in charge of the Colorado Fuel & Iron Co. (CF&I), at the time Colorado's largest employer. On the union side were hardworking men and idealists often characterized as dangerous immigrant radicals and anarchists.

Truth was an early victim as both sides churned out propaganda and bought off contemporary journalists. As a result, earlier explorations of these events have been heavily manipulated. One of the first books on the strike was *The Ludlow Massacre* by Walter Fink, a writer and union propagandist who approached strike leaders in March, before the massacre, seeking $450 to publish five thousand copies of a 160-page history.[3] The first serious book on the strike, aside from reports based on federal investigations freighted with their own political baggage, was Barron Beshoar's *Out of the Depths: The Story of John R. Lawson, a Labor Leader,* researched and written in the 1930s and published in 1942 with financial support from the Colorado Labor Historical Committee of the Denver Trades and Labor Assembly, which holds the copyright. Beshoar took over a project begun by Winnifred Banner, who died before she could complete the work she had called *Struggle Without End.* Beshoar, a journalist (he was *Time* magazine's Denver bureau chief), was the son of a Trinidad doctor who treated striking miners. As an adult, Beshoar became a close friend of Lawson, who directed the 1913–1914 strike during its critical, and most violent, stages. In Beshoar's telling, the strikers were the heroic victims of Rockefeller greed and the National Guard's excesses, a portrayal that has greatly skewed historic perceptions. Another key work, *The Great Coalfield War* by George S. McGovern and Leonard F. Guttridge, was published in 1972 as McGovern was running for president. The book is based on McGovern's more detailed but less compellingly written 1953 doctoral dissertation. Although the unpublished dissertation is footnoted, neither the published book nor Beshoar's accounting of the events is, and many scenes found in those latter works cannot be independently corroborated (some seem to be based on personal interviews with participants, but the details are lost).[4] In *Buried Unsung,* Zeese Papanikolas wrote of a personal journey through the history—he similarly wrote about the haunting experience of standing among the shadows of the Ludlow dead—but focused his work on the narrower perspective of slain organizer Louis Tikas and the role the coal war played in the lives of Greek immigrants in the American West.

Each of those books embraced the romantic notion of the resilience of the union men and women in the face of oppression, a hard narrative to resist. But most of the telling details indicate there was more at play than a simple act of resistance and solidarity. The point of engagement was a labor dispute, but the battles had more to do with class distinctions than with contracts. And while the involvement of such historic figures as Mother Jones was significant, it was the resolve and actions of everyday laborers that determined the course and pace of events.

The earlier books have had a tremendous impact on historical perception of the events in southern Colorado, in many cases affirming union publicity efforts. It is a given, for instance, that the deaths of the women and children in the Ludlow fire constituted a massacre. They did not. Rather than the intentional execution of a large number of people, the deaths seem most likely to have been the result of criminally negligent acts by the Colorado National Guard, private mine guards, and strikebreakers as they torched the camp. In the manipulation of the details of that fateful morning—an early, if not the first, cynical use of "spin" to establish public perception—the apparent summary executions by the National Guard have been cast aside for the more dramatic deaths of the women and children in their protective pit. And the histories ignore the numbers. Local records and verifiable newspaper accounts list at least seventy-five people killed during the strike. Of those, thirty-three were strikers or their families. Subtracting the thirteen women and children of Ludlow and a man who died after being jailed in harsh conditions, the miners lost nineteen men in battle. Another five of the dead were people not directly involved in the strike—in essence, innocent bystanders. The rest—at least thirty-seven—were strikebreakers, mine guards, National Guard soldiers, or others targeted by the miners, which means the operators might have won the strike, but the miners held their own in the war, killing nearly twice as many men as they lost. The efficiency of their guerrilla attacks calls into question the traditional treatment of the striking miners as victims. They might have been victims of an oppressive political and economic system, but they did not suffer their grievances meekly, and proved to be quite deadly.

Yet this is not a work of historical revisionism. The striking coal miners, whatever crimes they might have committed, were fighting for their lives and livelihoods in a tableau established by the mine operators, and against an overwhelming system of corporate feudalism in which the U.S. Constitution was trumped by greed and prejudice. Many of their acts might have been illegal, but they were operating in a lawless environment, conditions created by the coal companies and local law enforcement officials, then affirmed by the National Guard. The militia's behavior was particularly troubling as it cast aside the Constitution—martial law was never formally declared—and embarked on a campaign of oppression that seems stolen from another country's history, not America's. Scores of people were jailed without charge or warrant, and homes were searched and private property confiscated, again without warrant or anything close to the concept of probable cause. Their actions fueled the rebellion and stand as a chilling example of the potential backlash to a government that discards basic civil rights in the name of political expediency. Against that backdrop, the striking miners can be viewed as freedom fighters in the time-honored American tradition of rebellion against tyranny, and as men—and a few women—who helped crumble an egregious system of political corruption.

The drama that unfolded in southern Colorado came at a time of critical transformation for American capitalism, as the nation was still wrestling with its new royalty—the kings of industry. The agrarian economy that had dominated the country from its founding days was giving way to a new urbanization as workers—rural migrants and new immigrants alike—were drawn to industry-heavy cities in the East and around the Great Lakes. Census figures place the fulcrum of that change at around the time of the southern Colorado coal strike. In 1910, fewer than half of the nation's 92.2 million residents, 45.6 percent, were living in urban areas. Ten years later, most Americans, 51.2 percent, lived in urban areas.

That pivotal shift in population gave rise to massive social problems, from urban overcrowding to nativist animosity toward new immigrants pouring into American cities at a pace of up to one million people a year. Muckraking journalists, social progressives, and political activists—from communists to syndicalists to anarchists—attacked the problems from various standpoints, and the aggregate effect created a national mood hostile to big corporations even as the growing middle class sought to gain some of those riches for itself.

It was a time in which political passions ran hot and theoretical differences mattered, the left and the right often separated by picket lines and guns. In Europe, the old regimes were crumbling, and the United States was evolving into an international force. Robber barons and their scions still controlled the American economy, though public animosity toward the infamous trusts had given rise to reform movements that nipped at the ankles of the wealthy. Railroads and coal were still the lifeblood of the young industrial economy, but the future was being born in Highland Park, Michigan, where automaker Henry Ford was experimenting with his idea for an assembly line to crank out the vehicles of the coming economic revolution—the mass-produced car, which was about to transform the landscape of a maturing nation.

On the workers' side of the industrial equation, in March 1913 the U.S. Congress created the Department of Labor under outgoing president William Howard Taft, who signed the measure into law during the last hours of his presidency—and over his own misgivings.[5] Incoming president Woodrow Wilson named as the first labor secretary William B. Wilson—no relation—who was a former secretary-treasurer of the United

Mine Workers of America (UMWA) and who, as a member of Congress, had lobbied for the department's creation. The goal, the new secretary said early on, was to work "in the interest of the wage earners" but also to be fair to business and the public at large, a stance that presaged the department's current role as a defuser of disputes rather than a defender of labor.

More traditional war—the kind waged among nations—was bubbling under the surface, too. Europe was about to fall into World War I, and the Bolsheviks were gathering steam—both in Russia and in exile—for a final assault on tsarist rule. There was also a growing, and emblematic, crisis on the United States' southern border, where revolution and political assassination in Mexico drew President Wilson's attention. Relations deteriorated when Wilson refused to acknowledge the rule of Victoriano Huerta, a soldier "crude of manners, and bloodthirsty,"[6] who seized the country in a February 1913 coup. Without U.S. recognition, Huerta had trouble obtaining the arms he needed to maintain control against insurgencies by Pancho Villa in Chihuahua in the north and Emiliano Zapata and his Zapatistas in Morelos, south of Mexico City. On the day of the Ludlow Massacre, American sailors from the USS *Dolphin* were arrested after they went ashore in Veracruz without Mexican permission, a showdown that led to the shelling and eventual U.S. occupation of the city.

With all this going on, the state of Colorado was far from the minds of most Americans, and far enough from the centers of power and media to be generally ignored. Outside the region few were aware that the state had evolved into a massive company town, dominated by the will of the businessmen who ran the Colorado Fuel & Iron Co. and other mining firms.

The Colorado coal war would change all that.

The strike, with its months of tit-for-tat shootings, beatings, and squalid living conditions, edged into national prominence. A dismayed Congress, which had already established a U.S. Commission on Industrial Relations (CIR) to broadly investigate working conditions in American industry, added southern Colorado to its list of targets. But the killings at Ludlow turned the strike into a cause. Even anti-union newspapers like the *New York Times* editorialized against what they saw as violent excess by the Colorado militia—though the editorialists archly took the stance that the "crazily officered" state militia should not have lowered itself to the level of the anarchists.[7]

Some of this might seem like stale debate over stale disputes, but the issues involved in the Colorado strike—and countless others in that tumultuous era—laid the foundation for how most of us work today. In retrospect, the Colorado coal miners' demands seem quaintly simple: an eight-hour workday, the right to join a union, freedom to shop outside company-owned stores, and a system of checks to ensure that miners, who were paid according to how many tons of coal they dug out, received a fair weighing, among others. Many of these issues reflect working conditions we now take for granted, oblivious to the blood spilled to gain them. They support the view that employers buy their workers' time and expertise, not their souls, and that corporations do not have the right to imperil their workers' health and lives for the sake of profit. Admittedly, many of those battles are still being fought, as investor pressure on corporations to increase productivity and profits has led to cutbacks on safety measures, staffing, and maintenance in various industries. At the time of this writing, fourteen West Virginia coal miners recently lost their lives in two separate explosions, proof that these issues have not gone away.

Like many strikes, the Colorado dispute was more than a disagreement over contract terms. It was a clash of ideologies, powered by strong and uncompromising personalities on both sides. Union organizers and workers demanded they be allowed to band together to improve their bargaining power and their way of life. The mine owners held with similar doggedness that the only right wage earners had was to work on the company's terms or quit. Often the anti-union position was voiced in paternalistic terms as being in the workers' own best interests, an attempt by employers to guarantee that those who wanted to work could do so without interference by others. But the First Amendment was a cloak for reducing the issue to workers' right of free assembly even as the creation of blacklists and the summary deportations of union supporters indicted the employers' sincerity.

When blood is shed, there is a societal urge to find justice, usually defined as the conviction of the guilty and the quick meting out of a satisfactory penance. That didn't happen in Colorado. During the strike, hundreds of union organizers, strikers, and sympathizers were rounded up and charged with long lists of crimes, including the murders of mine guards and strikebreakers. After the violence ended, several National Guardsmen—or militiamen—were walked through courts-martial. But in the end, no one was held accountable for any of the deaths. Some of the dead were clear victims of willful murder. Others were simply caught by a stray bullet—collateral damage, in our modern parlance. Nearly a century later they are all but forgotten. It is telling that the monument at Ludlow is supported not by public funds but by the UMWA. One archaeologist involved in a project at the site reported being interrupted by tourists attracted by highway signs announcing a historical marker, only to be disappointed to learn that the Ludlow Massacre had nothing to do with Native Americans.[8]

Despite the passage of time, many of the social conditions that fed the violence in Colorado are surging anew. There is once again massive disparity between economic classes, a culture of intolerance for radical or contrary thought, the attempted marginalization of organized labor, and animosity toward fresh waves of immigrants. Yet America still remains a place for dreams, where the ambitious can build an empire and where an individual can control his own destiny. The question is, can we defy Hegel and learn from this brutal history, and find the corrective for the future in the mistakes of the past?

Prologue

TRINIDAD, COLORADO, AUGUST 16, 1913. Gerald Lippiatt, a stocky man with a bushy mustache, scuffed up little puffs of dust as he walked the slight rise of North Commercial Street between the Purgatoire River and the small buildings marking downtown's outer edge. It was a few minutes after eight o'clock on a Saturday night, and the late summer sun had given way to a full moon that bathed the prairie-edge city in gentle light. A dry easterly breeze slipping in from the Sangre de Cristo Mountains carried away the last vestiges of a hot and dry day. As Lippiatt, an organizer for the United Mine Workers of America, neared the heart of downtown, he was swallowed by the festive energy of people shaking off the exacting drudgery of a week working on the ranch or mining coal deep below ground. Blue sparks flashed from overhead wires as electric trolleys rumbled along brick-lined tracks, and at the city center, where Commercial Street crossed Main in front of the posh Columbian Hotel, a Salvation Army minister exhorted sinners to repent, his message stopping at the doors of busy first-floor saloons, pawnshops, and narrow gambling halls.

It was a busy weekend for union men. The State Federation of Labor had scheduled a two-day convention to begin Monday at Trinidad's new Toltec Hotel, a three-story brick building just down North Commercial Street from the Columbian. The convention's top agenda item: the UMWA's attempt to organize the mines around Trinidad in Las Animas County and farther north into adjoining Huerfano County. It was no easy task. Organizers had been jailed and some beaten by private mine guards and sheriff's deputies; sympathizers within the mines were summarily fired when found

UMWA organizer Gerald Lippiatt, third from the right in the back row of this undated family photo, was killed in a shootout in downtown Trinidad on the eve of the 1913–1914 coal strike. His death set the tone for the violence to follow. *Credit: Gerald J. Lippiatt family collection.*

out. Historically, strikes in the hard-edged mine camps ended under the barrels of state militia guns. The state labor federation had other issues on its agenda, too, including electing its top officers, industrial unionism—"the pet hobby of Charles H. Moyer" of the Western Federation of Miners—and an early version of globalism. "How to prevent the cheapening of Colorado labor, threatened by the influx of thousands of immigrants from Southern Europe with the opening of the Panama Canal, will be a vital question with the convention."[1] But the plight of the mine workers would be its prime agenda item. All day Saturday UMWA organizers and executives and representatives from other unions had been stepping off trains at the Colorado & Southern depot and following Lippiatt's evening path into Trinidad.

Lippiatt, thirty-eight, was an unlikely union organizer. He had immigrated from England with his family in 1891, landing in Ohio, where his father, a former miner, established successful farming and mining businesses. Why Lippiatt left the bourgeois comforts of Ohio for the wild and mostly lawless Colorado coalfields is unknown, but he was working in the northern coal district by April 1910, when the UMWA led the miners in a walkout after coal operators refused to negotiate a new contract. As secretary of the UMWA local in Frederick, north of Denver, with 125 members,[2] Lippiatt had had his share of run-ins with mine guards and the police, so confrontations alone—an elemental part of the job—didn't faze him. In June 1911, Lippiatt and several other union activists were sentenced to six months in jail in Lafayette, just east of Boulder, apparently for violating a judge's injunction against picketing.[3] He was sentenced to another six months in early 1913 after the Christmas Eve 1912 assault of Maggie Cox in Frederick.[4] His activities led to a temporary rupture in local solidarity. In June 1912, fellow unionists in the northern field voted to "send three delegates to Denver to the District office and make a request of our district officials for the removal of Brother Lippiatt as official organizer," a decision that was rescinded three weeks later without an explanation being entered in the records.[5] The turnabout may have been in recognition of Lippiatt's effectiveness in the field: The year before, he and a colleague talked more than fifty foreign-born strikebreakers into quitting the Northern Fuel Co.'s Alpha pit near Boulder and joining the union.[6]

When the UMWA decided to extend the strike to the southern field, Lippiatt was sent to help, getting his orders on August 7, 1913, along with three other organizers: Louis Tikas, M.V. Hibbs, and John Petron.[7] Lippiatt spent a few days in Trinidad, then went back home to Frederick for a brief visit before returning to Trinidad in time for the state labor convention. But he looked ahead at the assignment and saw death. A few hours before he boarded the 11:30 P.M. train on December 15, Lippiatt called John Lawson, president of UMWA District 15, which covered Colorado, Utah, and New Mexico, at his Denver home. "I am leaving for Trinidad tonight, John, and I want to tell you goodbye. . . . I think I'm going to be killed."[8] Lawson asked him why he thought that. "The gunmen have been pressing me pretty hard down there, John, but I am going back. I have a hunch they are going to get me this time." Lawson urged Lippiatt to stay in Denver. "We'll send someone else down," he said, but Lippiatt dissuaded him. "It is my job; I want to go." Around the same time, Lippiatt told his fiancée, Edith Green of Rugby, a small mining town twenty-five miles north of Trinidad, that she "might never see him again," she said. "I warned him to be careful."[9]

The gunmen Lippiatt feared were operatives for the Virginia-based Baldwin-Felts Detective Agency, a private police force for railroads, mine operators, and other businesses. Its primary function: to keep tabs on and harass union organizers and sympathizers through both direct confrontation and quiet infiltration. Baldwin-Felts men had been working in Colorado's northern coalfields since the start of the 1910 strike, and after the UMWA began making noise about expanding the strike, the southern

Colorado mine operators signed on, too. The agency had a penchant for hiring "professional bad men who were proud of it and anxious to show how bad they really were."[10] Many had recently worked in West Virginia and been involved in a series of high-profile gun battles and killings that occurred after coal miners walked out in April 1912, starting the Paint Creek–Cabin Creek strike.[11] It was a typically brutal affair that took a particularly vicious turn on February 2, 1913, when several Baldwin-Felts men joined Quinn Morton, owner of two Kanawha County mines, and Sheriff Bonner Hill in mounting a machine gun in a railroad baggage car. As the train rumbled up Paint Creek Hollow in the dark of night, the gunmen raked a striker's enclave with bullets. One striker was killed: Charles Estep, who had just ushered his wife and children into an "armored bulwark" beneath their cabin.[12] The strikers dubbed the company's new rolling weapon the "Bull Moose Special," and news of the killing—and the machine—spread widely. It was not lost on the miners of southern Colorado that six months later some of the same Baldwin-Felts men were walking the streets of Trinidad and company-owned mining towns like Berwind and Hastings. The threat could not have been clearer.

Two of the gunmen, Walter Belk and George W. Belcher, were hanging around outside the Toltec Hotel the night Lippiatt was making his way through the Trinidad crowd. Belk, thirty, had been in Colorado since December 1912, after directing a contingent of Baldwin-Felts gunmen in Paint Creek, where one confrontation led to his arrest on murder charges, although the case was dismissed before it reached trial. Belcher, twenty-six, was from West Virginia but had been in Colorado for several years and had not been involved in the Paint Creek strike.[13] He was the more flamboyant of the two detectives, known for wearing an underjacket of steel plates to ward off bullets. Both men had been deputized by Las Animas County sheriff James S. Grisham, giving them nearly unlimited power in the former frontier town. Standing there on Commercial Street, the men were an act of provocation, and of intimidation.

Around 8:15 P.M., Lippiatt walked past Belcher, Belk, and at least one other Baldwin-Felts detective, T. F. Douglass,[14] where they loitered outside the Toltec. Angry words were exchanged. Douglass, far from an impartial witness, later testified that Lippiatt threatened Belk that he would see him again when the detective didn't have "his crowd" with him. Belk, for his part, warned Lippiatt not to follow him around and said he had no intention of letting Lippiatt shoot him in the back, as had occurred in the northern fields. It was an intriguing comment, and when weighed with

Lippiatt's remark to Lawson about the gunmen "pressing me pretty hard down there" implies that Belk and Lippiatt had met before, or at least knew each other by sight and character, and that Lippiatt had a reputation with the Baldwin-Felts men.

Lippiatt decided a line had been crossed. He strode five doors north to the Packer Block of buildings and climbed the stairs between a hardware store and a small movie theater to the union offices on the second floor. He emerged moments later armed with a handgun and headed for Belk and Belcher, who had moved down the street away from the Toltec and were now standing by two wooden power poles in front of the Poliak Brothers pawnshop near the corner of Elm Street, a hundred feet or so from where Salvation Army minister J. W. Fleming was conducting a street service.[15] Five fellow organizers trailed Lippiatt as he cut through the Saturday night crowd, urging him to stop. As Lippiatt neared Belk and Belcher—Douglass had moved on—he began yelling. Accounts of the exchange vary but generally agree that Lippiatt dared Belk to repeat his earlier comments now that Lippiatt was armed and no longer alone. Lippiatt walked up to the two gunmen and pointed his gun at Belk's stomach. Belcher slapped at Lippiatt's gun as the union man fired, and the bullet struck Belcher in the left thigh. Belk pulled his own handgun and fired two quick shots that sent Lippiatt reeling backward and stumbling to the ground. Belk fired twice more, and the wounded Belcher added four shots of his own. Six of the gunmen's eight bullets hit their mark: One tore through Lippiatt's throat, and another burrowed through his back and lodged in a lung.[16] As the gunshot echoes died away in the shrieks of the crowd, Lippiatt's companions quickly picked him up from the street and hustled him into a nearby saloon, where he died minutes later. Belcher survived.

Although Lippiatt apparently pushed the confrontation, his killing enraged the miners. "Crowds of grim men loiter in the streets," the *Rocky Mountain News* reported the day after the shootout. "Armed deputies and police mingle in the crowds, disarming any who carry weapons." When the State Federation of Labor conference opened on Monday, the dead Lippiatt, who would have played a minor role at best, was the star. "Little bows of black crepe were attached to each official badge worn by delegates," a "mute tribute" to the slain organizer.[17] The room was filled with the inevitability of not only a strike but also more violence.

The mine workers' anger expanded dangerously the next day when the Las Animas County coroner convened a jury of six Trinidad businessmen, some of them owners and managers of the stores Lippiatt walked past the evening he died. After about three hours of testimony, the jury ruled the killing justifiable but recommended Belk and Belcher "be held for further investigation."[18] Both men were released on $10,000 bail, and lawyer Jesse G. Northcutt—who also owned the local *Trinidad Chronicle-News* newspaper and would soon represent the coal operators—signed on to defend them. The detectives' boss sought to portray the shooting as a victory for law over disorder. "Belk has been in the employ of our agency for 10 years, and in that time I have found him a cautious and conservative employee," A. C. Felts told a Denver reporter. "Information which comes to my hands is that Lippiatt was a dangerous man and that Belk, through his record, had reason to fear him."[19]

The killing—and the coroner's ruling that it was justified—transformed the miners, who "immediately denounced it as a cold-blooded and unwarranted murder," former U.S. senator Thomas Patterson said twenty months later, after the passions had burned themselves out.[20] "That incident did more to develop immediate bitterness and ill will and a disposition to retaliate than anything else."

For the miners, that Lippiatt apparently drew his weapon first was irrelevant. The general belief was that mine owners valued mules more than men, since they had to buy the mules and, in a sense, only rented their miners; if a miner died, another one could be quickly hired at the same pay rate. The ruling that Lippiatt's killing was justified was seen as just one more in a long series of judicial and bureaucratic decisions that affirmed the miners' belief that the structures of power and government existed for the benefit of the mine owners, not the mine workers, a conclusion built on feudal conditions in mine camps where basic civil rights were trumped by the operators' demand for cheap and docile labor.[21] What could have been a symbiotic relationship—the operators needed labor to dig out the coal; the miners needed work—dissolved under the pressures of greed, intransigence, and prejudice. And for seven months, it led to war.

ONE

Money in the Ground

To understand what happened in southern Colorado over the fall and winter of 1913–1914, it's useful to know something of the lay of the land. The Colorado Rockies and the Sangre de Cristo Mountains are, geologically speaking, mere toddlers. More than 300 million years ago, southern Colorado was an oceanside equatorial swamp of thick, lush jungles. As the plants died off they formed deep, carbon-rich peat bogs that, in an inexorably slow process, became buried under thick layers of sand and heavy sediments left by rising and lowering seas. The new layers pressed down on the old, turning the lower levels into sandstone and other sedimentary rocks, which in turn compressed the peat below into lignite, then bituminous coal, and finally anthracite coal. In something like a geologic distillation process lasting millions of years, each transition created a successively more efficient burnable source of heat and energy, with anthracite—the purest—consisting of about 90 percent pure carbon.[1]

As this transformation was taking place, the earth's surface continued its relentless bowing and heaving, shifting and grinding, until magma from below pushed segments of the crust upward. As the bulges rose, wind, rain, and ice slowly scoured away the softer sedimentary rock, leaving dramatic mountains: the Sangre de Cristos, one of the Rockies' southernmost ranges. Like two forgotten strays, the Spanish Peaks lie just to the east of the north-south main range, East Peak rising 12,700 feet in the sky and the West Peak soaring another 1,000 feet above it. The two mountains dominate the landscape along the border between Huerfano and Las Animas counties, holding snow well into the summer months. To the east of the Spanish Peaks lies a smaller range of foothills, then the prairie.

Beneath the mountains and foothills, the long-buried coal seams rest atop what is called the Trinidad layer of sandstone, the remnants of an ancient sea bed. But as the land heaved and the mountains rose, the coal veins did, too, in some places canting as much as sixty degrees.[2] Some of the fragmented veins now begin near the surface; others remain deep underground; a few stretch eastward from the mountains into the edge of the Great Plains, each a gift from nature to the kings of the industrial age.

They have been hard gifts to claim. The coal seams are firm enough, but the layers of rock immediately above them are "universally cracked and faulted owing to the geological disturbance,"[3] making them poor roofs for mine tunnels. During southern Colorado's mining heyday, roof falls were a constant occurrence, often with tragic consequences, despite miners' efforts to shore up the roofs with timbers. Even when the roofs held, the fractures often let methane gas seep in, ready to be ignited by a spark or the flame of a miner's unguarded lamp.

Coal was inextricably linked in the nineteenth century with the nation's expansive railroad system, one of the first technological steps toward shrinking the world by vastly reducing the amount of time required to move goods and people between markets and regions. Railroad companies fought bitterly over the right to lay tracks, crisscrossing the country with often redundant systems that eventually led to rapid consolidation. Like an army on the move, advancing railroads needed supplies—steel for the rails and coal for the engines. Entrepreneurs and rail directors looked at the coal and iron ore deposits in Colorado and Wyoming and saw riches waiting to be mined. With most of the existing supplies in the East, the new coal operators of the West had the advantage of proximity. It would be cheaper, they believed, to ship steel and coal for western rails and construction from the Rockies instead of the Appalachians.

As the railroads snaked through the countryside in the 1850s, coal mining became a commercial venture in Colorado. For several decades the mines were simple operations, with men using picks and shovels to scour coal from exposed seams on canyon walls.[4] In the 1880s and 1890s, miners began drilling holes and using dynamite to blast the rock loose. By the turn of the century, more elaborate operations, including deep tunneling, small-gauge rail lines, and tippling systems for dumping coal from cars, were the standard. Most of the coal seams ranged from three and a half feet to fourteen feet thick,[5] and despite the subterranean fragmentations some seams stretched deep into the mountains.

Where coal was found, mine camps sprouted. At first, these were meager clusters of shacks near the mine mouths, inhabited almost exclusively by men. A company saloon and a company store filled the basic needs at the larger settlements, and access was often strictly limited by the coal companies, whose owners preferred to operate out of the reach of union organizers, competing merchants, or muckraking journalists. Far from the sight of company executives and most law enforcement, life in the camps was dictated by the mine superintendent, who was in effect the master of his own fiefdom so long as the numbers—tons of coal mined, dollars of profit made—kept his absentee bosses happy.

Miners' wages generally were based on a tonnage rate, which meant they often were not paid for the "dead" work that keeps a mine operating, such as shoring up unstable roofs. Even the definition of a ton was subject to manipulation: Some companies in Colorado defined it as 2,400 pounds, not the standard 2,000 pounds.[6] And few other jobs were as dangerous as mining, where harsh living conditions aboveground and recurrent explosions and cave-ins below made for short and brutal lives.

Colorado's peculiar geology made its mines even more hazardous than those of the East and was partly responsible for a fatality rate nearly double the national average. In 1912, the death rate in Colorado's mines was 7.055 per 1,000 employees, or 8.9 deaths for every million tons of coal produced, compared with a national rate of 3.15 deaths per 1,000 workers and 4.29 deaths for every million tons of coal produced. Although the UMWA directed most of its organizing attention on the largest producers, Colorado state coal mine inspector James Dalrymple believed that the small operators ran the most dangerous mines and most frequently ignored state mine safety laws, sometimes hiring inexperienced foremen to oversee inexperienced miners—cases of ignorance leading incompetence with deadly results. Dalrymple placed some of the blame on the state, which had only three inspectors. "We can not do justice to ourselves or to anyone connected with the industry." The core responsibility, though, fell on the mine superintendents, particularly in the small mines. "We find some of them who apparently care about nothing else than to sit and see that the coal is coming out all right; very little attention is given to the men working under them."[7]

Safety regulations were considered a nuisance at best and expensive, time-consuming government meddling at worst. Owners—both the small operators and the large corporations—were content with a laissez-faire approach to local management so long as coal was dug out of the ground and loaded onto rail cars at the expected pace.[8] The responsibility for ensuring the codes were followed fell to the mine foremen, who were to have been certified by Colorado officials. But the state never scheduled the examinations, so the foremen were never certified. Thus such basics as properly shoring up roofs were subject to shortcuts even though "a great many accidents are caused by the falling of the roofs, and the roofs throughout the south are very treacherous, generally speaking."[9] And mine inspectors were stretched so thin they could only spend a few minutes at each mine per year, which meant there was virtually no enforcement of state codes. With a constant flood of new and inexperienced immigrant miners into the district, each swing of the pick was a metaphorical roll of the dice.

Although Dalrymple saw the most danger in small independent operations, the mass—and more dramatic—tragedies usually befell the large mines operated by large corporations. It was a function of scale. Big mines had bigger explosions that killed more men on bigger crews. Seven explosions between 1906 and 1910 in southern Colorado killed 272 miners, four of them occurring at CF&I-owned mines—two at the same Primero mine near Trinidad.[10] But most mining deaths came in small batches that often eluded broad notice: a small roof collapse in one mine, a mishap on the rail tracks somewhere else. Nationwide, only 12 percent of mine deaths were caused by explosions between 1912 and 1923, and about 50 percent were caused by rock falls.[11]

Unions could not eradicate the risks inherent in the work, but organized mines, particularly those in states where unions dominated, had 40 percent fewer fatalities than nonunion mines, such as those in Colorado.[12] In states where most of the mines were organized, even nonunion mines had a 32 percent drop in fatalities, suggesting increased statewide enforcement of safety laws and a local labor market in which mine safety entered into a man's decision on where to work. It is also likely that some of those nonunion mine operators adopted more stringent safety rules in their own shafts to remove an incentive for their workers to sign union cards.

In Colorado, it was clear that mining deaths, while routine, were not simply a matter of the risks of the trade. "Colorado has good mining laws and such that ought to afford protection to the miners as to safety in the mine if they were enforced, yet in this State the percentage of fatalities is larger than any other, showing there is undoubtedly something wrong in reference to the management of its coal mines," according to a 1914 report by the congressional Committee on Mines and Mining.[13]

The problem lay in a local culture dominated by politically powerful coal operators. "There was conclusive testimony," the report said, "that the miners worked under conditions that were in existence in scarcely any state except Colorado."

At the turn of the century, mine operators exerted almost total control over the physical and political terrain of the mining districts of Colorado, Wyoming, and Idaho, including silver and gold mining areas. If workers went on strike, mine owners responded with heavy hands, hiring fresh non-union crews, contracting with private detective agencies for gunmen to protect them, and pressuring local and state officials to arrest strikers, deport them as vagrants, and make life difficult for small business owners who sided with the union men. The National Guard was routinely deployed to help break picket lines. In the first half century of its existence, beginning in 1879, the Colorado National Guard was called out twenty-two times, and sixteen of those summonses were to handle domestic disturbances in strike zones.[14] In almost every instance the militia acted to end the strike, usually resorting to mass arrests of strikers under the guise of a military emergency and the suspension of civil authority. This use of the National Guard invariably was a class conflict, the immigrant-heavy, multiethnic, and impoverished miners facing off against troops drawn almost exclusively from the growing white middle and upper-middle classes.

Some strikes were successful in gaining small concessions, but not many. In September 1891, just two months after seven union men and three Pinkerton guards were killed in the bloody Homestead Steel battle near Pittsburgh, a series of violent run-ins and threats of dynamited mines in Idaho led Gov. Norman B. Willey to order the state militia to take control of the mining district. Backed by federal troops, martial law was declared and the mines reopened. The following July, the National Guard rounded up six hundred men—unionists, shopkeepers, and local sympathizers—and held them in a massive bullpen for two months without charge. The union drive was broken.[15]

Radicalized veterans of that and similar failed organizing drives came together in the summer of 1893 in Butte, Montana, to form the Western Federation of Miners (WFM). From its start the union leaders, including the legendary William "Big Bill" Haywood, believed that violence rather than the strike was the union's ultimate trump card, setting the stage for bloody showdowns across the mountain West.[16] The union was particularly strong in Colorado, accounting for about 27 percent of the WFM's 1903 national roster of 27,154.[17] The Colorado union men were almost exclusively "hard rock" miners—diggers of gold, silver, and other metals, as opposed to the "soft rock" coal miners—and they set hard picket lines.

Their reputation for recalcitrance and violence was built in the rich mines of Cripple Creek, where in 1894 local mine owners ordered their miners to lengthen the workday from eight hours to ten, without increasing the three-dollar day rate, or to accept fifty cents less a day for eight hours. The workers, not surprisingly, walked out when the owners imposed the ten-hour day on February 1. A few armed confrontations led the governor to send in the state militia, which pulled out after determining its presence was unnecessary. By late spring, the mine owners had built their own small militias to counter the armed WFM men, and battles resumed, including the dynamiting of the Strong mine on the aptly named Battle Mountain overlooking the mine town of Victor. Both sides were quick on the trigger, but the successful armed resistance of the strikers—they eventually won a return to the three-dollar, eight-hour day—established the WFM as a workers' force to be reckoned with, a reputation that stuck despite several ensuing lost strikes.[18]

In 1905, the WFM helped found the Industrial Workers of the World— the Wobblies—which similarly sought to gain economic power through direct action rather than negotiation. One of the marquee names at that meeting was Mary Harris Jones, known then and now in the labor world as Mother Jones. Jones is one of labor's few larger-than-life characters. Born in Ireland, she grew up in Toronto and lived and worked as a teacher in Michigan, then as a dressmaker in Chicago and Memphis, where she met and married George E. Jones, a member of the Iron Molders Union. After her husband and four children died in the yellow fever epidemic of 1867, Jones returned to Chicago and dressmaking, only to lose all her possessions in the 1871 fire that all but destroyed the city. Her losses were labor's gain. After the fire, Jones fell into union work and proved to be a skilled organizer.

Gifted with a strong voice, Jones was more performer than orator, a mesmerizing agitator who occasionally used small props, such as letters, and anecdotes from the lives of people in her audience to spin instant stories infused with both the history and rightness of the laborers' fight. Slightly built and invariably dressed in full-length black, she was an animated Whistler's Mother, up from the rocking chair and onto the stage, or the top of the capitol steps, or the platform of a railway station. Her power as an agitator led to countless arrests, deportations from strike zones, and smear campaigns by corporate bosses. One particularly vicious—and persistent—campaign was written by Polly Pry in her *Polly Pry: A Journal of Comment and Criticism,* which she founded after losing her job at the *Denver Post* over her inflammatory articles. Pry holds an odd position in U.S. journalism history: Something of a self-styled muckraker, she was also in the pocket of Colorado's coal companies. In January 1904, Pry wrote about a pending labor rally in Denver that was to feature Jones. Citing Pinkerton Detective Agency files, Pry detailed a history of Jones as a former whorehouse madam in Denver's notorious red light district. The allegation has generally been dismissed as agitprop against the mine workers' most efficient organizer, but the slur echoed until Jones's death in 1930 and even found its way into the *Congressional Record.*[19]

Although the WFM later broke with the Wobblies, the groups' radicalism helped further crystallize mine owners' perceptions that unions posed a mortal threat. As the 1913–1914 strike was being fought, the Colorado Mine Operators' Association released what it called the "Criminal Record of the Western Federation of Miners from Coeur d'Alene to Cripple Creek, 1894–1904." It was a red herring—the WFM was not involved in the 1913–1914 strike—but the list is telling. It detailed thirteen killings, dozens of beatings, and the occasional bombing—all evidence of what the mine operators described as the WFM's dangerous nature.[20] Reports cropped up elsewhere, too. In the July 7, 1906, issue of *Outlook* magazine, journalist William Hard described the killing of an Idaho strikebreaker, John Kneebone, by forty union miners when Kneebone returned to a mine near Coeur d'Alene after the miners had run him out of the district. The miners brazenly blamed the mine owners, arguing that if the companies had expelled the scabs as the union demanded, the killing wouldn't have happened. As spurious as that argument sounds, it was enough to keep a grand jury from indicting any of the mob, indicating that while the mine operators might have controlled most of the geography and local governments in the mining district, the miners had their own pockets of power and influence within sympathetic communities.

In August 1903, the WFM called a district-wide strike of the metal mines in Colorado. The UMWA, representing coal miners, joined in November, and the two unions ultimately led more than twenty thousand men out of metal and coal mines up and down the Rockies in demand of an eight-hour workday, an increase in tonnage rates, payment in U.S. currency, adherence to state laws establishing uniform weights, and other issues.[21] On September 3, 1903, Gov. James H. Peabody sent Brig. Gen. John Chase, a Denver ophthalmologist and father of six, and two other men to Cripple Creek to explore whether the National Guard should be deployed. It was a foregone conclusion—Peabody was virulently antiunion—and Chase dutifully reported back that the militia was needed to keep the peace, despite protests by the local sheriff (a former miner) that if strikebreakers were barred there would be no violence.[22] Peabody sent in the militia the next day under Gen. Sherman M. Bell, "an arrogant megalomaniac who thought that all labor problems involving the WFM were susceptible to a military solution."[23] Bell, a former Teddy Roosevelt Rough Rider, was also superintendent of the Independence mine and made no pretense about his role: He was there to break the strike.

Peabody ordered General Bell to supersede civil authority—in essence, to assume control of the district militarily. Bell delegated much of the groundwork to Chase. "Using force and intimidation to shut off debate about the advisability of the state's intervention . . . Chase, Bell's field commander, systematically imprisoned without formal charges union officials and others who openly questioned the need for troops."[24] The detainees included a justice of the peace and a county commissioner. "Not even the newspapers escaped harassment. When the *Victor Daily Record,* a strong voice of the WFM, erroneously charged that one of the soldiers was an ex-convict, its staff was imprisoned."[25] Separately, a civilian judge granted a habeas corpus petition and ordered Chase to turn over to civil authorities four men who had been detained by the militia. Chase, after filling the courtroom with his armed men, refused, and did not obey the civilian judge's order until Peabody directed him to. In Chase's perception of his role as a military commander, civil authority was second to his own, and the tenets of the U.S. Constitution—such as protections against illegal searches and detentions—did not apply.[26]

Between the company-hired mine guards and the state militia, security was tight but not foolproof. On November 21, Charles McCormick, superintendent of the Vindicator mine near Cripple Creek, and shift supervisor Melvin H. Beck stepped into the cage of the mine elevator and began the long, slow descent into the mine shaft.[27] Despite the security and the presence of strikebreaking miners, someone managed to stack dynamite in the passageway on the sixth level adjacent to the mine shaft. A loaded pistol was securely lodged in place nearby, and a string stretched from the trigger across the shaft. When the cage hit the string, it fired a bullet into the cache of dynamite. The blast killed the two men instantly.

A week later, operators of mines in nearby Florence and in Louisville, in the northern field, agreed to the union terms, and their striking miners voted to return to work. Most mine operators, though, held fast, and operations at the strike-bound mines picked up with imported scab labor. At the end of the June 5, 1904, night shift—a little after 2:00 A.M. on June 6— twenty-four strikebreakers at mines on Bull Hill, overlooking the small town of Independence, trooped down to the Florence & Cripple Creek Railroad Co. depot to catch a train to their homes in nearby Victor and Cripple Creek. As they and two other men—not miners—waited on the platform, they heard a short toot from the approaching train's whistle. At the sound, someone sitting about three hundred feet away moved his chair, intentionally pulling a thin steel wire that stretched to the trigger of a gun hidden beneath the train platform. The bullet was fired into a container of nitroglycerine next to about three hundred pounds of black powder.[28] "The earth seemed to heave under the platform and the station," H. W. Vanatta, a strikebreaking miner who was injured when the blast blew him about seventy-five feet, told a stringer for the *New York Times*.[29] The explosion was devastating, splintering the platform, destroying the depot, creating a twenty-foot-deep crater, and sending body parts flying in a macabre spray. Pieces of flesh stuck to walls five hundred feet away; everything within fifty feet of the blast was soaked with blood.[30] Eleven men were killed instantly; two others died later, and others had limbs amputated to save their lives. As the bomb went off, another twenty men had been making their way to the platform from the mine. A minute's delay in the blast and the death toll might have easily doubled.

The next morning hundreds of people, many of them armed, massed on the streets of Victor. Flyers were circulated at about 11:00 A.M. announcing a public meeting for 1:00 P.M. at a vacant lot at the corner of Fourth Street and Victor Avenue, close to the Armory Building and the WFM hall. "Near the center of the lot was a large float, a wagon ordinarily used for handling scenery," which was mounted by a handful of officials from the Cripple Creek Mine Owners Association (CCMOA). Clarence Hamlin, one of the operators, railed before the crowd of about 2,500 people that the blast was the evil doings of the WFM; the bombers should be hanged, and the union should be purged from the mine district. "I want to hear what the boys in the mines have got to say about this trouble," Hamlin concluded.[31] William Hoskins, a union miner, spoke up but was hissed down by the crowd and then beaten, which sparked a broad melee and gunfire.[32] More than forty shots were fired, killing two people and wounding five or six others. The incident drew even more people to the streets, thickening the crowd to five thousand, and a riot broke out. By the time the militia arrived the violence had subsided, but the commanders decided that the gunmen involved in the shooting were union men who had sought refuge in the WFM hall. When the miners refused to surrender, the soldiers took cover in a building across the street and opened fire, sending more than 250 bullets through the thin wooden walls.[33] The miners tossed a white handkerchief down the hall steps. About forty union men, six of them seriously wounded, surrendered and were arrested. But the violence wasn't over. A crowd of about eleven hundred soldiers and mine owners' supporters rampaged into the night, until nearly every union-friendly business in town was wrecked.

The CCMOA, backed by the militia, used the bombing to effect a local coup d'etat. Before the street riot began, Teller County sheriff Henry M. Robertson, a former union miner, was taken by force to the CCMOA headquarters, where Hamlin and others asked him to resign.[34] When he refused, someone threw a coiled rope at his feet, the threat of a lynching implicit. Robertson signed the resignation that had already been written out for him, and the owners appointed one of their own ranks, Edward Bell, as sheriff. Bell, in turn, replaced the sworn deputies with the operators' men. Over the next few days other labor-friendly politicians quit under threat of lynching and were replaced with vigilantes who set to work arresting miners, union organizers, and sympathizers—including some of the deposed political leaders—and imprisoning them in open-air bullpens. Some four hundred men were arrested and another five hundred warned to leave town. About one thousand men ultimately left on their own. A week after the confrontation began, 170 men remained in custody, and on June 8 thirty-seven of them were loaded aboard a train under armed guard. Once the train was underway, their head keeper, Col. Leo W. Kennedy, opened a sealed envelope detailing their destination: the Four Corners, where Colorado, New Mexico, Arizona, and Utah come together, about as desolate a stretch of desert as can be found in the American Southwest.[35] No one was ever tried for the bombing itself,[36] but the WFM was, for all intents and purposes, done in Colorado.

The WFM and the Indianapolis-based UMWA were distinctly different unions, often at odds over strategy and influence, but in the eyes of Colorado's capitalists they were interchangeable. For individual miners, the extralegal response by the mine owners in Cripple Creek—with the collusion of the state militia and support of Colorado's political leadership—

signaled that the U.S. Constitution had been usurped. By early 1905, when the strike was formally called off, morale was low, the sense of defeat heavy.[37] For organizers and union sympathizers, the loss represented both precedent and omen. Violence became less a fear than an expectation, as much a part of the union-building process as negotiations.

The strike also marked a key demographic shift. From the early days, Colorado coal was dug mostly by English speakers: American-born or immigrant miners from Cornwall, Scotland, and Wales. After the 1903 strike, the ethnic makeup of the miners changed radically. In that year, CF&I alone employed sixteen thousand people in both its mining and steelmaking operations, only 5,300 of whom were native-born Americans—a number that included Mexican American and African American men at a time when segregation and racism were part of the white-dominated social and economic structure.[38] The payroll reflected thirty nationalities, with Italians forming the largest group. Labor activists believed the shift was a strategic attempt to fill the mines with groups of workers who would be difficult to organize into a union: people who could not communicate easily with each other and in some cases brought regional biases from Europe into the Colorado mining district. Edwin V. Brake, Colorado's deputy labor commissioner, claimed that "the highest official" of one of the coal companies admitted to him that it was intentional. "The purpose was, of course, to produce in advance a condition of confusion of tongues, so that no tower upon which they might ascend the heavens could be erected."[39] Perhaps more significant, many of the new hires had no background in mining and thus were "not conversant with the rate of wages or the conditions that prevail in this country, and they will submit to conditions that men will not tolerate who have had experience as practical miners."[40] And the inexperienced miners often were ignorant of the dangers they faced— or the danger they posed to other miners—when they entered subterranean labyrinths whose ceilings were suspect, whose walls seeped noxious and explosive gases, and whose passageways were coated with highly flammable coal dust.

Colorado's coalfields were divided roughly in two, north and south. The northern field, centered in Boulder and Weld counties just north of Denver, was the smaller of the two. Miners there dug lignite and sub-bituminous coal, which burned hot enough for heating homes and firing boilers but not for coking steel.[41] Many of the mines developed within or near small towns perched at the edge of the plains or in the foothills, allowing miners to live off site in their own homes, or to rent from property owners other than the coal operators, and commute using "interurban" trolleys. That gave the coal towns more stability and the miners more freedom to shop and socialize where they liked.[42] Coal companies still exerted considerable control, but elections were less susceptible to open fraud, and union organizers could mingle freely with workers on public streets and in bars and meeting halls.

The southern field was a different story entirely. In the empty lands between Colorado Springs and the Raton Pass into New Mexico, towns were few and far between and isolated by harsh roads. As late as November 1913, physician Julian Lamme made the drive from Trinidad to his home in La Veta, some fifty miles away, in three hours, fast enough to warrant a mention in the local Walsenburg newspaper. Because of the remoteness of many of the coal seams, CF&I and other mine owners established camps—little more than shanty towns in some cases—of low-grade housing, saloons, and company stores. Quality was uneven. In some camps, "houses in the main are good. This applies more particularly to those built recently. They are usually frame, but the most recently built ones are of brick or concrete block. They are of the square cottage type of three or four rooms," cost $200 to $700 to build, and rented in 1913 for two dollars per room per month.[43]

Most closed camps were also closed economic systems. Mine operators paid workers in company scrip, forced them to live in company houses (or at least on company land in jerry-built shanties), shop at the company store, worship in the company church to sermons uttered by the company-hired minister, and drink in the company saloon, where—as in the mines themselves—company spies kept close track of what was done and said. The mine superintendent was the highest local authority, overseeing camp marshals who were deputized by the local sheriff, though there was no court system within the camps. Serious crimes were turned over to the sheriff. Petty crimes were handled by the marshal as investigator, judge, and jury. "Within these towns a man has no rights. He is granted a certain amount of freedom and given a certain number of privileges, but there is no machinery that he could call to his aid in redressing a wrong. If he doesn't like it, he can quit."[44] It was not the kind of environment upon which a healthy community is built.

On October 11, 1910, state labor inspector Eli M. Gross arrived in Starkville, three miles into the canyons southwest of Trinidad, to investigate an explosion that killed fifty-six miners. "[T]he residences or houses and living quarters of the miners smack of the direst poverty. Practically all of the residences are huddled in the shadow of the coal washers and the smoke of the coke ovens making the surroundings smutty with coal dust and coke smoke. Not all of the houses are equipped with water, and practically none have sewerage; they depend for their water upon hydrants on the streets. The people reflect their surroundings; slatternly dressed women and unkempt children throng the dirty streets and dirty alleys of the camp. One is forced to the conclusion that these people must be very poorly paid, else they would not be content to live in this fashion."[45]

Those conditions were not unique to Starkville. Victor Bazanelli moved into the Gray Creek mining camp northeast of Trinidad in 1906 after emigrating from Tyrol, Italy, to join his father, who had found work near Forbes a year earlier. Some of the houses were wooden shacks cobbled together from discarded lumber and crates. The better ones were built of concrete, square in shape, one story divided into four rooms. "Ours was cement blocks, but the inside was just rough. They had floor but of planks, no linoleum or carpet. . . . Some didn't have the [plank] floor, just cement. We used dynamite boxes for chairs." Poverty was pervasive but meat was cheap and readily available, ensuring that the workers would have the strength for the physical demands of cutting and hauling hundreds of pounds of coal during a ten-hour day. "Only one kind of soup—meat. Meat was plentiful at five cents a pound, or three pounds of steak for twenty-five cents. So you had meat."[46]

Little medical help was available, and death from what now seem like minor health problems was a regular occurrence. Las Animas County coroner records for the first nine months of 1913—covering the first week of the strike—list 120 deaths, including Lippiatt and mine guard Robert Lee (more on him later), who were killed in strike-related acts of violence. Of the 118 nonstrike deaths, about two-thirds were from illness, accident, or suicide. Twenty-five of the dead were age eighteen and under, mostly toddlers suffering from ileocolitis or other gastrointestinal problems, stillborn infants, or victims of the occasional gunshot accident. One youngster, Elias Duncan, age eight, died of peritonitis after being kicked by a calf. Angela De Paulo, age three, fell into a fire and burned to death. Mine accidents—thirty-two in all, eighteen caused by rock falls—accounted for about one out of every four fatalities during that period. And some of the seven recorded murders were indirectly related to the mines, as workers in bars and the coal camps shot and stabbed each other over insults and threats both real and perceived.

The "open" town of Aguilar, north of Trinidad, seemed one step removed from the Wild West of myth and legend when Nick Bisulco, four years old, and his family emigrated from Italy in 1900. Bisulco grew up in Aguilar during the 1903–1904 strike and the lead-up to the 1913–1914 strike. The town was all rough edges, with seventeen saloons on the main street, each with its own gambling area. Jim Gregg, an African American, and his wife, "one of those beautiful women you just want to look at," opened a "sporting house" in a two-story building with seventeen rooms upstairs. Gregg's wasn't the only whorehouse in town, but he might have had the best marketing idea: "They had a jitney bus, five cents for a round trip," to shuttle customers back and forth from the mine camps. The gambling rooms were usually heated by central stoves in the winter, and as the gambling and drinking intensified so did the room temperature. "[T]hen it [would] get so hot they had to take their coats off and . . . [you could see] everyone had their six-shooters."[47]

The miners might have had weapons, but they did not have a political voice. The courts and the local political structure in the south were directly controlled by, or friendly to, the interests of the mine owners. In elections, local mine superintendents often cast their workers' ballots for them while excluding outsiders from the polls, clinching political control. Union organizers were spotted by the operators' undercover detectives—at CF&I, run by William F. Reno, chief of security—and pointed out to mine superintendents across the district as though sending a weather warning. "A new organizer for the U.M.W. of A. from Illinois has shown up in this district in the last few days for the purpose of doing organization work," read one such missive, signed by Reno. "He goes by the name of Kreilrat, age about 45 years, 6 ft. 3 inches, weight 250#. Run this man out of your camp if he shows up there and notify undersigned. Show this letter to your superintendent and acknowledge receipt." Other letters went out unsigned. "All superintendents: Look out for Jack Nelson, commonly called the Big Swede. He has been working at Wooten and he is an organizer for the U.M.W. of A. Sandy Allen may apply to you for work; we do not want him."[48]

The legal system belonged to the coal operators, too, and they were rarely faulted for any injuries to the workers, either below or above ground. In Pueblo County, sixty-six men were killed in CF&I's steel mill from 1905 to 1910, but only twenty-four of those deaths were the subject of inquests, which usually blamed the victim. The local coroner saw no reason to probe the others. After three men were killed and nine injured in one explosion at the steel plant, coroner Patterson explained why he didn't find an investigation necessary: "That accident destroyed property of tremendous value. It will cost the company thousands and thousands of dollars to repair the damage done. It stands to reason that they would not want that accident to happen, so there is no question of blame involved. It was just an accident. Don't you see?" Of ninety Huerfano County coroner investigations into mine deaths over a ten-year span, only one found the mine operator at fault. All the others—with causes ranging from cave-ins to runaway coal cars—were found to be accidental or the fault of the dead miners.[49]

CF&I mine superintendents routinely ignored recommendations from state mine officials, often issued after investigating fatal disasters, on how to lessen dangers to the miners. They also ignored laws designed to improve working conditions, relying on local authorities to absolve them of liability. "The attitude of this company toward their employees is one of lawlessness, fraud, and corruption," Brake, the state's deputy labor commissioner, wrote in one report. "The system, as employed by C.F. & I. Co. in Las Animas county, is not only in open defiance of all the laws of the state of Colorado, but it maintains, under the guise of law, an armed force consisting of deputy sheriffs, in all its camps, who are used to not only violate all of the laws, but to maltreat any one who attempts in any way to assert his rights as an American citizen."[50]

In Huerfano County, the mine operators—particularly CF&I—were supported by the legendarily corrupt Sheriff Jefferson B. Farr, whose sins bordered on caricature. Farr, a native Texan, was one of three sons of a Texas Ranger who established themselves as powerful figures around the county seat of Walsenburg in the 1890s. They owned buildings, bought farms to raise alfalfa and hogs, and moved into politics. Jeff Farr was appointed sheriff in July 1899 after the previous sheriff—his brother Ed— was killed leading a posse after the Sam "Black Jack" Ketchum Gang of train robbers.[51] Jeff Farr quickly established himself as a powerful political string puller, drawing comparisons to New York's Boss Tweed and Tammany Hall.[52] Political beliefs seemed not to figure into his vision of public service. Raised a Texas Democrat, he switched his registration to Republican, the majority party in Huerfano County, to more easily consolidate power—and to the great aggravation of his Democrat father. "When he ran for sheriff the first time his father . . . found out he was running on the Republican ticket, and he was going to whip him, and the other boys had to get the old man out of the state."[53]

Already active in local business, Farr continued to buy retail properties and set up several corporations with local partners. Through the Great Western Land and Investment Co. and the Spanish Peaks Mercantile Co., co-owned with Mayor James B. Dick, Farr controlled some sixty properties in and near Walsenburg. Some were rented out as saloons, and at least three houses on Walsenburg's Eighth Street were brothels, though Farr denied knowing that—or knowing that there were slot machines in his bars—during an unrelated trial in August 1913.[54] Farr eventually monopolized liquor supplies and saloons across the county, forcing competitors out of business.[55] "No one can get a license unless they buy their beer, cigars, and other things for their saloons from these parties, and that gives them a power in politics over all the saloons in this county."[56] Farr also described himself as a stockholder in a local bank and personally owned three properties, including his family home at 207 Rito Street, just outside the Walsenburg city limits, where he lived with his wife, their three children, and a servant.[57]

Significantly, Farr also was the president of the *Walsenburg World*, one of two local newspapers. And he directed a jury system rigged to ensure verdicts for whatever interest he had. Farr would draft the jury pool by walking Walsenburg's business district "selecting jurors here and there and frequently holding his thumbs up or down to indicate whether or not the juror was to vote for acquittal."[58] In March 1914, Malloy Ball, head swathed in bandages, testified in Walsenburg before a congressional committee investigating conditions in the coal district that Farr deputy Louis Miller had recently beaten him, breaking his jaw. Miller was acquitted by a jury that included seven fellow deputies.[59]

One of Farr's business partners in the liquor business was John T. Kebler, who ran CF&I's fuel division until he died in 1907, which meant Farr's interests often aligned with those of CF&I and the other coal companies.[60] "He makes a brag that anything they want, he will do," said John McQuarrie, who served as Farr's undersheriff from 1903 to 1909. Reno, CF&I's security chief, was also a business partner of Farr's, and Farr paid close attention to Reno's letters and telegrams warning of union agitators in the district. "Sheriff Farr would always have his men look out for them and run them out of the county and make things disagreeable for them the moment they would spot them," McQuarrie said. The "disagreeable" conditions included being beaten before being loaded onto a train or forced out of town on foot. Farr's favors to the coal companies extended to forming coroner's juries after mine deaths. "I was always instructed, when being called to a mine to investigate an accident, to take the coroner, proceed to the mine, go to the superintendent and find out who he wanted on the jury."[61]

Farr's office was in the granite county courthouse, and the jail was housed in an adjacent smaller two-story granite building to the west. But Farr ran his fiefdom from a saloon farther down Main Street. Fat, with red hair and mustache and a permanent blush from booze, Farr would sit in the dark and have his deputies round up people for mandatory audiences. Mike Livoda, a UMWA organizer, received one such summons in March 1912 after he finished a late-night sandwich at a Walsenburg diner. When he stepped out into the street, four men were waiting for him. One told Livoda that Farr wanted to see him, and they escorted him to a bar.

"We walked in and there was a big fat man, oh, I suppose he weighed over 200, good 250 pounds, and he used the wild language, " Livoda recalled. Farr turned to the escorts and said, "Is this the son of a bitch?" then asked Livoda if he knew who he was and answered for him: "I'm Jeff Farr and I'm the king of this county and if you want to do any of your dirty work, you going to have to do it down in Las Animas County." Farr told Livoda to be out of town by the next morning. When Livoda and his escort reached the sidewalk, the four men said, "Let's put him out of town tonight." It was after midnight. The men escorted Livoda to the Colorado and Southern railroad track where one of them told him "to get on that track and walk back towards Trinidad" nearly forty miles to the south. Livoda walked three miles in the moonlight to the Ravenwood mine, then spotted three men on horseback trailing him, so he kept going another two miles to the Globe mine camp, where he evaded his watchers and found a refuge with friends. The next day, Livoda returned to Walsenburg, determined that Farr would not run him out of town. He was followed wherever he went, but Farr made no more moves against him. Three months later, though, Livoda was savagely beaten and nearly killed.[62]

Much of Farr's power came from his control of the ballot box. County precinct lines were redrawn to make the company-owned camps individual precincts, and election officials would delay delivering returns until the first legitimate ballots were counted and the trend in a particular election discernible. Then the precinct vote would be adjusted to ensure the outcome Farr desired—invariably the election of fellow Republicans. Sometimes passing herds of sheep were counted, each sheep a ballot for Farr's favored candidate.[63] "Political discussions or political meetings were not permitted within the limits of these closed precincts. . . . Many of those who voted in these precincts were illiterate, and in numerous instances the judges of the election marked their ballots for them in violation of the law; and the companies distributed, during the day of the election, cards, so printed as to indicate to the illiterate voters the names of the Republican candidates as the proper ones to be chosen."[64]

Farr was never prosecuted for his crimes. He died in March 1920. By the time his estate was settled ten years later, it held $59,772.50 in assets—just over $1.2 million in 2006 dollars—mostly property around Walsenburg, stakes in three local firms, and some cattle. With some $46,000 in "claims and deductions," his wife, son, and two daughters split $13,516.25, or just over $250,000 in 2006 dollars.[65] There is no mention of the liquor supply business, the whorehouses, or whatever cash he had accrued during more than two decades of reign.

The bigger question is why the people of Huerfano and Las Animas counties put up with this modernized version of feudalism, salted through with classic American corruption. In the midst of the coming strike, Ethelbert Stewart, a federal mediator, would travel to Colorado to investigate the cause of the labor unrest. "I heard the cry of the suffering of the innocent public, but I confess I was not deeply impressed, or convinced of the massive innocence of a public that sits supinely by for thirty years, and sees the fungi of medievalism overspread the industries of the state without a protest," Stewart wrote in a report to his bosses at the U.S. Department of Labor. There was some protest against political corruption, he noted, but not against the oligarchy of coal, or the brutality of life in the coal camps engineered by the coal operators. "The evils that are permitted to generate, unmolested in industry, must always, sooner or later, assert themselves in politics."[66]

In other words, southern Colorado had the government, and the economic system, it deserved.

TWO

Company Men and
Union Leaders

John C. Osgood was a young man of thirty-one when he arrived in Denver in 1882, stepping out of Union Station into the dusty streets of a fast-growing city of thirty-five thousand people just two years after Colorado attained statehood. The trip was made at the request of the Chicago, Burlington & Quincy (CB&Q) rail line to investigate whether enough coal could be had in Colorado to support expanding the rail line across the Great Plains. Osgood was about to make a decision that would affect the trajectory of history.

Born in Brooklyn, New York, in 1851, Osgood was the son of a wholesale druggist who "became infected with the Western fever" and moved his family to Iowa in 1857.[1] After the father's death two years later, Osgood was raised by relatives in Providence, Rhode Island, but left school at fourteen to work as an office boy in a local cotton mill. At sixteen he moved to New York City to clerk for a Produce Exchange firm. Precocious at business, by the time he was nineteen Osgood was working as cashier for the Whitebreast Fuel Co., in Ottumwa, Iowa, a coal supplier to the CB&Q. Four years later, Osgood shifted to the First National Bank of Burlington, Iowa, where he completed making the connections he used to finance his 1876 takeover of Whitebreast when he was only twenty-five.

When Osgood stepped off the train in Denver, he immediately saw potential—but rather than establish a beachhead for the CB&Q, his client, he set out to build an empire of his own, creating a partnership with several Iowa colleagues and two Denver lawyers to form the Colorado Fuel Company.[2] Ten years later they merged with another firm and became the

Colorado Fuel & Iron Co., controlling sixty-nine thousand acres of coal land, fourteen mines, and eight hundred coke ovens spread over four sites with a capacity of twenty-five thousand tons of coal per month, as well as steel mills and rolling plants.[3] Osgood's stake was worth millions, and he liked to spend it. He built a $3 million castle called Cleveholm a mile outside the mountain village of Redstone near his first coal mine and marble quarry. Still standing, the forty-two-room estate initially was set in the 4,200-acre "Crystal Park" along the Crystal River, a bucolic spot with a stable for twenty-five horses and a game preserve holding deer, elk, and bighorn mountain sheep.[4] Construction began shortly after Osgood married his second wife in 1899, and over the next two decades the estate would host the likes of John D. Rockefeller, J. P. Morgan, and Teddy Roosevelt, who occasionally shot game from the mansion's portico.

A classic self-made man, Osgood also, not surprisingly, was virulently anti-union but had a paternalistic compassion for the people who worked for him. He approved the creation in 1901 of CF&I's Sociological Department under Dr. Richard W. Corwin, who already ran CF&I's medical department and hospital—another innovation that placed CF&I ahead of its competitors. Osgood professed to believe that a worker's physical environment affected his productivity and took benevolent steps aimed at enticing worker fealty, including letting Corwin set up a program to make CF&I responsible for the education and health of its workers and their families.[5] Medical buildings and schools were erected, and company housing was improved. But benevolence can be relative. Since the miners lived on company property, they could never own their homes, were forced to shop in company stores, and were billed for medical services whether they needed them or not—and whether or not they could get to the hospital in Pueblo for treatment.[6]

Since living conditions in each camp varied depending on the outlook of the local superintendent, it was hardly a workers' utopia. Eugene Gaddis, a Methodist Episcopal minister who worked in the camps as a preacher and, for a time, as CF&I's Sociological Department director, wrote a scathing report on conditions, his department's failure to improve the workers' lives, and the CF&I managers' culpability for the miners' miseries. Gaddis was one of the key witnesses in the U.S. Commission on Industrial Relations investigation, describing lives of desperate oppression leavened only by drunkenness. Gaddis quoted an anonymous member of CF&I's board of directors as admitting to him that "[w]e might as well confess it, we have not given them anything but the saloon for the past 25 years."[7]

Despite Osgood's role in pioneering Colorado industry, business problems dogged him. Production delays forced Osgood to scramble continuously for money to stay afloat. Given capitalism's cannibalistic nature, Osgood's problems were a blood scent. In 1902, Osgood precipitated a crisis by suspending CF&I stock dividends, leading to a showdown with legendary corporate poacher John W. Gates, aligned with Union Pacific's Edward Harriman and other eastern investors who, with an eye on CF&I's coalfields, wanted to force Osgood out and take over the company.[8] Osgood, relying on boardroom maneuvers and a strategically timed court injunction, held off Gates, but not for long. By the end of the year he turned to George Jay Gould for help, warning that if Gates succeeded, competitors of the Denver & Rio Grande Railroad (D&RG)—in which Gould was the principal shareholder—would reap the benefits. Gould didn't have the $3 million Osgood needed, so Gould turned for help to John D. Rockefeller Sr.,[9] who was flush with cash after selling his vast Mesabi Range iron ore fields and Great Lakes shipping fleet to J. P. Morgan for $88.5 million.[10] Morgan merged them with Carnegie's former steel mills to create U.S. Steel.

The Gould-Rockefeller relationship was "mystifying," as Rockefeller biographer Ron Chernow described it.[11] Gould had assumed control of the estate of his father, Jay Gould, when the legendary robber baron died in 1892. The son proved to be better at squandering money than at making it. By 1909, Rockefeller refused to be involved in any venture with Gould unless his own people controlled the board. Less than a decade later, Gould had lost his father's empire[12]—and Rockefeller's goodwill—through a combination of woefully bad investment decisions exacerbated by the 1907 recession.

In 1902, though, when Osgood was looking for a cash infusion, Gould still enjoyed the trust of Rockefeller, with whom he had invested in several railroad properties. Osgood blamed CF&I's problems on an engineering firm hired to design and build new facilities, which led to cost overruns of more than 100 percent. Gould apparently believed Osgood and went to bat for him, sending an overture to Rockefeller's office at Twenty-six Broadway in New York, an address as famous then as 1600 Pennsylvania Avenue in Washington, D.C. Rockefeller, coincidentally, was traveling in the West with his son, John D. Rockefeller Jr.,[13] an 1897 graduate of Brown University and understudy to run the family empire. The office had been left in the charge of Frederick T. Gates, one of Rockefeller's closest business advisors (no relation to John Gates), who saw the potential and agreed to an emergency $1.25 million loan. For Osgood, it was a devil's pact. CF&I's problems were deeper than a few cost overruns, and Rockefeller eventually sank $6 million in the venture.[14]

By June 1903, Rockefeller had a controlling interest in CF&I, and within two months he had packed the board with his own and Gould's people. Osgood was out.

After losing CF&I, Osgood went to Europe for a month, then returned with a new plan. Buying up smaller mines, he formed the Victor-American Fuel Co. in December 1903 and began competing with CF&I, eventually owning mines in Fremont, Huerfano, and Las Animas counties. By 1913, CF&I controlled three hundred thousand acres of coal lands as well as the steel works at Pueblo; Osgood's Victor-American controlled fifty thousand; and the Rocky Mountain Fuel Co., the state's third-largest operator, had thirty-one thousand acres.[15] Osgood shifted from competition to collusion, working with CF&I and other mine operators in showdowns with union organizers.

In what was typical fashion for Rockefeller, he bought into CF&I based on underlings' recommendations without having a clear sense of what it was he was getting into—in this case, a regional powerhouse that dominated local politics, bought judges, and controlled its work force through a mix of deprivation and intimidation. At the time, he and Gates did not know—though Gould apparently did—that CF&I was riddled with rogue midlevel managers who had been bleeding the firm, lying about its local operations, and exerting feudal control over squalid mine camps.[16] To manage the business, Rockefeller and Gould turned to Frank J. Hearne, who had been president of the National Tube Co. until the firm disappeared into Carnegie's U.S. Steel. Four years later, Hearne died a week after suffering a heart attack and was replaced by Jesse F. Welborn. Born and raised on a Nebraska farm, Welborn had joined CF&I almost at the beginning, hiring in as a clerk for Osgood's Colorado Fuel Co. in 1890 after working for a few years as a bookkeeper at a Nebraska bank.[17] He rose through the ranks of CF&I's sales division, winning the general manager's job in 1899. At the same 1903 meeting in which Rockefeller and Gould's CF&I directors hired Hearne, Welborn was named vice president for sales. Welborn was a popular choice within CF&I to succeed Hearne, but not within the boardroom. Frederick Gates, a board member, wrote to Welborn congratulating him on the presidency but also informing him that he would soon have company. One of Rockefeller's personal advisors had recently moved to Denver for family reasons and would be "looking over the work and the field of the Colorado Fuel & Iron Company in their larger aspects."[18]

There was a lot to assess.

The man the Rockefellers picked to untangle the mess in Colorado was Lamont Montgomery Bowers, a farmer's son from rural south-central New York who had recently built the Rockefellers' Great Lakes shipping fleet into a monopoly. Tall, balding, and a quick study, Bowers had amassed his own comfortable fortune in the late 1800s through retail and real estate businesses around Binghamton, New York, and in Nebraska, where he had been a land speculator. Bowers's business background, though, was less important than his family connections: His nephew (the age difference was only six years) was Frederick Gates, Rockefeller's advisor. All three men believed in the benevolence of wealth, a corporate structure built upon independence among proven managers in the field, and a disdain for unions.

Gates's emergence as a key executive reflected Rockefeller's unconventional method for attracting and retaining his lieutenants. Rather than look for underlings skilled in a specific industry, Rockefeller focused on broad competence and the ability to get jobs done. In the early years, as he built Standard Oil into a simultaneously admired and reviled corporation, he exhibited a soul of cutthroat ruthlessness, and he reaped the benefits—tens of millions of dollars in dividends from his holdings. Rockefeller believed that his wealth was a combination of lucky timing and something akin to divine stewardship, and he intended to use much of the fortune for benevolent causes. He began to surround himself with younger advisors who would help him disseminate his wealth. This new generation, Gates key among them, had little grounding in Rockefeller's past with Standard Oil, which allowed the tycoon to re-create himself in the eyes of the new acolytes.[19]

Rockefeller believed that success grew from paying attention to details, and he recognized that ability in Gates, a minister who as executive director of the American Baptist Education Society authored, in response to a burning issue of the time, an exhaustive 1888 study that recommended a major Baptist college be established in Chicago. Leading Baptists—including Rockefeller and Gates's patron, Minnesota grain baron George A. Pillsbury—were seeking ways to counter what they saw as the growing dominance of Harvard, Yale, and Princeton (curiously, JDR Jr.'s alma mater, Brown University, founded by Baptists, did not enter into their analysis of

A 1913 photograph of Lamont Montgomery Bowers, a businessman from Bing-hamton, New York, who ran John D. Rockefeller's Great Lakes shipping fleet. Bowers, who was tapped to oversee the magnate's investments in the Colorado Fuel & Iron Co., shared with Rockefeller a deep philosophical antipathy to unions. *Credit: The Papers of Lamont Montgomery Bowers, Glenn G. Bartle Library, State University of New York at Binghamton.*

the influence wielded by the Ivy League schools). They sought to give young Baptist scholars an alternative that would in turn foster a Baptist-based intellectual elite. Gates saw that placing the school in Chicago was the equivalent of putting the magnet close to the iron filings, in this case the explosive population growth underway in the Midwest.

Rockefeller agreed with Gates's ideas and appreciated his understated way of handling himself, a personality sympathetic with his own. In 1889, Rockefeller donated $600,000 to the cause, with $400,000 to be raised from other sources, and the University of Chicago was born. Two years later, Rockefeller's health began to fail, and he realized that guiding his financial empire with one hand and his philanthropy with the other was more than he could handle. He invited Gates to take over the philanthropic side of things, and the young man slowly became one of Rockefeller's closest advisors.

Wealth begets wealth, and it was no different for Rockefeller. In the financial panic of 1893, iron prices tumbled and the owners of the Mesabi iron range in Minnesota were on the verge of failure. Rockefeller bailed them out in a controversial maneuver that eventually gave him control of the iron fields and affiliated rail business in the upper Great Lakes.[20] Getting the ore to the steel mills proved to be a challenge, though. Great Lakes shipowners, knowing it was Rockefeller ore they would be moving, quoted the tycoon exorbitant rates. Rockefeller's solution: build his own fleet and move his own ore. But he needed someone to run it. Gates recommended his uncle.

Rockefeller and Bowers met in 1895, separated by a fortune but united by a common background. Rockefeller could well have seen flashes of himself in Bowers, eight years his junior. Both men were born in the first half of the 1800s to underachieving fathers in New York state's rural Southern Tier. Both men spun lives of personal success—Rockefeller legendarily so—from the threads of hard work, innate intelligence, ambition, and the luck of timing. And each man was a bridge between eras. Bowers came of age during the Civil War, made his fortune in the tumultuous years afterward, and went on to usher in the twentieth century as an elder in the church of capitalism.

Bowers was the youngest of six children born to Gardiner Sawin Bowers and Achsah Taylor Bowers in 1827 near Binghamton, New York. He summarized his childhood in an unpublished 1923 memoir written after he had retired to his farm in Maine, New York.[21] Both a portrait of his boyhood neighborhood and the autobiography of a successful businessman explaining his life to his sons, the memoir is revealing in the details Bowers chose to include. He wrote of early jobs tending sheep and cattle and of hoarding the first quarter he ever earned, as well as youthful mistakes that evidenced both his drive and his occasional failure to understand the likely consequences of his actions. The memoir portrays a man confident that his conservative view of the world is the correct view, anchored in pragmatism, and nurtured through experience.

The derivation of Bowers's anti-union beliefs is unclear, but he held them deeply and as part of a broader philosophy that businessmen were the leaders and caretakers not only of the economic system but also of society. He regarded business owners and managers as benevolent paternalists who were better at determining the interests of their workers than the workers themselves—or those who sought to lobby on their behalf, from unionists to journalists to wealthy labor sympathizers. In a 1912 letter responding to a public campaign to reduce the steel industry workday from twelve hours to eight, and the week from seven days to six, Bowers ridiculed the scions of wealthy industrial families who supported labor reforms. Calling them "goody goody, milk and water sort of men" drawn into the "labor agitators' net," Bowers contemptuously dismissed reformers as "pious frauds." "It will be a happy day for the business men, who are the only true friends the laboring men have, when a lot of these social fanatics are placed in lunatic asylums, and the muckrakers, labor agitators and the grafters are put in jail."[22]

Bowers's drive and faith in his own worldview dominated his personality. As a young man, he worked as a salesman in Binghamton, then became a partner in a soap business and later a grocery. The hard work took its toll on Bowers's health. At the urging of his doctors, he moved west around 1878 with his wife and their young son, Franck Taylor Bowers, then three. Bowers sounded out opportunities in Kansas and Nebraska before settling in Omaha, where he entered the about-to-boom real estate business. He and a partner bought up land on Omaha's outskirts, an area that with the extension of railroads was becoming a center for both stockyards and meatpacking. After a year, Bowers began selling farm implements and other heavy machinery. New arrivals drawn by both jobs and outlying farmland available for homesteading created a regional boom that left Bowers comfortably well-off though plagued by chronic appendicitis and indigestion that flared during times of stress.[23] When his health failed again around 1883, Bowers, who "had saved a pretty handsome little fortune," was able to retire "in a modest way" to a newly built farmhouse back in Maine, New York, where their second son, Clement Gray Bowers, was born in 1893.[24] Bowers was not yet forty years old.

While there were obvious advantages to working for Rockefeller, Bowers was not eager to join his nephew in the Rockefeller fold, despite their close relationship, which included shared vacations at Lake George in the Adirondacks. The first overtures came shortly after Gates set up shop in Rockefeller's office at Twenty-six Broadway. Bowers was offered a salary of $15,000 "to take an important place in Mr. Rockefeller's iron ore development in Duluth."[25] He declined "for several reasons" and later rejected another overture for an unspecified job on the Pacific Coast, where Rockefeller—at Gates's recommendation—was buying up vast swaths of timber forest.

In 1895, Bowers accompanied Gates on a trip to Cleveland to inspect Rockefeller's nascent Great Lakes shipping fleet. Although Bowers had no experience in shipbuilding or sailing, Rockefeller accepted Gates's recommendation that they entice him to run the operation. Exactly why Bowers took the job, after rejecting the earlier offers, is murky. The endeavor reeked of risk, which the conservative Bowers routinely avoided. Fear of failure led him to demand an unusual contract that "put my salary so low that in event I wanted to quit or I should fail, there would be no inducement in way of a big salary to remain."[26] He also arranged a schedule that allowed him to spend half his time on his own investments and business partnerships back in Binghamton, where his family remained; Bowers stayed at rooming houses when in Cleveland.

For all the uncertainty, Bowers proved to be a stunning success. Known as the Bessemer Steamship Co., and later the Rockefeller Fleet, the new ships were the largest on record for the Great Lakes, stretching longer than five hundred feet. Bowers made a habit of flouting conventions about workable ship sizes and construction methods, using his sharp analytical mind to see things that seasoned shipbuilders and designers often overlooked. Among them was replacing cast iron with lighter cast steel in the frames of the ships. Every ton of weight lost to the lighter material was replaced with an additional ton of ore, "which in the life of a ship amounts to a big sum of money. . . . We reduced something like a hundred tons on some ships, adding the same tonnage to their capacity."[27] Bowers also introduced performance bonuses for the captains, effectively co-opting their loyalty.

Across his career Bowers developed a reputation for scrupulousness. As an observant Baptist, he was offended by graft at a moral level, and he adhered to his belief that businessmen should behave ethically. Yet he was not above using power ruthlessly to force others to acquiesce to his wishes, and in fact saw such acts as necessary in the pursuit of ethical behavior. Confronted with rampant bribery to offload ships on Sundays at certain Great Lakes ports—particularly Buffalo's grain yards—Bowers forbade any Bessemer ships to be loaded or unloaded on that day. He further refused to give up berth space to companies that would pay the bribes and offload, effectively shutting the ports on the Sabbath. "I never paid one dollar nor did we ever unload a ship on Sunday, but won out every time and made good."[28] Bowers also found the opportunity to enrich himself, though apparently with Rockefeller's blessing. He designed a new anchor, which became an industry standard, eventually used worldwide. Bowers formed the separate, private L. M. Bowers & Co. to make the anchors and continued to invest in real estate, including in New York City.

His core work, though, was running Rockefeller's ships. Bowers eventually amassed a fleet of fifty-six ore haulers, the largest on the Great Lakes and the biggest single ore fleet in the world.[29] Rockefeller, as in most of his other businesses, soon monopolized Great Lakes shipping. But when Morgan bought out Rockefeller and Carnegie in 1901, Bowers was out of a job, or at least an assignment. He took on occasional projects for Rockefeller—including overseeing construction in Cleveland of the seventeen-story Rockefeller Building—but tended mostly to his own affairs until 1907, when he decided to move to Denver for health reasons. For once it was not his own health at issue but that of his wife, who suffered from tuberculosis. They hoped the dry air of the high plains would help her recover.

In November 1907, JDR Jr. and Gates completed Welborn's transition from power to figurehead. Gates wrote to Bowers in November informing him that he would become the vice president of CF&I, a title that was more cover than description. Gates was already secretly sending copies to Bowers of all his communications with Welborn, and he warned his uncle that CF&I officials would likely treat him as an "interloper." It was clear that Bowers was in charge, and within a year he had the official labels: vice president, treasurer, and chairman of the board.[30]

Bowers's first task in Colorado was to try to grasp the scope of CF&I's operations. As he did in Cleveland, Bowers tried to overlay his ethical template on the organization. One of the first programs to go, or at least to have its budget slashed, was the Sociological Department Dr. Corwin had established, "a change in policy that reflected . . . Bowers's conviction that employee benefits were unnecessary frills."[31] Conditions in the camps, already difficult, became worse. Bowers embraced the Rockefeller management philosophy of hiring people then leaving them alone to do their work, which had a deleterious effect on the mine camps, given the absolute power of the mine superintendents.

Bowers and other officials at CF&I's home office in Denver's Boston Building rarely, if ever, traveled into the coalfields, relying on the superintendents' reports passed up through district managers. It seems, in retrospect, to have been a function of willful ignorance. Complaints lodged over superintendents' conduct were ignored; dismissed miners found deaf ears for their appeals. Bowers, said Gaddis, the minister and one-time

CF&I sociological director, "told me his men in the Boston Building did not take complaints over each other's heads; and that the camp regime was the same. . . . [Bowers felt] that to grant the right of appeal with the types of characters whom they had to deal was to invite chaos." While Welborn disagreed with Bowers's approach, the Rockefellers' man in Denver set the tone. That placed near-ultimate authority in the hands of the mine super-intendents, "blasphemous bullies" who could "easily erect a wall between himself and the division manager. . . . At the bottom of the pit with pick and shovel, the miner frequently found a grafting pit boss on his back."[32]

Bowers also quickly moved to dismantle the company's political division, seeing in its structure both an opportunity for thievery and a misplaced use of power. In the 1904 election, Hearne had handed out $80,605 in CF&I cash. "So far as I can discover, not one particle of good was accomplished for the company; but Mr. Hearne was an aspirant for the position of United State[s] senator and devoted a vast amount of time and money with this end in view, I have no doubt." Bowers did not mention Farr by name but acknowledged CF&I's involvement with him. "A sheriff, elected by the votes of the C.F.&I. Co. employees, and who has been kept in office a great many years, established himself or became a partner in sixteen liquor stores in our coal mines. To clean up the saloons and with them the gambling halls and houses of prostitution, has been one of the things Mr. Welborn and I have devoted an enormous amount of time to. . . . The decent newspapers everlastingly lampooned the C. F.& I. Co. at every election; and I am forced to say the company merited, from a moral standpoint, every shot that was fired into their camp."[33] Bowers also reduced the company's spy network under Reno.

Bowers claimed to have ended CF&I's political maneuverings, yet he also bragged about pushing the state legislature to adopt during the winter of 1912–1913 a new mining law "almost entirely written" by a CF&I official and four other men. Still, CF&I's reputation for overt political string pulling led Bowers to advise Rockefeller against accepting an overture to invest in the *Pueblo Star-Journal;* its general manager, Frank S. Hoag, had asked Rockefeller for a $75,000 investment, at 4 percent interest, to help him buy the paper. Bowers warned his boss to stay away from the deal. "The C. F. & I. Co. would be immediately accused by the other newspapers of Pueblo, and of the southern counties of the state, as having taken a new tack in the control of politics."[34]

The letters that flowed between Denver and New York reveal Bowers's icy worldview. Bowers wrote to JDR Jr. in April 1909 recommending a 10 percent drop in wages at the Pueblo steel mill "whether the United States Steel Corporation do so or not." The letter comes close to evidencing at least covert collusion in fixing wages. Bowers also argued that a similar reduction in wages at CF&I's coal and iron ore mines would not be advisable unless unionized mines elsewhere in the country—the competition for laborers—dropped wages, too, which Bowers acknowledged was unlikely. The letter went on to display Bowers's disdain for his immigrant workers. "We can do this without violence to our sympathies because 66% of the employees at the mills are not Americans or American citizens by adoption but are over here for the purpose of selling their labor in the highest market in the world, and when they have a few hundred dollars to their credit in the banks of the countries from which they came, they will go back there to enjoy their bread and beer. . . . I always regret cutting the wages of laborers who have families to support and are trying to pay for homes and educate their children but considering these foreigners who do not intend to make America their home, and who live like rats in order to save money, I do not feel that we ought to maintain high wages in order to increase their income and shorten their stay in this country."[35] That Bowers felt comfortable adopting such a tone to JDR Jr. suggests an expectation that the scion of Twenty-six Broadway shared, or at least was sympathetic to, his own views.

Bowers drew just as firm a line in keeping union organizers on the outside, as though fending off a siege, and he was ready to see the invisible hand of international anarchy behind any event. On October 8, 1910, some six months after a strike in the northern fields had begun, an explosion at CF&I's Starkville mine near Trinidad killed "upwards of 30 men" working in "one of our oldest and safest mines," Bowers wrote to Gates—the loyal man on the ground letting the home office know about significant developments.[36] His count was premature: Fifty-six men ultimately died in the blast. Eight months earlier a blast had ripped through the company's Primero mine, killing seventy-five workers.

Bowers wrote to Gates two days after the Primero blast that it was "probably caused by some miner smuggling in pipe and matches, the use of which is prohibited. The mine was thoroughly ventilated, but, like most soft coal mines, has pockets of gas that are struck which causes explosions, and then the dust ignites and havoc follows. The latest reports indicate that the mine is not damaged, and work will resume as soon as the miners get over the excitement." But after the Starkville disaster, Bowers was seeing union saboteurs in the shadows. "There has been a suspicion in our minds that the disaster at Primero was the work of enemies of non-union miners," Bowers wrote to Gates. He cited the dynamiting of the *Los Angeles Times* building a week earlier by the McNamara brothers, killing twenty-one, and a recent fire at a mine tipple owned by the Victor-American Fuel Co., which "increases the suspicion lurking in our minds."[37]

In a later letter to Twenty-six Broadway, Bowers was even more direct in discussing an explosion at the Model mine operated by the American Smelting & Refining Co., which Bowers said had taken steps to dampen explosive dust within the mine. "No cause has ever been discovered for the explosion, so far as we have been able to learn. I will say confidentially, however, that it is the opinion of a good number of men that that disaster, as well as the one at Starkville, was caused by dynamite being placed in the mines under the direction of the gang referred to in this letter." The "gang" was union organizers, "little less than desperadoes." An Idaho jury's acquittal five years earlier of the WFM's Big Bill Haywood and other union leaders in the bombing death of former governor Frank Steunenberg "has made these murderers bolder than ever before. They are in politics and with pen and voice are whooping it up for their pal Roosevelt, who is a thousand times more dangerous in his un-American and anarchistic utterances than Herr Most and all of the other anarchists that have ever landed on American soil. I wish I had one-tenth part the hatred for the devil that I have for this infernal blatherskite."[38]

Bowers went on to say that he would update Gates when "we have found out the loss of life and the condition of the mine. The men were probably working about two miles and a half from the Starkville entrance, and as the wreckage is generally most serious at the entrance, and as we have been able to go in over 7,000 feet, we are hoping that the damage to the mine is not extensive."

Nowhere did he express concern for the fate of the miners, or the families of the dead.

Around the time Bowers was moving west to Denver, a Pennsylvania-born miner named John R. Lawson was moving from Denver to the southern coalfields. Lawson wasn't going to dig coal, though. A member of the UMWA's international board, he was heading south to organize the miners.

Standing over six feet, three inches, Lawson was precise about his appearance, "always perfectly groomed," his close friend the journalist Barron Beshoar recalled. "Every hair was just always in place. John Lawson never needed a haircut." In later years, Lawson often sent his suits ahead on trips to keep them from getting creased in his luggage, an odd touch of dandyism for a man accustomed to life in the dirt and grime below ground and the deprivations of coal camps above. Lawson's precision extended to his demeanor—smart and unflappable even during intense negotiations or at flashpoints of violence. "He was an extremely soft-spoken man. Some, when they lose their tempers, shout and yell," Beshoar said. "The madder John got, the softer his voice became. When he had gone to where it was barely audible, that was time to get out."[39]

Lawson came to the Colorado coalfields by a circuitous route. He was born in Mahanoy Township in Pennsylvania's Schuylkill County in 1871, the third of nine children born to coal digger John Lawson Sr. and Margaret Lawson, who had immigrated from Scotland two or three years earlier.[40] The elder Lawson began working in Pennsylvania's anthracite district during the infamous Molly Maguires' campaign of terror; the younger Lawson was born two years before McParlan, the Pinkerton detective, infiltrated the group. The father worked first around Mahanoy but within a few years had moved his family to Mount Carmel, in nearby Northumberland County. It's unclear whether the father supported the Maguires, but he was clearly a union man. When the Knights of Labor arose after the Maguires collapsed, the elder Lawson signed on.

At the age of eight, young John Lawson quit school and followed his father into the Mount Carmel coal mines as a "slate picker" in the Reading Railroad's Alaska Mine coal breaker, earning fifty cents a day in a six-day workweek plucking rocks inadvertently mixed in with the coal as it traveled down a chute. Two years later Lawson took his place below ground, signing up at the Reliance mine as a trapper boy tending subterranean ventilation doors. Lawson dreamed of becoming a mining engineer, and at night he studied math and coal mining through a correspondence course from the Scranton School of Mines.

Lawson was exposed to broader ideas through Sunday school at the family's Presbyterian church, where the teacher maintained a small library from which Lawson was allowed to borrow books. Like many other immigrant parents, Lawson's mother and father wanted a better life for him than he could expect from mining, and just before his seventeenth birthday Lawson was shipped off to Philadelphia to join his older brother, Colin, as an apprentice to a stonecutter. But Lawson had mining in his blood, and in 1895, at age twenty-four, he moved with his father to Roseburg, Oregon, where they joined a handful of other coal miners to buy a lease on a mine outside of town, an attempt to seize control of their own work lives. As they readied the mine for opening, one of the landowners backed out and refused to sign the lease. The project collapsed. The Lawsons, out of cash, moved on to Rock Springs, Wyoming, where they signed on as miners with the Union Pacific Coal Co.'s Mine No. 9, before heading south to Walsenburg to work in CF&I's massive Walsen mine.

Jeff Farr was just assuming his self-built throne as Huerfano County sheriff, and Walsenburg was an open town, offering the miners more of a semblance of normal life than the quasi-prisons of the remote mine camps. Still, coal, and the coal bosses, prevailed, reflecting coal's importance to the city's economic health. Maps of the mine detail a deep labyrinth below the dirt streets of Walsenburg, as though the city were laid out both above and below ground. Other, smaller mines also dotted the landscape, dominated by a large rise of land called the Hogback just north and west of the heart of the village, separating it from a wide bowl of land that held yet more independent mines.

Lawson chafed at conditions in the corporate-owned Walsen mine, and he and his father soon left for a small independent mine in New Castle, a remote Western Slope mining town hugging the banks of the Colorado River about 170 miles from Denver. There, he met Olive B. Hood, the daughter of a Scottish landscaper.[41] They married October 2, 1898, in New Castle; the elder Lawson returned to Pennsylvania.

The next spring, Lawson and his wife traveled to Philadelphia and stayed through the summer and winter. The couple's only child, daughter Fern, was born January 13, 1900. With added responsibilities, Lawson returned to Colorado and in June was living with his wife's father in Cripple Creek, trying his hand at gold mining.[42] He soon moved on to New Castle, where he hired on as a coal miner at Perry Coryell's Slope mine.[43]

Coryell, who also published a local newspaper, the *New Castle Nonpareil*, was a regional figure of some ambition and had a sneaky violent streak. In September 1892, Coryell was embroiled in a local campaign for county commissioner when he and the editor of a rival newspaper attacked each other in a series of tit-for-tat articles. Coryell escalated the dispute one night when he walked up behind the rival editor, Henry J. Holmes, as he was talking with someone on a Glenwood Springs street and cracked him across the back of the skull "with a loaded cane. Holmes fell to his knees when Coryell struck him again felling him to the ground. Holmes staggered to his feet and grappled with Coryell, wrenched the cane away and gave him a beating. They were fighting like demons when parted."

Both men were arrested, but Coryell was adjudicated the instigator—"the court characterizing the assault as a brutal, cowardly one"—and was fined thirty-five dollars plus costs.[44]

In a small mining town like New Castle, it is unlikely Lawson signed on with Coryell blind to the mine owner's questionable nature. Lawson and a friend quit over unsafe conditions and fears that Coryell did not know how to run a mine. The two-man walkout proved to be prescient, if not lifesaving. A few weeks later, Coryell's mine was wracked by an explosion that killed two miners and injured half a dozen more. But Lawson needed to earn money, and prospects were slim. He signed on with another Coryell mine farther up in the mountains above New Castle; that mine was hit by a strike after Coryell cut the rate he paid the miners for shoring up the mine roofs with wood. In 1901, Lawson gave up on Coryell and went to work for the Boston Colorado Coal Company's Mine No. 7 in South Canyon, about seven miles east of New Castle.

In 1903, when the statewide mine strike began, Lawson emerged as one of the local leaders. Lawson, his wife, and their three-year-old daughter were living in a standard miner's cabin at the time. The bedroom was small, so Olive Lawson had moved the bed and other bedroom furniture into the dining room, where the family slept. At 4:47 A.M. on Thursday, December 17, just over a week before Christmas, the family was blasted from its sleep by a bomb left outside what the bomber likely assumed was the bedroom. Lawson recalled that "the entire side of the building . . . was blown out, or blown in, as the case may be."[45] A photo of the house shows the damage to have been less extensive: The windows were damaged and the outer layer of clapboard sheared off. Still, the attempt to kill was clear. It was one of five bombs detonated that morning, placed under or against the outside walls of the poorly built homes of strike leaders. No one was injured seriously despite the power of the blasts, and the miners quickly appointed Lawson and others to a committee to investigate the crimes. The committee in turn hired an investigator, and together they compiled evidence and a list of suspects connected with Coryell, who was missing some eighty-five pounds of dynamite from one of his mines. The motive: Coryell blamed the UMWA for an earlier explosion at one of his mines, even though state inspectors ruled the blast an accident.[46] The strikers' committee presented its findings to Garfield County district attorney John C. Gentry, who Lawson later said told him there was enough evidence to charge some of the men.[47] Yet no one was ever arrested.

When the strike ended, Lawson found himself targeted. Shortly after he started working at one mine, the works were sabotaged and he was fired. It happened again at a second mine, and then a third, sabotage trailing him wherever he went. Soon no one would hire him. Leaving his family behind, Lawson tried his luck in Nevada for a few months but returned to New Castle to find that Coryell had published articles in his *Nonpareil* newspaper criticizing him, including one that Coryell apparently wrote himself claiming that he had driven Lawson from the district. Lawson encountered the author of another of the articles, whom he described as "a little fellow that weighed about 230 pounds," on the street.[48] Lawson demanded an explanation, and "he struck me." After the fight, Coryell wrote another article that "challenged me to meet him." Lawson and Coryell crossed paths at a New Castle barbershop about four days later, though it is unclear whether it was prearranged or by chance. Coryell "invited" Lawson to step out into the street, where he pulled a shotgun from beneath a lap robe in his buggy and shot Lawson in the lower abdomen, critically wounding him. Coryell was arrested but never prosecuted. Word of the shooting spread through the mine camps, though, cementing Lawson's image as a tough and dedicated union man willing to face down a mine owner's shotgun.

Lawson recovered slowly, and it was several months before he could return to work. When he did, it wasn't much of a job, digging away at a small, foot-wide coal seam in the Palisade mine some sixty-five miles west of New Castle. But Lawson also immersed himself in union politics, and in the fall of 1905 he won election to the UMWA's international executive board representing District 15. He left the mines to become a full-time organizer. His first assignment was the Durango Field in La Plata County, in the southwest corner of the state, where he organized three locals in two weeks and successfully negotiated a two-year contract.

When not working out of the Denver UMWA office, Lawson spent most of his time floating among the coalfields, talking to miners and trying to organize union locals. One of the places he visited in 1907 was Walsenburg, near the CF&I Walsen mine in which he worked when he first arrived in Colorado. After a few days of surreptitious meetings with miners, a "Mr. Johnson" approached Lawson on the street, claiming to have been appointed by a committee of local businessmen, and warned him to leave town. Lawson laughed him off, though another unidentified organizer heeded the implied threat and left on the next morning's train. A few days later, two of Sheriff Farr's deputies accosted Lawson on the street. One of them pressed a small silver-plated revolver against Lawson's coat and then charged him with possessing a concealed weapon. Lawson was jailed overnight, denied access to a lawyer or a telephone, and convicted in a speedy court appearance the next morning. He spent a week in Farr's jail before a union lawyer could spring him by appealing the conviction. The case languished; the appeal was never scheduled for a hearing, and the matter apparently was never resolved.[49]

Lawson changed his base to Trinidad, in neighboring Las Animas County and out of Farr's direct reach. But confrontations continued there, and Lawson closed up shop and headed back to Denver in 1908. He moved his family into a small, six-hundred-square-foot house in a working-class neighborhood on Xavier Street, northwest of downtown. Lawson worked out of the District 15 offices in the downtown German-American Trust Company Building at Seventeenth Street and Lawrence. But he spent much of his time in the adjoining Weld, Boulder, and Jefferson counties, where the dynamic was somewhat different than in Huerfano and Las Animas counties. If the UMWA was going to bring Colorado under the union banner, the place to start, union leaders decided, was in the northern field.

THREE

Trouble in the Fields

The same year Lawson moved his family to Denver, the UMWA won a rare contract at the Northern Coal and Coke Co.'s lignite mines in the northern fields, where different mines paid different rates depending on how hard or easy their coal beds were to mine. When the contract expired in 1910, the UMWA pressed for a 5.5 percent raise and standardized rates across the mines. Northern rejected the demands, viewing them as the UMWA's stance at the opening of negotiations, and waited for a response. But the UMWA wasn't in a negotiating mood. The union had already set up a strike-benefit fund of $400,000, and on April 1 the miners walked off the job, emboldened in part by recent strikes that gained a 5.5 percent raise for one hundred thousand miners in Illinois, Kansas, Missouri, Arkansas, and Oklahoma.[1] The strike quickly spread to other, smaller mines across the northern field.

In response, Northern hired the Baldwin-Felts Detective Agency—A. C. Felts, brother of one of the founders, was dispatched to the strike zone—for protection and reconnaissance and began importing scabs.[2] Northern also hurried to fence off its mines, creating in essence guarded mine camps in Lafayette, Louisville, and Superior.[3] When strikers began accosting strikebreakers as they arrived at the train station, Northern had trolley tracks extended into its Lafayette compound. "In some instances, the miners took their wives with them, in many instances their families. And the women folks would undertake to leave the enclosure to go to the Post Office for their mail, or to go to church, or the children would undertake to go somewhere—to school. They were all assaulted [the youngsters by strikers' children]. They were called vile names. A state of insurrection existed."[4] Northern approached Boulder County sheriff M. P. Capp for protection. When he refused to make any efforts beyond basic law enforcement, company officials branded him a labor supporter and went to court seeking an injunction against the strikers.

Insurrection, though, lies in the eye of the beholder. After hearing strike reports, Colorado secretary of state James B. Pearce, who by nature of his office was also the state labor commissioner, traveled to the northern fields on August 19, 1910, to investigate.[5] He concluded that there was no "state of insurrection" and that Capp, rather than being a union supporter or the opposite, like Farr, a coal operators' tool, was a "real sheriff, and that he was fearlessly and impartially giving his time to preserve the peace." Pearce concluded that the mine operators had seized on minor acts and embellished them for political ends. Working miners with cash in their pockets gravitated to local saloons; miners on strike tended to stay home. "Officers of the union were exercising their best influences over the men, constantly urging them to obey the law, keep sober, and do nothing that would injure their cause with the general public, well knowing that they had everything to lose and nothing to gain by unlawful acts." Reports of children harassing each other were inflated to seem like mass upheaval. "A few instances of where children called 'scab' at different people as they were passing by a street or alley was exaggerated into the most dangerous condition of lawlessness, and designing persons were using these instances as a basis for a demand on the Governor to send the State militia into the field to preserve order where nothing but the best order already prevailed."

Forcing the governor to dispatch troops would achieve two ends: The public would perceive the act as proof that the miners were riotous and needed quelling, calling into question their reasons for walking out in the first place, and the presence of the militia would shift the cost of maintaining security to the state. But Pearce made it clear that the biggest threat to security in the region came from Baldwin-Felts, which "had shipped in a number of gunmen, who constantly went armed, and, from their general demeanor in some instances, where I observed them, appeared to invite trouble. . . . There were instances where some of these men would go into the towns with their arms conspicuously displayed, which served as an irritant, and was not conducive to good feeling."

Not all the bad feelings were engendered by the gunmen. Strikers were responsible for repeated altercations, beatings, and acts of intimidation as they sought to force scabs from the field. The Baldwin-Felts gunmen and company mine guards used similar tactics to try to demoralize the strikers. The company's strategists used any interaction between strikers and strikebreakers as evidence that the strikers were a threat to law and order, even as company spies acted as instigators. The Northern Coal and Coke Co. found a sympathetic judge, Greeley W. Whitford of Denver, who in November 1910 issued an injunction against the striking miners "that forbade us to do anything, in fact, but eat or sleep," one man recalled.[6] Specifically, the injunction barred the strikers from accosting strikebreakers, gathering in large groups, picketing, or using signs, placards, or any other means to try to intimidate strikebreakers into quitting the mines. When altercations continued anyway, the judge issued broad warrants to round up strike leaders on contempt charges even though they were not involved in the actions themselves. After a fight on the streets of Lafayette on December 17, 1910, warrants were issued for sixteen uninvolved strikers, mostly union leaders, on charges of violating the injunction. Another round of arrests came July 14, 1911. In both cases, many of the miners were sentenced to a year in jail. They had only served a few months when Whitford ordered them released as his initial order moved up through the appellate courts; the release made the appeals moot and ensured that no other judge would rule on Whitford's actions.

One of the men arrested was Ed Doyle, a union coal miner from Spring Hill, Illinois, who moved to Lafayette in September 1907, joining a brother in Colorado's northern field.[7] The next year his father, also a coal miner, was killed by a runaway tram in an Illinois mine, and Doyle moved his mother, three sisters, and another brother to join him in the Colorado coalfields. Doyle, who had served as a union vice president and a mine check weighman in Illinois, quickly assumed a leadership role in UMWA Local 1388 as a weighman. When the strike began, Doyle, the family's sole breadwinner, moved west to Washington state and worked there for four months, but the rain drove him back to Colorado in August, and the next month he was elected president of the on-strike UMWA local. Doyle also kept a journal, detailing a near-daily regimen of fights and gunfire, reports of scabs leaving the mines or scabs signing up for work, and mine fires, accidents, and death.[8]

In one entry, Doyle records that around dusk on October 5, 1910, striking miner Robert Davis rushed into the dusty heart of Lafayette sounding the alarm on horseback like a modern Paul Revere. A detachment of armed scabs and mine guards was headed for town, he warned. The strikers scrambled for their own guns and gathered at City Hall, awaiting the parade.

"About 30 scabs on foot came into town with some guns in their belts, an auto with Baldwin thugs acted as guides," Doyle wrote. "The auto contained several rifles. All the scabs were herded into [the] Bermonts and VanDerberg Store. In the meantime, the citizens spread along the sidewalk from the City Hall to the union hall (one block)." After a short time, the scabs left the store and walked silently back down the street. "They come to the walk guarded by the gun-auto, marched right through, and neither side uttered a word," Doyle wrote. "In about 10 minutes they again passed the [City and union] halls." A county sheriff's deputy hailed the gun car and spoke quietly with the Baldwin-Felts men. "The scabs and auto then moved on and out of town." The strikers dispersed.

The next morning, a union sympathizer living about a mile outside of town "told us that just at dark a huge body of men gathered at the Capitol boarding house and with their guns, came to the outskirts of town and laid down in the field. It was then plain to see that the plans were that we would drive the small bunch out of town, and meet our deaths by being shot from ambush."

The UMWA was not the "one big union" the Wobblies advocated, but it was large and powerful. From its headquarters in Indianapolis, the union deployed organizers, agitators, and the occasional high official to work toward contracts in various places, which created a small but significant cadre of people who knew conditions in coalfields across jurisdictions. Similarly, the mine operators were not operating in vacuums. Some mining companies were individually held, but many were owned by financial consortiums that included investors with stakes in Colorado, West Virginia, Pennsylvania, and Indiana. That they shared information is a safe conclusion, and with the transience of union people, strikebreakers, and corporate agents, there developed something of a floating community of competing activists who moved from flashpoint to flashpoint bringing news of other showdowns with them. Local newspapers in mine districts also routinely carried wire-service stories about goings-on elsewhere, a rich stream of information. For the kind of intelligence that didn't make the papers, both the mine operators and the unions used networks of spies and sympathizers—many of whom, like the union organizers and private detectives, moved from coalfield to coalfield as union drives waxed and waned.

Charles E. Lively played a minor role in the southern Colorado strike, but his path through the coal mines illuminates the extent of the spying over a number of years. Lively became a miner at age thirteen in his native West Virginia, around 1902, and eventually joined the UMWA. By 1912, he was collecting a second paycheck from Baldwin-Felts for "secret service" work, flitting from hot spot to hot spot to spy on the union and its organizers in Illinois, Oklahoma, Kansas, and Colorado.[9] He ran for and won election as vice president of the UMWA local in La Veta, just west of Walsenburg, where he "was working on a murder case" during the 1913 strike when he killed a man and was arrested. Rather than pull strings to have the case dismissed—an easy task even for an undercover Baldwin-Felts man in Jeff Farr's Huerfano County—Lively let the case languish and spent sixteen months in the county jail and secretly reporting to his Baldwin-Felts handlers on jailhouse conversations with and among other incarcerated miners. Lively eventually pleaded guilty to involuntary manslaughter and was sentenced to time served and released.[10]

After the Colorado coal war, Lively returned to West Virginia so deeply undercover he was fired by a Mingo County mine boss who believed him to be too friendly with a known union agitator. Lively then rented space on the ground floor of the UMWA offices in Matewan and opened a restaurant catering to organizers, union officials, and local supporters such as police chief Sid Hatfield, a union sympathizer and one of several men involved in the infamous 1920 Matewan shootout in which seven Baldwin-Felts men—including A. C. and another Felts brother—and the mayor and three other local men were killed.[11] Lively's role as a spy did not become known until he began testifying against union members and sympathizers, including Hatfield, in trials related to the Matewan massacre. Lively defended his role as similar to that played by Pinkerton's McParlan when he infiltrated the Molly Maguires.

In his own testimony, Lively described a cloak-and-dagger existence in which he would occasionally mail reports to post office boxes in Bluefield, Virginia, where the agency was based, using the names of nonexistent companies. Other times he would send reports to fake names for ersatz girlfriends in another town, all designed to avoid arousing suspicions among possible union sympathizers in the post office. Once Lively began testifying, the UMWA suspended him "for 99 years," a better fate than Lively suspected he would have met had the union discovered his spying while he was still within their reach. "I think they would have turned me over to the undertaker."[12] In 1921, Lively and an array of other Baldwin-Felts gunmen assassinated Hatfield and another man, Ed Chambers, as the unarmed men climbed the steps for a court appearance in nearby Montgomery County. Lively and two others were acquitted of those assassinations, but the general perception was that they had killed the two men at the behest of Baldwin-Felts and local mine owners.

For some, trouble in the mines was seen as a financial opportunity, and they offered themselves out for bid. Union officials bribed an unidentified Denver journalist seventy-five dollars a month to get stories about union activities into print in hopes of riling mine operators.[13] Doyle and other union officials believed that goading the mine operators into acting against the miners would help persuade the workers that they needed the union.

Other opportunists came to the union. On October 13, 1910, a Robert S. Scott of Florence, Colorado, wrote to the UMWA's secretary-treasurer, William Crawford, in Denver offering his services.[14] "I want to inform you that I am a special agent for a rail road. But while I am a detective I am neither a scab nor a scab herder. A certain agency in Denver [the Globe Inspection Co.] who knows me and knows of my position, offered me a job the other day as a side line. It would seem as though this outfit has a gang of thugs in their employ who would do Detective work if someone would do the clerical work for them. The offer made me was, keep a lookout for places where those thugs could be used to the best advantage to keep tab on certain secret organizers, and keep in touch with the general union move." Scott wrote that he had not yet responded to the offer from Globe. "I just thought I would write you, and see if their offer could be used to advantage in any way."

It isn't clear whether the union signed him up, but Doyle's personal records include several reports from spies within the detective agencies. One letter seems to be an internal report from the Burns Detective Agency office in Denver to the Atlanta headquarters arranging a meeting between CF&I's Bowers and W. J. Burns.[15] Another letter, coincidentally dated the day Lippiatt was killed in Trinidad, was to A. C. Felts and is signed cryptically: "Yours truly, From the one who conferred with you August 12. Should you desire my services, give me a number." The substance of the letter was a request for a raise from an unspecified amount to sixty dollars, citing the work as "a very risky business."

The companies had the advantage in the spy competition, gauging by the ranks of some of their moles. Doyle wrote a detailed prestrike letter to UMWA president John White on March 11, 1913, accusing Frank Smith, former UMWA District 15 president, of being a company spy.[16] After describing several suspicious incidents, Doyle reported that even while Smith was out of work and on two-dollars-a-day union relief, his family patronized Denver theaters and other entertainments and "he continued to drink and keep company with lewd women . . . in the same manner he had while District president." Doyle included details from a letter found near Smith's home (the location was not specified) that was neither signed nor addressed by name but was clearly a communication from a handler to a spy and included a receipt for $150 deposited in the First National Bank "for salary and expenses for February, 1913." Rather than expose Smith, Doyle suggested the union should set him up an as unwitting conduit of disinformation the union wanted to spread to the mine operators. Doyle also recruited spies of his own from outside the district.

Given the number of spies, operatives, and organizers involved, cross-pollination was no surprise. In West Virginia, Walter Belk, the Baldwin-Felts man, worked with a private detective by the name of Coates in an ultimately failed attempt to find evidence to get a local judge indicted. Coates reappeared in Trinidad during the 1913–1914 strike with C. D. Elliott, another West Virginia alum. All three men were staying in the Toltec Hotel. Belk recognized Coates, who was using the name R. W. Carruthers. Elliott "was posing as a writer for an eastern magazine and Carruthers—Coates—was posing as working on the same line. They only remained in Trinidad about a week or 10 days. I talked with Elliott shortly after his arrival there. He was making a very close inquiry of George Tittsworth," a notorious mine guard and Las Animas deputy sheriff. Belk stumbled across Coates a few days later in Walsenburg. "In a joking way I told him that I was very much surprised to see him out here fighting with the dynamiters and cut-throats, when in West Virginia he was on the other side, and he just said that he would unearth something some day that would be quite a surprise."[17] There is no indication that Belk ever outed either man.

The strike limped along in the northern field. Union miners were unable to keep the coal operators from replacing them; statewide coal production had dropped 20 percent after the strike began but quickly regained about half of the loss. Many strikers, broke, were living in tents and shacks. In towns like Frederick and Boulder, strikers struggled to pay bills and sought other jobs, some leaving the district to take up with mines elsewhere.

Edwin Brake, the deputy labor commissioner, watched the strike from Denver, staying out of the fray for most of the summer in the belief that the public welfare was not at risk during the warm months. But as fall neared, and the strike continued without negotiations, Brake tried to draw the two sides together. On August 24, 1910, he wrote a letter to Smith, the UMWA District 15 president in Denver, and to F. F. Struby, president of the Northern Coal and Coke Co., and three other companies under strike, asking if each side would form a negotiating committee to meet with the other. Smith responded the next day, writing in a conciliatory tone that the union had been willing to negotiate from the beginning—ignoring the fact that the strike began when the UMWA refused to extend the previous contract while talks continued.[18]

Struby took his time, finally responding August 30 in a letter cosigned by the presidents of other companies under strike: the National Fuel Co., the Parkdale Fuel Co., and Evans Coal and Fuel Co. The operators denied they had any disputes with the workers, taking an almost childish tone. "We beg to state that no differences exist between us and our present employees. . . . We assume, however, that your communication has reference to the United Mine Workers of America, who were in our employ prior to April 1st, last." The operators then accused the UMWA of walking out without giving them the opportunity to negotiate "arbitrary and unreasonable demands . . . because we would not concede the same." So they replaced their workers. Brake urged arbitration. Smith of the UMWA agreed; Struby responded that since the companies had no quarrels with their current workers, they had no need to seek arbitration. After more back and forth, the operators agreed that, as they recruited fresh nonunion miners from the East they would give preferential hiring for future openings "to our former employes who are capable and desirable."

If the operators seemed intransigent, the UMWA's own recalcitrance was made clear in a letter from an independent mine that had been hit by the strike. M. P. Fox, owner of the Matchless Coal Co., wrote to Brake that he had met with Smith at Fox's home on August 26 and agreed to meet the union demands for a wage hike. On September 14, the union voted to reject the offer, "declining to permit their men to go to work in our mine, or any other, until all the operators of the northern field had accepted their terms." But with the main operators holding firm, and mine operations nearing prestrike levels, it became clear that the union needed a fresh strategy if it was to avoid a debilitating defeat similar to the 1903–1904 strike. So in December 1911, UMWA officials meeting in Chicago agreed to expand the strike to the southern field, hoping to close down nearly all of Colorado's coal mining operations to bring added pressure on the mine owners.

The union decided to open an office in Trinidad, and sent John McLennan, who would soon become president of UMWA District 15, to set it up, a difficult task in a tense environment. CF&I officials got wind of the union's plan and persuaded the local chamber of commerce to convene a special a meeting to hear the mine operators' plea that local businesses keep the organizers out of town. "The chamber of commerce refused to accede."[19] But McLennan still had trouble finding office space: Once landlords found what the rooms were needed for, advertised space was suddenly unavailable. The UMWA finally found room on the second floor of the Packer Block, two blocks north of the city's main intersection, and got to work with four organizers.

The coal operators continued to track the union's moves, and Bowers was planning for the likelihood of the strike spreading to the southern fields. "While we hope to avoid a strike, it is the part of wisdom for us to be prepared should it come. It will be either a long, bitter fight, or submission to unreasonable demands and dictation" by labor radicals. At the time, CF&I was pulling in money at a comfortable clip, and rather than increasing dividends to shareholders Bowers recommended investing in a new open-hearth furnace, presumably at Pueblo, to be ready to meet the increased demand he believed would come with the next upswing in economic development. And it would be wise, he counseled, to stockpile cash until the labor troubles were resolved. If a strike did occur, "[t]his would deprive us of income from our coal operations and partially or entirely close our steel works temporarily. . . . [W]ith a large cash surplus and a million or two invested in our own bonds and securities, we could pull through a strike or business depression."[20]

The union was similarly making plans and began looking for organizers among its ranks to work the southern field. Lawson tapped Mike Livoda, a Croatian immigrant working in the Lyden mine near Golden, outside Denver. By March 1912, Livoda was attracting Farr's attention in Walsenburg, and he was savagely beaten.[21] A few months later, CF&I officials drafted a fake letter discrediting Livoda and circulated it among its mine superintendents, with instructions they show it to Slavic and other

Eastern European miners in an effort to marginalize Livoda. Lawson learned of the ruse, and CF&I quickly withdrew the letter before he could expose it.[22]

If Bowers knew what was happening in the mine district, he didn't share it in any great written detail with Twenty-six Broadway. "We are always fearful of strikes on the part of the miners, as the lawless agitators are on the alert and we never can tell when trouble will come, their effort to unionize our coal miners being unceasing," he wrote to JDR Jr. at the end of a letter updating his boss on CF&I's financial performance. "Our men are well paid, well housed, and every precaution known taken to prevent disaster. So far as we can learn, they are satisfied and contented, but the constant dogging on their heels by agitators, together with the muckraking magazines and trust-busting political shysters, has a mighty influence over the ignorant foreigners who make up the great mass of our ten thousand miners. Still, everything now seems to be favorable and the outlook good."[23]

The UMWA thought the outlook was good, too, and it made its intentions clear. In early December 1912, just after Elias Ammons was elected Colorado governor, Lawson warned him that labor trouble was on the horizon. "I was told that very likely there would be a strike during my administration. . . . [H]e casually told me that. He said a strike would be called whenever they thought it was opportune, or something to that effect."[24]

Earlier that fall, UMWA vice president Frank J. Hayes had persuaded fellow union leaders to hire Adolph Germer as an international organizer, beginning November 16, 1912, to help in the southern district.[25] A Zelig-like figure in the American labor and socialist movements—he eventually would become a top official with the Congress of Industrial Organizations—Germer immigrated with his family from their native Germany in 1887, when he was six. They settled in Mount Olive, Illinois, where he eventually went to work as a coal miner.[26] An early union supporter, by the time of the 1912 presidential election he was an avid Socialist and backer of Eugene V. Debs's quadrennial presidential campaigns. Germer ran for office himself in that election, seeking an Illinois legislative seat, but lost.

By February 1913, Germer was meeting with miners in Colorado's southern field under a false cloak: "I was billed as a 'National Lecturer of the Socialist Party' . . . to disconnect the local organization." Germer found "things are rather delicate to handle. I feel confident that quite a percentage of the miners can be gotten into the organization, but I fear that the very moment we press organization work, it will mean the discharge of the most active members and this might involve the Union in a strike."[27] In a letter to a friend, Germer distilled the stakes more succinctly. "With the right kind of work those men can be organized, but the probability is that if we organize the men, we will organize a strike, for the very moment we press organization, the most active men will be discharged and of course the organization will then have to come to their rescue."[28]

Yet the southern mine operators were already responding. They brought in Baldwin-Felts detectives to fight the nascent organizing campaign, with the help of local officials like Sheriff Farr in Huerfano County and Sheriff Grisham in Las Animas County. In the first six months of the year, Farr swore in sixty-two new deputies, many of them Baldwin-Felts men, including Walter Belk (January 16), A. C. Felts (February 19), and a C. W. Belcher (June 20)—the initials likely an error referring to George W. Belcher, who with Belk killed UMWA organizer Gerald Lippiatt five weeks before the strike began. Farr also swore in three of his own relatives.

The pace was startling. Between January 10, 1911, and January 10, 1913, a span of two years, Farr deputized a total of 144 men. But in less than nine months between January 10, 1913, and September 1, 1913, the start of the strike, he deputized 326 men,[29] often in groups and rarely knowing anything about their pasts or whether they were the kind of people who ought to be running around with a gun and a badge of authority.[30] In fact, Farr and Sheriff Grisham in Las Animas County deputized anyone Baldwin-Felts hired. Farr was in daily talks with CF&I officials about the strike threat and sent the freshly deputized men to guard mine camps. None of his men was ever paid by Huerfano County; Farr assumed the mines were paying them even though they were his deputies.

Union backers recognized the threat that the newly deputized gunmen posed. In early August, the Trinidad Trades Assembly formally asked Sheriff Grisham to disarm the detectives and limit law enforcement to locals, which would effectively remove the Baldwin-Felts men from the field. Grisham did not respond publicly, and after Lippiatt's killing the Trades Assembly urged that the sheriff be recalled in a special election. Meanwhile, the union was arming its own organizers, getting them commissions as game wardens, which gave them official clearance to carry guns in the event a temporary ban was ordered.

Mine operators also sought to take the steam out of the organizing drive by complying with state laws they had previously ignored and granting a slight wage increase. In April 1912, CF&I and the other operators raised the basic tonnage rate by 10 percent, and in the spring of 1913 they instituted an eight-hour workday.[31] CF&I also announced it would no longer pay miners in company scrip (finally adhering to state law), though it instituted a "debit" system at its stores, advancing purchases and then taking the debt out of wages before they were paid.[32] Welborn and Osgood portrayed their companies' changes as the acts of caring and benevolent managers.[33] But Bowers, for one, was clear in his intent in a letter to Gates. "I know of no better way than to anticipate demands and do a little better by the men than they would receive if they belonged to the unions. This keeps them in line and reasonably happy."[34]

At the mines themselves, superintendents closely monitored their men. Germer and the other organizers had long been tagged as agitators and were poison for the miners to talk to. "Little or no active work can be done by myself or any other organizer among the men. Any association that we have with the men may mean their discharge. For the time being, in my opinion, all that is needed is a man in charge of the field who will stay here and take care of the office work." Germer believed the organizing would have to be clandestine. "Let the man in charge employ men of different nationalities to work in the mines and in a quiet way talk to the men. Then when the time comes to carry on the fight in the open, put a force of organizers to address meetings."[35]

Doyle had a similar idea, a simple yet extremely effective strategy of using the mine guards' and superintendents' zealotry to their own advantage. Beginning in May 1913, the union sent twenty-one two-man teams of organizers into the southern field. While one organizer worked openly to entice workers at a mine to join the union, the other got a job in the same mine and ingratiated himself with the bosses as an anti-union man, offering to pass along names of miners who were signing union cards. When the active organizer encountered a miner hostile to the union, he would give the name to the secret partner, who would lie to the bosses and identify the anti-union miner as a union supporter. Those who were sympathetic were left alone, unsigned but loyal.

Slowly, the bosses did the work for the organizers, unwittingly firing anti-union miners as the ranks slowly filled with secret supporters.

The lead-up to the strike itself seemed less a drama than a march to a preordained outcome. In July, the union appointed a strike policy committee of four men: Lawson; McLennan; Frank Hayes, the UMWA vice president; and Doyle, the journal keeper in the northern fields in 1910 who was now

District 15 secretary-treasurer. The committee was given broad authority to organize miners, negotiate with the mine operators, and call and direct a strike. Lawson and Hayes immediately announced plans to organize all twelve thousand miners in the southern field and lead them out of the mines.

In early August, the policy committee sought a meeting with the mine operators, using Governor Ammons as a go-between.[36] Ammons tried, but the session was a parody of a conference. The operators refused to meet the union officials face-to-face, holding to their view that any such meeting implied a recognition of the UMWA as the bargaining representative for the miners the coal operators employed. And the union refused to look at any proposal that did not include that very recognition.[37] Ammons promised to keep working on the problem and sent Brake, the deputy labor commissioner, to Trinidad on a fact-finding mission. "I want you to make a thorough investigation as to the probabilities of doing something to stop the strike."[38]

After Ammons's inconsequential efforts, the policy committee drafted a letter to miners in the district and flooded mailboxes with the announcement that "today is the day of your emancipation," encouraging all miners to join the UMWA.[39] Organizers also slipped into the camps at night, or met with miners out in the countryside away from the mine guards. Livoda and another organizer "come in somehow" to the mine camps in the canyons west of Ludlow—Hastings, Forbes, and Berwind— urging miners like Victor Bazanelli to pay seventy-five cents in monthly dues to ask the bosses to "quit those cruelties."[40] The organizers found eager audiences. "Ninety percent of the people signed up, secretly like." Bazanelli joined in July. Charles Costa, who was already working in the mines, became an on-site secret representative. "The union was trying to help us to get at least four dollars a day, and raise coal to seventy-five cents a ton, eight-hour [workdays] and less cruelty. That we could help each other out if one was fired for nothing."

Increasing wages was not an insignificant desire. But to many miners, daily indignities with no way to redress them seemed to matter more. Complaints fell on deaf ears—or got the miner turned out of his job. At one point, Brake assigned a labor commission inspector to visit a mine outside Aguilar after local miners formed a committee to demand the mine adopt a check weighman, as required by law. When the state inspector arrived and joined the committee in a meeting with the mine operator, the miners were summarily fired as agitators—a brazen response in front of a state labor official.[41] In the pits, supervisors rarely bothered to use miners' names, usually just ethnic slurs. "I know a guy worked in the mines for four years and never was called by his name," said Bazanelli. Miners' wives were easy prey for sexual predators among the guards and supervisors: To tell would mean to starve the family.

One guard, Robert Lee, was particularly notorious for targeting miners' wives and daughters, and for general brutality against miners. "He had never hesitated to beat one up, knock them in the head, abuse them and use them for his own conveniences." Around October 1912, while working as a deputy sheriff in the Segundo camp during a campaign to force saloonkeepers to obey Sunday closing laws, Lee became drunk and forced his way into the home of an Italian family who lived behind a saloon they operated. It was a Sunday, and the husband wasn't home. Lee forced the wife to open the bar for him to "help himself and some friends to drinks." During the binge Lee "insulted the daughter of the house." Toward evening, when he stepped outside and moved toward the rear of the building, someone hit him over the head with a heavy mining drill, nearly killing him.[42]

On August 7, the UMWA ratcheted up its efforts, deciding to move even more organizers—including Lippiatt—to the southern field. Camp social events such as dances were used as organizing meetings, the loud songs and merry-making a cover to deceive the guards and Baldwin-Felts men. One of the prime attractions was Mary Thomas, a young Welsh mother with a golden voice. Her husband had abandoned her and their two children in Wales three years earlier to make his fortune in Colorado. In the summer of 1913, with no prospects in Wales, she and the children arrived in the coal district planning to wring support from him until Thomas could open her own small business. Costa and his wife, Cedi, immediately swept Thomas into the organizing campaign without her knowledge; they invited and escorted her to parties and tent gatherings, where she would lead songs as organizers moved surreptitiously among the miners, proselytizing the cause.[43]

As the UMWA pushed its organizing drive, deputy labor commissioner Brake decided to make a personal survey of conditions in the southern field, timing his fact-finding trip to coincide with the State Federation of Labor convention planned to begin Monday, August 18. He arrived by train a little before eight on Saturday night. As Brake checked into the Toltec, he heard a commotion outside on Commercial Street. With others from the hotel, he ran out to see what the commotion was about. "I found that two deputy sheriffs had shot and killed Gerald Lippiatt," whom Brake described as a striking miner from the northern field. "The streets were filled with people and the shooting created quite a furor."[44]

Sunday morning, Brake met with officers of the Trinidad chamber of commerce. "They informed me of the terrible unrest that existed in the county, stating that they were very much dissatisfied themselves with the industrial condition, that they did not entirely blame the miners, but that they wanted to avoid a strike if it were possible." They urged Brake to use his influence with the State Federation of Labor to head off a showdown. Brake remained in Trinidad for a week, well after the labor conference ended, talking with miners, local residents, and anyone one else he thought might be able to offer some insight. Brake returned to Denver and met with Governor Ammons and Secretary of State Pearce, his direct boss, outlining his fears and expectations in the southern fields. He urged the governor to summon Sheriffs Farr and Grisham and order them to disarm both sides immediately. "I told him that the feeling was very intense, that the town of Trinidad was filled full of armed men, guards and detectives." Lippiatt's killing, he feared, had lit a fuse. "I apprehended if something was not done and done quickly, that there would be an outbreak there that would be disastrous."[45]

Ammons saw parallels to the Paint Creek strike. He wired his counterpart in West Virginia, Gov. Henry D. Hatfield, a Republican and backer of the region's coal giants, for a hint of what outcome he might expect. "Kindly wire me if recent miners' strike, your state, resulted in recognition of Miners' Union."[46] Privately, union organizers saw parallels to the West Virginia strike, too, and believed a walkout in southern Colorado was unavoidable. "The men are eager for the word [to strike] to be issued, in fact, they are getting restless," Germer wrote to White, the former UMWA president. Germer was part of a lineup of organizers and other union officials to speak at a Labor Day rally in Walsenburg that drew six hundred people, "the largest meeting of any kind ever held in town. . . . Quite a number of bosses and superintendents were present as well as several of the Baldwin-Felts. The meeting was originally billed in the open but I was told that sheriff Farr and his gang were organizing to break it up so I decided that we would have it indoors." After the site was moved, Farr's men sought to downplay the event, spreading word that no one would show up. "Now the gang is circulating the report that we are only bluffing, that we will never call a strike and that our only purpose in holding the meetings is to get members in order to get their money."[47]

Publicly, the union still tried to show that it was more interested in talking than striking. As rank-and-file miners seethed over the Lippiatt killing, the strike policy committee sent a letter to the mine operators individually asking them to meet with the UMWA to negotiate contracts, hoping to divide the alliance of owners. The tone was solicitous and sought to establish a common interest in labor peace. "We are no more desirous of a strike than you are, and it seems to us that we owe it to our respective interests, as well as to the general public, to make every honest endeavor to adjust our differences in an enlightened manner." The letter argued that formerly anti-union companies in other states had seen the light and entered into contracts with the UMWA, "and we are much pleased over the security and stability given to the industry through the medium of the trade agreement." It urged the operators to "meet now as friends and proceed to settle this entire controversy with honor to ourselves, with credit to our people, and with faith in each other."[48]

Only two operators, both small, responded. The three major players—Bowers and Welborn of CF&I, Osgood of Victor-American, and David W. Brown of the Rocky Mountain Fuel Co.—ignored the overture. The newspapers were filled with articles speculating about the likelihood of a strike. Both sides were preparing for a fight, not a conversation. On September 2, some eighteen miners were fired from the Delagua mine for attending Labor Day meetings the day before, the same day Mother Jones arrived in Trinidad, her first trip to the region in the present campaign.[49] The coal operators' heavy-handedness proved to be a good organizing tool for activists like Germer. "The companies here have resorted to the same tactics as the operators in West Virginia, discharging men whom they suspect of belonging to the union. . . . [T]o-day I was informed that thirty-five Greeks were marched out of another camp because they had expressed themselves in favor of the union. I fear that unless something is done within the next week or ten days, the men will come out [on strike] of their accord."[50]

While the union men were celebrating Labor Day, the company thugs were busy. The union office in Trinidad was burglarized that night, and thirty-five completed membership applications disappeared, though Germer did not link that act to the dismissal of the thirty-five Greek miners. Germer, who kicked himself for leaving such sensitive material unsecured, saw the crime as more evidence of the operators' fears of the union. "I did take the ledger and the organizers' reports so they got the names of only a few of our members. Every day the force of spotters [company spies] is increased and several of them have come to me and told me what good union men they are. The barons and their gang are more worried than we." Germer felt that support for the miners—or, at the least, opposition to the way coal operators were treating their men—was growing among local noncoal-business owners. "There was never a more hopeful situation in this state and we cannot afford to let the opportunity slip by such as presents itself now. We have the chance of a lifetime to do something for the Colorado miners and bring them to a place where they will be credit to their fellow workmen everywhere."

Bowers either was oblivious to what was happening in Trinidad or sought to hide it from Twenty-six Broadway. While vacationing in Binghamton, he wrote to the home office about the year's financial performance, expressing pleasure that the $1.65 million in net profits for CF&I's recently closed fiscal year were close to the previous record year and "would have exceeded 1912 if wages had not been advanced" to try to stave off the union organizers. He mentioned the labor situation as an afterthought. "There has been a group of labor-union agitators in southern Colorado for more than a month and threatening to call a strike for the purpose of securing a recognition of the western Federation of Miners," Bowers wrote, misidentifying the union. State political and business leaders had protested and "the matter has quieted down, though their national officials are still in Colorado. . . . This has kept us all in a state of unrest, so that my vacation has been a season of worry. A disaster of this sort would put us up against a fight that would be serious indeed."[51]

The "disaster" was closer than Bowers knew. Around the time he was writing his letter, the UMWA was shipping to Colorado the tents used to house evicted workers in the Paint Creek strike, and on September 10 the union bought another 150 tents from a local supplier. The union was also arranging for places to put those tents. Doyle's files show several payments to a man identified only as J. F. Smith for rents on a number of unspecified properties. It is likely Smith was either a union member or a sympathizer acting as a go-between with owners of pastureland near the mines, where the union planned to create tent villages once the strike began and the miners were evicted from their company-owned homes. On September 1, while the UMWA policy committee was still nominally seeking negotiations, Smith was paid $75 for "lease on land." The next day he was paid $100 for another lease, and on September 3 he received $150 more for leases identified as near the Segundo and Forbes mines. On September 6, Smith received $175 for a lease at Ludlow. Four more payments were made over the next two weeks, for a total of $785 on nine pieces of property, as well as $131.90 for "salary and expenses."

The Ludlow tent colony would become the strikers' main settlement, erected on a lot owned by John M. Dotson, a "stock raiser" and former postmaster at Ludlow.[52] It lay east of the C&SR rail tracks connecting Denver to Trinidad, and a few hundred yards north of a strip of buildings that formed Ludlow itself—the train depot, a post office, a saloon, a store, and a small cluster of houses. The colony was bordered to the north by the deep-cut Del Agua Arroyo, a seasonal creek that ran from Del Agua Canyon—home of the Hastings and Delagua mines—out onto the plains toward the Black Hills, a mound of land covered with scrub brush east of Ludlow.

From the distance of time it is impossible to judge the motives of those who agreed to lease land to the miners, or even whether Smith told the property owners—mostly ranchers or townspeople with small stakes of ranchland—that the union, rather than grazing cattle, planned massive bivouacs of the displaced. Though the coal companies controlled the politics of the region, they didn't control its soul. Many small business owners—retailers who recognized that the miners, not the operators, were their customers—backed the union miners, often extending credit when money was tight.

So southern Colorado offered a mixed tableau in the late summer of 1913, with mine operators virulently opposed to recognizing the union, union supporters dead set on gaining that recognition, a local political structure that backed the operators, and a mercantile class that was split. Mine operators believed they had minimized the union presence in their mines and could, as they did in 1903, simply repress the activists and wait as whatever strike might occur played itself out. The organizers, confident that their cause was just and that their tactics had won the souls of the vast majority of workers, believed shutting down the mines would bring the operators to the negotiating table.

Each side severely underestimated the resolve of the other.

The Wilson White House and the new federal Department of Labor kept a close eye on developments in Colorado, concerned about both the effect on the nation's coal supply and the potential for violence. In some ways, the looming strike was as much a test for the Wilson administration and the Labor Department as it was for the union and mine operators, and for

Ammons, in his first term as Colorado governor. Labor Secretary Wilson dispatched his deputy secretary, Ethelbert B. Stewart, to New York to talk with JDR Jr. about defusing the strike. If Stewart and his boss were hoping for a cordial reception, they were overly optimistic. At Twenty-six Broadway, President Wilson was viewed with deep skepticism, and his new labor secretary—a former UMWA official—with open suspicion. Wilson had slipped into the White House in 1912 through a political back door, thanks to a deep divide within the Republican Party created by Teddy Roosevelt and his Progressive "Bull Moose" Party. It was a unique moment in modern American politics.[53] The two-party system expanded to four as growing dissatisfaction with the consolidating power of the rich fed support for the Socialist Party and its quadrennial candidate, Debs, as well as Roosevelt's fellow Bull Moosers. By the time the votes were counted, Wilson won with 42 percent of the popular vote, to Roosevelt's 27 percent, incumbent Republican William Howard Taft's 23 percent, and Debs's 6 percent— the apex of the Socialist Party's political support.

In the all-crucial electoral college, Wilson won only twelve of the then forty-eight states with a majority of the votes—eleven southern states and South Dakota—which gave him only 131 electoral votes of the 265 needed to win. It is clear that had Roosevelt not run, splintering the Republican vote, Taft likely would have won reelection. And the split continued down the ticket. With the Republicans in disarray, Ammons, a former journalist turned rancher and Republican turned Democrat, won the Colorado governorship over Republican and Bull Moose rivals with 47 percent of the vote.

Wilson's win did not sit well at Twenty-six Broadway, which believed the president-elect was aligned with labor against capital. "I wish some day that we might have a real businessman as President," Rockefeller lamented.[54] So when Stewart, the federal mediator, arrived at Rockefeller's offices, he was shunted aside like an unwelcome solicitor. Starr J. Murphy, who handled legal affairs on Rockefeller's executive committee, finally met with Stewart but took the position that given the physical distance between New York City and the Colorado fields there was little they could know about conditions in the West. Murphy did not mention the regular correspondence between the CF&I offices in Denver and Twenty-six Broadway, or JDR Jr.'s letters offering encouragement and support for whatever actions Bowers and Welborn deemed best. Stewart told Murphy that CF&I was the central player on the owners' side and that the other Colorado operators had said they would follow CF&I's lead. While Stewart understood Rockefeller's stance that the details of the negotiations would be best handled in the field, he hoped the policy governing CF&I's approach would be established in New York. But Stewart made no headway.[55]

On September 12, White, the UMWA president, announced a conference to begin September 15 in Trinidad to "decide whether a strike shall be called and, if so, [the conference] will shape the policy to be pursued by the officials in charge."[56] Union officials invited the coal operators. "We are making this last endeavor to settle our differences peacefully and with the hope of preventing a strike. If you will kindly come to this joint convention we feel sure we can adjust all points at issue between our respective interests in a satisfactory manner." The conference—which took place the day before Stewart met with Murphy in New York City—was not a sudden decision; it had been in the works for several weeks. The announcement seemed geared more toward gaining news coverage for White's other comments: The union had set aside $1 million for strike support; it had leased the land to build its strikers' colonies, and it was shipping tents westward from West Virginia. He also acknowledged that the union had been using secret operatives to organize the mines. "The men are prepared for war, if war is to come."[57] The same day White made his announcement, Germer, the Socialist organizer based in Walsenburg, drove to James Holmes's Pueblo hardware store with E. L. Neelley and arranged for an unspecified number of revolvers to be shipped to the union at the Neelley-Caldwell hardware store in Walsenburg.[58] Welborn later claimed that Germer had bought "a large quantity of arms and ammunition" from a Pueblo gun dealer—some fifty-eight rifles—and had them "shipped to the southern coal fields."[59]

White then left Colorado for a business trip to the East. The active strike preparation was left to Hayes, the international vice president sent in from the UMWA headquarters in Indianapolis to help direct the organizing campaign, and to Mother Jones, Lawson, and others, who traveled through the mining district fanning the flames of discontent. In Walsenburg, 600 miners jammed into the Palace hall for an update speech by Hayes. "Before God, we will win this strike and it seems that a strike is certain. Nothing on earth can keep us from winning."[60] Hayes and Jones later addressed miners at Ludlow and Hastings, then ended the day at Trinidad's West Opera House, one of the gems of the Rockies. Its wide, deep stage faced three tiers of seats that overflowed with more than two thousand miners, their families, spies, journalists, and curious townspeople

Strike leader John Lawson, left, legendary union organizer Mary Harris "Mother" Jones, and UMWA lawyer Horace Hawkins in an undated posed photograph, likely taken in Denver during the strike. *Credit: Denver Public Library, Western History Collection.*

who had come out to see Jones. The back of the auditorium was open to the lobby, and the crowd stretched from the seats through the lobby out the front doors and into the street.

The session began with a few preliminary speeches before Jones was introduced, applause and whistles showering down as she made her way from the wings to the front center of the stage. The crowd still cheering, Jones removed the pins holding her hat in place and tossed it to a man in the front row to hold, then smoothed her white hair back and adjusted the white shawl over her black dress.[61] Jones began calmly and matter-of-factly, slowly working herself and the crowd into a cheering, stomping frenzy. For two hours, she paced back and forth, savaging the mine operators and Baldwin-Felts detectives for colluding to keep the workers under the mine owners' collective thumb.[62] "Her strong, foghorn voice was just as commanding as were her gestures," Thomas wrote years later. "She held us all spellbound."[63] The performance was vintage Jones, sounding alternately like a supportive maternal figure and a steel-boned agitator, building up to a fiery, screaming ending: "If it is strike or submit, why for God's sake, strike! Strike until you win!"

The next day the miners convened their meeting and listened to a litany of complaints about working and living conditions in the mine camps, low wages, unpaid "dead" work such as shoring up the mine roofs, and weighmen cheating them on the amount of coal they turned in. The meeting adjourned for the morning after a few words from Mother Jones, pushing the theme of solidarity across the unions. "I want to ask you to please remember while you are in town that the Pells Brewery Workers are on strike. They did not strike without a cause, I am sure. The Brewery Workers Executive Board are about as able men as we have in the labor movement and I am pretty sure they would not endorse a strike without a cause. Be sure you don't touch that Pells Brewery beer; if you drink it you will be full of scabs, so I want each and all, if you do get beer, get union beer, get beer made by men working under decent conditions, and don't patronize those places. If you get hold of any fellow who does, hammer him good."[64]

After lunch and more testimony from miners, Jones again took the stage and delivered a long, rambling monologue about the responsibility of workers to fight for their own rights and dignity. "I wanted to come here sooner, but I have been busy," Jones said, citing the West Virginia strike. She came back again and again to the Baldwin-Felts detectives and scabs, two related evils, and what she described as acts of courage by West Virginia miners in the face of grave danger. It was Mother Jones at her best—or worst: part righteousness, part self-inflation, part homespun shtick, and all agitation.

"Don't be afraid, boys," she said. "Fear is the greatest curse we have. I was never anywhere yet that I feared anybody. I do what I think is right and when I die I will render an account of it. These miners have suffered, but it will have to come to an end, my boys. If your operators do not give to you that which is fair, then I say strike, but let the strike be the very last move you make. . . . The time is ripe now."

The next morning the miners continued their meeting, and Mother Jones was conspicuously quiet for most of the day. In late afternoon she again took the stage and read aloud a telegram that Frank S. Hoag, the new publisher of the *Pueblo Star Journal*, had sent the delegates urging the miners to consider the effects of a strike on the industrial health of Colorado. Hoag was the same publisher who had sought a $75,000 investment in his paper from Rockefeller. Like a motivational speaker with a prop,

Jones brandished the telegram and asked the miners about their own lots in life and the considerations that Colorado's captains of industry had given them. She reminded them again of the Baldwin-Felts detectives, of the deadly conditions in the mines, of the primary role the miners played in creating the wealth that the operators enjoyed. The UMWA had asked the operators to sit down with them and talk over those grievances, she said, but had not even received the courtesy of a reply.

For more than an hour Jones railed against the mine operators and the near-feudal conditions under which the miners lived, again building to a climax. "Rise up and strike!" she bellowed. "If you are too cowardly to fight there are enough women in this country to come in and beat the hell out of you. If it is slavery or strike, why I say strike, until the last one of you drops into your graves."

Moments later the miners adopted the list of demands the policy committee had drafted in August and declared that if the operators did not respond they would walk out a week later—September 23.[65]

The mine operators did respond, in a fashion. About thirty-five operators representing 95 percent of the coal produced in the southern coalfield gathered at the Rocky Mountain Fuel Co.'s offices in Denver to discuss strike contingency plans. They agreed to work together to keep the mines running, splitting the costs based on the tonnage of coal each company mined, though in fact most of the bills were paid by the Big Three—Rocky Mountain Fuel, Victor-American, and CF&I, by far Colorado's largest company and employer.[66]

The operators held firm to their belief that the UMWA had not organized their mines, and did not represent their miners. There would be no strike of any consequence. "There is no good of talking now, anybody can see for himself on Tuesday what the strike will amount to and how many men will go out," Osgood said.[67] Privately, some of the company men were less cocksure. In a letter to John H. McClement, a New York–based CF&I director and a former associate of Gould's, Welborn reiterated CF&I's opposition to the UMWA. "We know that only a small percentage of our men belong to the union," Welborn wrote, going on to claim that Colorado miners earned more than miners elsewhere. "In spite of this, however, it is probable that in the event of a strike call most of the men would respond, although we believe a great many would later return to work when they found that we were determined in our opposition to the organization and were successfully operating our mines. We are very much concerned and on the anxious seat, yet there is nothing to do but wait."[68]

Publicly, the operators, through Osgood, argued that the Trinidad convention that called the strike involved few real miners and that most of the attendees were union plants from afar—the classic "outside agitators." "There were no delegates from any of the principal mines in southern Colorado, and the men who claimed to represent these mines were selected by the organizers themselves, and not by the miners, and many of them have never seen the mines they were supposed to represent." Osgood went on to claim that "the actual mine workers of Colorado do not desire a strike" and that the UMWA was mounting a power grab for its own benefit, not that of the miners. Osgood touted the operators' recent wage hikes and denied that the camps used a "guard system"—a rather bold claim given the evidence—except in the northern field, where striking miners "are constantly committing acts of violence." The statement was clearly aimed not at the miners but at the public and state power brokers, in hopes of consolidating support for the mining industry against the UMWA's organizing campaign.

Yet the intent of the miners could be found in telling moments. E. H. Weitzel, CF&I's general manager, asked workers at the firm's Rockvale mine in Florence, north of Denver, to attend a meeting at the local opera house so he could discuss the strike call and argue the company's position. The workers refused to go, and the meeting was canceled.[69] At Ludlow, the UMWA had scheduled a strike meeting for the future site of its tent colony and strike headquarters for the Sunday before the walkout. Saturday was usually payday, but at the nearby Berwind mine the superintendent pushed payday back to Sunday, thinking that would keep the interested miners at home—or at least in the saloons. And those who collected their pay and tried to make their way down the canyon to Ludlow found a cordon of mine guards stretched across the canyon mouth.[70]

The only communication the operators had with the UMWA itself was indirect, through the newspapers.

"If a strike is called," Welborn said, "it will be to the finish."[71]

FOUR

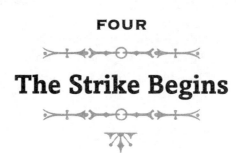

The Strike Begins

The coal camps emptied in a snaking line of misery. A heavy storm had developed over northern Mexico a few days after the Trinidad convention, a monsoonal flow that chilled as it moved up the Rockies and overwhelmed the lingering heat of summer. Cold, driving rain and occasional sleet ebbed into a steady drizzle, then strengthened again into torrents. By the morning of September 23, the official start of the strike, rain cascading down treeless slopes formed shallow rivers on the dirt pathways. As the water saturated the ground, the usually bricklike crust of sand and gravel dissolved into silty swamps that sucked at the wheels of the striking miners' wagons and carts and at the feet of horses and men, women, and children. Still, they came, upwards of twelve thousand people, young and old, the committed and the uncertain, a flow of humanity trading one level of poverty and insecurity for another.

Most of the miners who walked out did so in the drenching rain that morning, although some union men jumped the gun. In Huerfano County, the mines had been all but closed for several days as the miners followed their own schedules for striking.[1] The effectiveness varied widely from camp to camp. Operators claimed that overall fewer than half of the miners walked out; the union claimed near-total unity. Stewart, the federal labor mediator, amassed yet another batch of numbers, presumably from the mine operators.[2] While some of the numbers seem inflated—particularly the staffing levels the operators claimed were at work—the key statistic of coal production indicates that the strike, while not complete, certainly was deep and wide. In October 1912, Las Animas County mines produced

420,086 tons of coal. A year later, the first full month of the strike, county mines produced only 121,680 tons of coal, or about 29 percent of the October 1912 level. For Huerfano County, the decline was less sharp, with 70,926 tons produced in October 1913, about 43 percent of the previous October's 164,712 tons. Stewart counted twenty-eight mines "not in operation" in October 1913, and another thirteen specifically closed because of the strike, out of 164 on an incomplete list of the county's mines. In all, a quarter of the mines Stewart tracked were completely shut down; the rest operated at varying levels of output.

Privately, Welborn estimated that 70 percent of the miners had joined the walkout—about half the company's total mining workforce, separate from its steelmaking workforce—for reasons ranging from open support of the UMWA to fear of reprisals if they crossed the picket line.[3] Publicly, the operators, while denying the union successes, said many of those who had left did so because they feared reprisals for defying the strike call. No doubt there were some miners who joined the strike more out of fear than out of solidarity, and many kept walking once they left the mine, clearing out of the southern district altogether.

For nearly all the miners, to go on strike was to fall into homelessness. Those who lived in the closed camps lost access to their homes once the strike began, with guards at some mines rousting strikers who did not immediately leave their company-owned homes. This has been painted in the past as forced evictions by the mine companies, a union-busting act of retaliation. But Lawson, other strike leaders, and the miners themselves knew that to go on strike meant to give up their company-owned homes, and most miners left willingly.[4] In a few places, guards forcibly removed strikers and tossed their belongings into the dirt streets.[5] In some camps, guards refused to let strikers take their belongings with them, sparking showdowns that added even more tension to the already brittle atmosphere. Most of the miners didn't go far, settling into the new tent colonies being erected at the edge of the plains near the canyon entrances, while others fled to Trinidad and elsewhere seeking shelter and jobs.

The rain made the exodus difficult. "When steep hills came—and the roads about Trinidad mostly stand on end—the men and women got out and pushed through the thick, greasy mud. Sometimes the children pushed too," journalist Don MacGregor reported in the *Denver Express,* a paper sympathetic to the strikers' cause. During an hour's drive between Ludlow and Trinidad, he saw fifty-seven wagons "and uncounted others" on foot making their way along cross-country paths to the main road.[6]

Many of the miners had reserved spots in the tent colonies. Mary Thomas, the singing miner's wife from Wales, was estranged from her husband even though they shared the same quarters in the Berwind mine camp (she slept alone in a room with a chair propped under the doorknob).[7] Thomas requested a tent for herself and her children in the Ludlow colony; her husband was to bunk in a separate tent with a male colleague in the single men's quarters in another part of the camp. Thomas's friend Cedi Costa arranged for the two families and the Gorci family to have their tents near each other, condensing the social connections from the spread-out mining camp into the tight constraints of Ludlow. Thomas hired a deliveryman to take her family and their possessions to the tent colony, a process made miserable by the weather. "It was a rough trip down the canyon in the soft mud. The wheels bogged down to the hubs, and the horse steamed as the rain fell on his straining body." The colony was still taking shape, and Thomas's tent wasn't ready yet, so they stacked the possessions on the ground. A sympathetic Colorado & Southern (C&S) rail worker, Milford G. Low, who had stopped by the tent grounds with his wife and young daughter, offered the Thomases shelter for the night at their home a few hundred yards northwest of the tent colony.

Thomas returned the next morning to the tent colony, which was still being slapped together in the pouring rain. The Lows had offered to keep Thomas's daughters for an extra day, giving her time to settle into the camp. Many of the tents had yet to arrive from West Virginia, a delay the strikers blamed on CF&I machinations, and the union quickly bought replacements. Whether CF&I was responsible or not, the widespread belief that the company had that kind of power and would use it underscores the miners' fears of the lengths to which the mine operators would go to break the strike.

When Thomas arrived at the camp the second day, only one large tent and four smaller ones were in place. Anticipating a long stay on the prairie, union officials sought to make the tents as stable as possible. Each was large enough to hold a wood-burning stove, and floors were cobbled together from boards to protect the strikers from the cold ground. Camp organizers converted the first large tent into a temporary canteen for the arriving strikers. Thomas volunteered to hand out coffee as the miners arrived, seemingly carried out of the canyons by the storm runoff. "Most of them were completely exhausted. It was still raining, and they were cold and soaked to the skin. Lawson was mud from head to foot as he pushed and pulled the vehicles which inched along at a snail's pace. Some of the

The Ludlow tent colony in winter, apparently taken as a triptych from a water tower adjacent to the Colorado & Southern rail line. The view is to the east, the horizon marked by the Black Hills where strikers regrouped after the Ludlow Massacre. The "death pit" was beneath one of the tents in the second row from the right edge of the camp. *Credit: Courtesy Colorado Historical Society, ID No. 10027993. All rights reserved.*

miners came in wagons piled high with their cheap, rickety furniture, their small children perched on top. Others had carts, the husband pulling and the wife pushing as children trudged along behind through the sticky mud. Hundreds walked, the husband with a pack on his back, his wife carrying the baby."

The quick evolution of Dotson's ranchland from prairie to small, temporary village was repeated up and down the eastern Sangre de Cristo foothills. Beginning in the north, tent colonies went up at Cameron, Walsenburg, Lester (near Main, a stop on the C&S line, covering the Rouse, Lester and Pryor mines), Rugby (which covered the Rugby and Primrose mines), Aguilar, Ludlow, Forbes, Suffield, Cokedale, Sopris, and Morley.[8]

Ludlow was the largest of the encampments, eventually housing five hundred striking miners and their families, a total of about twelve hundred people.[9] That many people required organization, and Lawson established a colony police force, a sanitation department, a grounds commission, and other committees geared toward keeping the camp running. It was strategically located to monitor the main (north-south) rail line from Denver, and, when twinned with Forbes about four miles to the south, monitored traffic in and out of two canyons leading to the Victor-American mines at Delagua and Hastings and the CF&I mines at Berwind and Tabasco, the busiest mine canyons. Between Ludlow and Forbes stood Water Tank Hill, an overnamed rise of land that offered a clear view of two main rail lines and the connecting spurs, both Ludlow village and the tent colony, and the road to Trinidad. The centrality of Ludlow led union officials to make it their de facto field headquarters, and its importance to the strikers made it important to the mine guards and, later, the state militia, which kept the colony under close surveillance.

Lippiatt's killing on the dusty Trinidad street was the strike's first violent death, even if it preceded the actual walkout. The second to die, though the circumstances are murky, was Mike Driscoll, fifty, who failed to return from a day trip to Trinidad to visit his sister on the first day of the strike. Driscoll had once been a loader in the local mines; he and his wife ran a boardinghouse in Rugby, between Aguilar and Walsenburg, where they put up six miners and, for a time, a "servant" at a local hotel.[10] When Driscoll didn't return on that Tuesday, his wife wasn't immediately concerned, but by Friday she had dispatched searchers. Two boys, Emmett Locke and Vincent Lynn, found Driscoll's body about 7:30 P.M. in a shallow arroyo alongside a county road midway between the Southwestern and Jewel mines. His neck was broken, and he had blood on his hands. The death was ruled an accident, but with an asterisk: The coroner report noted that Driscoll had died "unattended" and might have been beaten and tossed into the arroyo.[11] It was unclear whether Driscoll had any direct connection with the strike—either supporting it or flouting it—and whether his boarders stayed in or joined the walkout.

There is no uncertainty over the next death.

Around 11:00 A.M. on the second day of the strike, miner Tom Larius, thirty-five, met with at least four fellow miners, all Greek immigrants, at the Namino saloon in Segundo, up the Purgatoire River west of Trinidad. Though a small settlement, Segundo was divided into Old Town and New Town, separated by the Colorado & Wyoming Railroad tracks. The Old Town consisted of privately owned houses and other buildings and was dominated by striking miners who assigned several armed men to stand watch from a hill above the settlement.[12] The New Town was the mine camp, guarded by fifty-nine "rifle-armed gunmen of the Colorado Fuel and Iron Company" who demanded a company pass before allowing anyone into or out of the camp. Larius wore a bright red sweater—the unofficial color of the strike—against the morning chill and drizzle. He was new to Segundo, having been kicked out of a CF&I mine camp in Frederick, in the northern field, the previous weekend for disorderly behavior (it is unclear whether he had been scabbing).[13] The men talked for a while and, a little before noon, left the bar, walking to a new footbridge built across an arroyo the day before to make it easier to cross from the closed mine camp to the open post office and school. It also limited the strikebreakers' exposure, making it easier both to protect them and to keep them from defecting.

But the footbridge was left unguarded that morning. Larius and the other miners paused to pry at some of the boards. Someone spotted them and informed mine guards in CF&I's nearby mine office. Robert Lee, forty-eight, the hated guard who preyed on miners' wives and daughters, took the job of stopping the men.[14] He left the mine office with his rifle and went to his horse, sheathed the gun in a scabbard attached to the saddle, mounted up, and cantered to the footbridge. Witnesses said Larius and three of his companions carried long guns but apparently did not brandish them.[15] Yet it is difficult to believe that Lee approached them alone if they were armed, unless he possessed a huge personal reservoir of hubris. In any event, Lee, still on horseback, began herding the miners off the bridge. When they had moved about two hundred yards to the west, nearing a set of beehive-shaped coke ovens, Larius dropped back, and as Lee reared his horse around, Larius raised his shotgun, "a single-barreled weapon of ancient make," and fired. The pellets shredded Lee's throat before he could pull his rifle from its scabbard. Larius dropped his gun, and the "miners ran like hell for the hills. The marshal, he is dead at once."[16] Other mine guards emerged from the office and shot at the fleeing men; one stumbled but, if wounded, wasn't hurt badly enough to stop his dash for sanctuary in the hills. Lee's killing gave the mine operators the rallying point they were hoping for. "One of our best Marshalls (or deputy sheriffs) was shot at noon today, while arresting some Greeks, who were destroying a bridge," Bowers wrote to his son. "This is a bad thing for the strikers, as it has aroused the officials and they will be ruled with much more vigor."[17]

Fred Herrington, general counsel for CF&I, issued a statement that the miners had been overheard in the saloon talking about "getting" Lee.[18] The claim seems spurious, and the coroner's jury gave it no credence, ruling the killing a murder but not part of a plot.[19] The miners could well have met over a beer to discuss plans to dismantle the bridge, or discussed other matters entirely and vandalized the bridge on the spur of the moment, but it stretches belief that they could have known Lee would be dispatched to stop them, a necessary element of any conspiracy to "get" Lee that morning. It seems more likely that the miners were up to mischief, Lee interceded, and Larius took the opportunity to either settle an old score or register a new one. In an example of the kind of "spin" that was to come, Herrington described the hated Lee, a ten-year CF&I employee, as "mild tempered and a pleasant man to meet . . . a Virginian and a gentleman, and he was highly thought of by the company." Herrington also apportioned some blame to "the incendiary utterances" of Mother Jones, "who has been urging the men to acts of violence in her addresses."

The mining camps and tent colonies remained mostly peaceful, though, and Ammons rejected the operators' requests that he call out the Colorado National Guard, believing that local authorities were handling the situation. Still, there were flare-ups. At the Walsen mine at the western edge of Walsenburg, women and children thronged the main gate at quitting time, urging the strikebreaking miners to walk out. Tracklayer John Hale refused—one suspects rudely—and was set upon by the women, who chased him down the street and knocked him to the ground, "rolled him in the mud and kicked him." As mine guards ran up to help Hale, the women scattered—save one, who "jumped astride of Hale and beat him over the head with a heavy bucket, breaking his nose and cutting his face in several places."[20] At the C&S rail depot in Ludlow, a band of strikers armed with boards and ax handles intercepted three strikebreakers whose train was met by a wagon heading for the Hastings mine. The strikers detained the three men, ordering the wagon to continue on without them. The strikers persuaded two of the scabs to leave the district; the third eventually made his way to the mine. And in Trinidad, two bands of gunmen shot at each other late on September 24, but apparently no one was wounded and no one arrested—a phantom exchange in the dark of night.

Federal and state officials had not given up hope that a settlement might still be reached. In Denver, Stewart, the federal mediator, had taken Starr Murphy's point and met with Bowers in CF&I's Denver office the day after the strike began. Bowers complained later that Stewart had no interest in hearing the coal operators' position on the miners' demands concerning wages, hours, and other conditions, which Bowers claimed had already been granted. He said Stewart only wanted to persuade him to accept union recognition. "I told him that I would refuse, as would all of our officials, to recognize the union or the official representatives of the union in which 90 to 95 percent of our employees had no relation or interest; that these officials had come here for the sole purpose of forcing the issue, and that, in my opinion, they had no interest whatever in these miners except to secure several hundreds thousands dollars a year for their treasury."[21]

Bowers was venting directly to President Wilson, whose new labor secretary was viewed by the coal operators with unveiled cynicism. "I was not aware at the time of Mr. Stewart's visit here," Bowers wrote the president, "that the officials of the United Mine Workers of America had been in conference with Commissioner of Labor Wilson some time before the strike was called, neither did I know that Commissioner Wilson was for years the secretary and treasurer of this union, nor that Mr. Stewart was a leader in union circles." Bowers went on to scold the president about his administration's choice of Stewart to try to bring the two sides together. "My notion of a mediator is that he should have an open and unbiased mind, which I have never known a man long connected with labor unions as an officer to possess. My sense of fairness prompts me to say that an independent man should have been selected to act as mediator, providing there was any dispute existing between ourselves and our miners, demanding mediation, which there was not."

Privately, Bowers crowed to his son about meeting "with a man sent from Washington by the Secretary of Labor to see if he could not get both sides to bend. We have no trouble with our men and the thing is to force us to employ union men only. Not while L.M.B. is in the saddle." Bowers described Stewart as large, "250 or 275 pounds, with grey hair like Mark Twain's and a red face to match." Stewart, Bowers acknowledged, was "altogether a rather agreeable man," but "[w]hen excited he has to stutter." He wrote with self-congratulatory glee: "I wound him into kinks and beat him at every point. All his arguments were silly and amounted to no more than a busted bubble. Gosh he was a big chap, but his cause is too plainly in behalf of unionism and I had him sweating and hamming like a half choked calf eating pumpkins." But the executive was also shrewdly assessing the potential personal effects of the strike. He confided in his son that he feared the walkout "might stampede our stocks and bonds." In an act of opportunism that could not have been popular within Twenty-six Broadway, Bowers sold off some of his CF&I holdings and invested in the New York Central, Pennsylvania, and Union Pacific railroads. "I think I can buy [the CF&I bonds] again at a lower price if the strike lasts any length of time."[22]

Stewart had a different view of the session with Bowers. From Room 305 of the Shirley-Savoy Hotel, at the corner of Broadway and Seventeenth in Denver, Stewart handwrote a three-page letter to Secretary Wilson, reporting that he had met several times with UMWA District 15 president McLennan, and at Ammons's office with the governor and Brown of the Rocky Mountain Fuel Co. Then he met Bowers. "He had evidently had instructions from New York to meet me. Mr. Bowers is very bitter. The situation here is very tense, and unyielding. Governor Ammons says he could have got the miners everything they asked for except recognition of the union. This is the essence of the struggle, I fear, and you know what an ugly problem it presents."[23]

Emotions, and violence, simmered. There were threats and taunts, beatings and gunshots as mutual antagonism between the strikers on one side and the scabs and mine guards on the other played out in countless minor frictions. In late October, the operators took out ads in local papers detailing what they considered to be acts of violence by the strikers—sixty-four incidents over twenty-one days. Some of them seem laughable, such as when two nonunion miners were rousted "from a picture show at Walsenburg and compelled to take out union cards." But there were bombings and rifle assaults, too. On September 28, the home of Charles Lagresto in Walsenburg was dynamited after his eldest son "refused to obey a strike order."[24]

Union officials either denied the violence or tried to blame it on company agitators who slipped in among the ranks of the strikers, Baldwin-

Felts wolves dressed in union sheep clothing. "These men go into the camps, even into the tent colonies, and excite our men to acts of violence," Hayes said. "This is a hard matter for us to control. It is one of the many tricks used by the operators to injure our cause."[25] Each side sought to portray itself as the law-abiding victim of the other's evil ambitions. The operators were simply trying to exercise their rights as businessmen to harvest their investments while under attack by outside radicals who did not represent their employees. Union officials were defenders of the defenseless, dedicated to peacefully conducting an economic strike until the operators promised to improve the working conditions of the men who built their wealth. Both claims were wanton distortions. While preaching peace, the operators were instructing the Baldwin-Felts agency to procure machine guns, including some of those used in the recently concluded West Virginia strike, and were importing gunmen from outside Colorado. The striking miners were cleaning out gun shops in Trinidad while union officials imported weapons from outside the district. The growing stockpiles weren't for show.

At dawn on September 29, strikebreakers at the independent Oakdale mine in Oakview, some twenty miles west of Walsenburg, were finishing breakfast and preparing to head below ground. Before the strike, some two hundred men worked the mine, but only forty-seven men remained on the job. Some of these miners were Japanese, segregated in a boardinghouse near the mine or in huts set apart from the rest of the miners' lodgings, a function of the pervasive racism of the era.[26] The camp was a short distance from another independent mine in the same canyon, where the operator had agreed to the miners' demands and union men were at work. The close proximity of the two mines, overlaid with racism against the Japanese strikebreakers, made run-ins inevitable.

About 6:20 A.M., as daylight washed into the canyon and the strikebreakers moved toward the mine, a barrage of rifle fire swept the camp, pinging off the ground, shattering windows, and drilling holes through the thin wooden walls of miners' homes, the camp office, and the Japanese quarters. None of the strikebreakers was hit, an incredible stroke of luck—or, more likely, the assailants weren't shooting to kill. The Japanese boardinghouse and huts, which seemed to be the prime targets, were shredded by rifle fire, but the mine office took its share of hits, too. The attack continued for more than two hours and ended when about ten mine guards maneuvered to the bottom of the hill and, at a signal, charged up the hillside, shooting as they ran. By the time the guards reached the top, the attackers had fled into the dense brush. One striker was reportedly wounded in the shoulder, but his fate afterward went unreported. The details of the attack all came from mine guards and mine officials, as reported to Farr's Huerfano County sheriff's deputies. Union officials laughed it off, claiming that strikers were not involved. Germer said mine guards had used similar ruses in West Virginia, shooting up the property they were meant to protect to justify their own jobs. "If the mine was shot up the way they said it was, someone else [other than strikers] is responsible."[27]

The operators used the incident as evidence that the violence in Las Animas and Huerfano counties had grown beyond the local sheriffs' abilities to control it and that the National Guard was needed to restore order. Still unable to believe their miners were actually revolting against them, the operators thought that calling out the National Guard would encourage lukewarm strikers to break ranks with the radicals and cross the picket line.[28] Farr, his company loyalties unwavering, added his voice in a four-page telegram to the governor. "My dear sir;—In light of the very recent and deplorable outbreaks in my county during part of the mine strike of the coal miners of southern Colorado, I feel it my duty to advise you officially of the conditions of affairs as they obtain here."[29] He detailed the violence and argued that the strike was too spread out for his deputies to maintain control.

Governor Ammons had been hearing similar appeals since before the strike began, a chorus that included business owners in the district, elected officials, local residents, and the coal operators themselves. He viewed the demands with a certain amount of skepticism, and was wary of being drawn into using state money to intercede in a private labor dispute. Colorado's unions and their supporters opposed deploying the militia, too, fearing it would severely curtail the UMWA's ability to picket—officially against state law—and to interfere with mine operations. Protected strikebreakers would be more effective workers.

Ammons enjoyed the support of many union leaders, including Lawson, whom he had appointed during the campaign to represent him on the state Democratic Party's executive advisory board.[30] Yet the coal operators had backed Ammons, too, in the 1912 election, after reading the political tea leaves and realizing that the Republican split meant the Democrat would likely win.[31] Presuming political support from both sides, Ammons sought to bring them together, aligning with neither though he gave enough credence to the UMWA's demands and interests to raise suspicions among the operators. Several privately ridiculed Ammons, and Bowers referred to him in letters to Twenty-six Broadway as "our cowboy governor."[32] Ammons, though, did not rise to the call to send in the troops, not through any overarching sense of its appropriateness but because the demands were divided both ways. Rather than lead, Ammons sought to conciliate, not understanding that a weak and indecisive governor could do little to quell the passions and the violence.

Ammons appeared before the Commission on Industrial Relations when it took testimony in Denver on December 2, 1914, after the strike was over, and still seemed flummoxed by the demands made on him as the strike began. "The general condition was bad from the beginning; that the operators wanted protection and demanded protection for their property, and that the United Mine Workers were just as insistent that they [the militia] were not needed, and that they ought not be called on. The people there that did not belong to either side were at first somewhat divided, but before the troops were called out I think they were practically unanimous."[33]

What united them was a rapid escalation of violence. On October 1, strikers and mine guards exchanged more than thirty shots in the dark outside the Suffield mine, just north of Trinidad. Hayes again claimed the incident was "a frame-up" by the mine guards. Two days later in Lafayette, in the northern field, six bombs were heaved over a stockade protecting Bulgarian strikebreakers at the Rocky Mountain Fuel Co.'s Mitchell mine. Only one bomb detonated, blowing the end off one of the workers' huts, but it was followed by a fusillade of about five hundred gunshots. The attack was timed for when most of the scabs were working underground, part of a near-nightly campaign to terrorize the nonunion miners.[34]

The same evening, a blast heard up to five miles away disintegrated a powder storage shed at the independent Primrose mine, midway between Walsenburg and Aguilar, and also caved in the rear and side walls of the adjoining company store.[35] The blast sent debris a hundred feet into the air, blew wall sections more than two hundred yards, shattered windows across the camp, and knocked out both electricity and telephone connections. Once again, blame was hard to figure. Mine officials speculated someone had sneaked up to the unguarded powder house, drilled a hole, and dropped in a slow-burning fuse, but there were no witnesses and little evidence left to analyze. Though it is believable that strikers were responsible, it's hard to understand why such a valuable and volatile storehouse was left unguarded, suggesting either that Primrose guards were in cahoots with strikers or that Baldwin-Felts agitators blew it up in hopes the striking miners would be blamed.

In Denver, Bowers gathered reports from the field and the local papers and sent an update to Twenty-six Broadway, asserting that most of CF&I's striking miners would rather be working and that those who had joined the strike "would be back at work if it were not for fear of assassination or violence." Bowers enclosed a newspaper clipping about the Oakview shootout and pointed out that the attacks did not involve CF&I mines. "Our armed guards so far have been able to protect our miners. We have eight large electric searchlights established, and each sweeps the surrounding country for five or six miles." JDR, Jr., apparently liked what he read. "We feel that what you have done is right and fair and that the position which you have taken in regard to the unionizing of the mines is in the interest of the employees of the company," he wrote back three days later. "Whatever the outcome may be, we will stand by you to the end."[36]

Nowhere do the records indicate that Bowers was giving Twenty-six Broadway details about exactly how the mine guards and Baldwin-Felts men were working outside of the mines. The Denver-based director of the Mountain Division of the American Red Cross, S. Poulter Morris, was in Trinidad on October 6 to see whether the relief agency might have a role to play. The overt displays of weaponry stunned him. Around 4:00 P.M., when the sidewalks of Trinidad "were so filled with men that at times it was necessary to go into the streets in order to make any progress," Morris saw a three-man parade that astounded him. "A Mr. Belker [*sic*; it is unclear whether this was Belk or Belcher], one of the Baldwin-Felts detectives, walked up the Main Street with two of his associates accompanying him, one of whom walked in front with what appeared to be a Winchester, a .30–30, and the other in the rear with the same type of gun." Given the confrontations that had already occurred, and the constant tensions in the strike district, Morris interpreted the display as "an open invitation to violence." The miners were equally obvious. "Within a few hours, I saw a large seven-passenger automobile draw up in front of the Headquarters of the Miner's Union, and six men, in addition to the chauffeur, two of whom I recognized as the officials of local miner's unions, each of them armed with what appeared to be a high power rifle, get in the machine and start in the direction of the Ludlow Tent Colony."[37]

The sighting turned out to be a prelude. The next day, October 7, a pitched gun battle broke out about 3:30 P.M. near the Ludlow tent colony as a car bearing Belk, Belcher, and four other people veered off from the Ludlow road south of the colony to take a short cut to Hastings in Del Agua Canyon, a route that would let the car steer clear of the tent colony.

"When we got over the hill in sight of the colony, we noticed a bunch of men—I supposed it was boys playing ball—running across the prairie in our direction," Belk said.[38] As the car drove within eight hundred yards of the men, there was a loud bang from the underside, near the right front wheel. "The chauffeur thought it was a blowout; so did I." The driver halted the car. "As soon as the noise of the engine stopped, you could hear the rifles spitting and the dust raising up and the bullets whizzing over our heads." Four of the men, including Belk and Belcher, jumped out of the car and drew their guns. "Mr. Belcher fired two shots." Belk said he ordered Belcher to stop firing, afraid that they might strike women and children on the far side of the strikers—a self-serving and hard-to-believe act of chivalry. The four men armed with handguns, unprotected on the open prairie, facing off against thirty-five to forty men armed with high-powered rifles, decided to move, and move fast. They jumped back in the car and sped off, finding shelter behind a row of steel rail cars, which they used as a shield as they drove out of rifle range.

The car made it to Hastings, and a few minutes later a squad of about thirty guards swept out of the Del Agua Canyon toward the tent colony, where armed strikers had taken up positions on rail cars and the canyon walls and along the arroyo. Many were Greek and Montenegrin immigrants, veterans of Balkan wars and armed with high-powered rifles—a much tougher force than the riffraff the mine guards likely thought they were facing.[39] Hundreds of shots were fired over the next three hours, ending only when the setting sun kept the fighters from seeing each other. Three men were reported wounded.[40] The mine operators said unidentified strikers in the tent colony started the fight by firing on the car as it drove past. Lawson and other union leaders said that someone inside the car fired first and that later that night, after Sheriff Grisham's deputies had finished their inconclusive investigation and left, snipers along the hillside rained more bullets into the tents, though again no one was reported injured. The presence of snipers led some of the families to begin digging trenches under the wooden floors of their tents, ersatz foxholes that could give them and their families low places to hide when the bullets started flying. The excavation went further at a tent near the southwest corner of the camp, where strikers dug a deep underground bunker to be used as a birthing chamber for the colony's pregnant women.[41] And Lawson ordered rifle pits be dug along the arroyo to the north of the colony.

Around 1:00 P.M. the next day, gun battles again broke out between strikers and mine guards. A car carrying R. L. Harrison north from Trinidad had just passed Rameyville, near the entrance to Berwind Canyon, when gunfire erupted from the hillside, riddling the car with bullets. One grazed Harrison's head. The car sped on to Ludlow as Harrison tried to return fire with his handgun, the bullets falling harmlessly short of the strikers on the hillside.[42] A half hour later, a caravan of twenty-five CF&I mine guards emerged from Berwind Canyon, four armed men on horseback leading three wagons, two holding mine guards and the third empty. They were headed to the Ludlow depot to pick up a searchlight shipped in for installation at the Tabasco camp. Strikers had been slipping in under cover of darkness to threaten strikebreakers, and the operators hoped the powerful searchlight would keep the intruders out. It also could be used to sweep the tent colonies, making sleep difficult inside the thin white-canvas walls.

As the caravan passed a concrete culvert, a ranch hand named Mack Powell, thirty-five, working in the surrounding fields, rode past on horseback and on out ahead. Seconds later gunfire erupted between the guards and a force of about fifty strikers hidden up a hillside some five hundred yards away, likely the same men who had shot up the car carrying Harrison. Powell, a striking miner who had moved out of the Ludlow tent colony three days earlier to take the ranching job, almost immediately toppled from his horse.[43] A few strikers slipped down the hillside and took up positions on a steel rail overpass as "the bullets of the guards beat upon the steel framework like hailstones"[44] The rail bridge gave the strikers two angles of attack against the mine guards, who had taken shelter in a deep cut along the road. Several of the guards hid behind their horses; one of the animals was killed. With bullets flying, one of the guards rode off on horseback to Ludlow to summon help while people living in nearby ranch houses scurried for cover. Powell's wife and mother and other women and children at the Green ranch ran to the rail section house, seeking protection in its basement.[45] A quickly formed detachment of thirty-five National Guardsmen from Trinidad was rushed by special train to the Rameyville stop, where they detrained and marched toward the gun battle. As they came within sight, the strikers faded away, disappearing over the hilltop and ending the battle some two hours after it started. An estimated thousand shots had been fired.

In the calm, another ranch hand was able to reach Powell and found him dead from a bullet that sliced into his left arm and all the way through his chest.[46] As usual, each side blamed the other for starting the battle, but it seems unlikely the mine guards would open fire from such an exposed position—assuming they had even seen the strikers hiding on the hillside.

The strikers claimed the mine guards had killed Powell, but the Las Animas County coroner's inquest, though inconclusive, made it seem more likely that strikers had shot him. The fatal wound came from the left, where the strikers occupied the hillside; had the mine guards killed Powell, he probably would have been shot in the back, since he was riding away from them. The most likely scenario is that one of the strikers mistook the fast-riding ranch hand for a mine guard out ahead of the column and brought him down with a long-distance shot. The death was ruled "felonious."[47]

Sheriff Grisham saw it as ominous. He wired Governor Ammons the day after the battle admitting to a growing sense of helplessness in maintaining the peace as he anticipated receiving arrest warrants for some of the strikers involved in the shootout. He wanted the governor to send in the militia before he tried to serve them. "I sincerely believe that an attempt to execute this process without the aid of the militia of the state will lead to wholesale bloodshed and riot."[48]

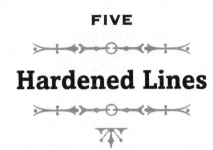

FIVE

Hardened Lines

Stewart, the federal mediator, was still trying to find a way to end the stalemate, and failing at every turn. He saw invisible hands reaching out from Twenty-six Broadway to Denver despite assurances from Starr Murphy, the Rockefellers' legal counsel, that the Colorado executives of CF&I—Bowers and Welborn—were in charge. "I had become convinced that the local mine managers were not empowered to settle except on terms dictated from New York."[1] Bowers, in a letter to Twenty-six Broadway thanking JDR Jr. for his support "in fighting this unjust, uncalled for and iniquitous strike," confided that he saw Stewart and his boss, Secretary of Labor Wilson, as no more than union agitators in government suits. Stewart "came here under false colors, representing himself as being appointed as mediator, while he has been spending weeks with the labor agitators . . . and refused to listen to the operators' side unless it was in conference with the union officials, which, of course, the operators flatly refused to consider."

Bowers's words burned on the page. "When such men as these, together with the cheap college professors and still cheaper writers in muckraking magazines, supplemented by a lot of milk-and-water preachers with little or no religion and less common sense, are permitted to assault the business men who have built up the great industries and have done more to make this country what it is than all the other agencies combined, it is time that vigorous measures are taken to put a stop to those vicious teachings which are being sown broadly throughout the country." Bowers saw something of an approaching Armageddon, a battle between business good and labor evil in which the future of the country hung in the balance ."[I]f the business men do not awaken from their indifference and take aggressive measures on a large scale to right the wrongs that are being inflicted upon the business of this country, we will see a revolution, we will be under military government and our Republic will end where so many others have ended."[2]

In a letter to Milford B. Streeter, a Brooklyn brewery-parts dealer and CF&I stockholder, Bowers's exasperation bubbled over again. "The union labor agitators have run in sluggers from the east and armed them with Winchester rifles, and the black-hand assassins are terrorizing the miners by their threats of death." Bowers refused to accept that the UMWA was trying to organize the mines for any reason other than to glean protection money. "Our men are perfectly satisfied and would not strike but for fear of death threatened by these back-handers and armed sluggers, supplemented by the murderous Greeks who are now back here from the Turkish war. These Greeks are nothing but bloodthirsty devils, and the labor leaders are back of them, supplying them with guns and ammunition. At every important mine in the coal region strikers are encamped in tents, and they fire upon everybody and everything that comes within sight."

But Bowers was also adamant that the union would not prevail. Like Welborn on the eve of the strike, he saw it as a battle the coal operators must and would win. "A man of my age, peaceably inclined, does not fancy such warfare, but knowing that we are right from every legal and moral standpoint and being endowed with pretty substantial fighting qualities, I shall not yield one inch, but will fight them to the finish."[3]

Powell's death did nothing to dampen the passions in the field. On October 11, the day the coroner ruled on Powell's death, two Baldwin-Felts detectives near Aguilar were surrounded by armed strikers who disarmed the men, roughed them up, and released them, bloodied from head cuts, to authorities in Walsenburg. In La Veta, a gun battle erupted when a group of strikers ambushed several mine guards as they escorted strikebreakers from a rail car to the mine. Again, no one was wounded, but the escalation of violence led to a run on gun shops in the district, with shelves cleaned out in Trinidad. The mine operators decided rifles were not enough and began ordering in machine guns.[4] They bolstered their legal team, too, by hiring Jesse G. Northcutt, who was a Taft Republican, a former district court judge with a history of being friendly to the coal companies, and the publisher of the *Trinidad Chronicle-News*.

Northcutt, an avuncular man, heavyset with an unruly shock of gray hair, would seem to be an uneasy ally. In a political speech in 1912, he blasted the region's closed political system, complaining that at nominating conventions if a candidate "isn't right with the company and they don't want him, he goes off the slate." Political skills and devotion to public duty were irrelevant. "[F]rom bottom to top, the candidates are selected, not with a view to their ability to discharge their duty. Not with a view to their integrity, but 'Are they satisfactory to the company?' If they are, that settles it." Northcutt, testifying two years later, said that those conditions existed at the time leading up to his speech but had changed since then, a remarkable shift of the political earth that coincided with his going to work for the coal operators a couple of weeks into the strike.[5]

Northcutt would come to play an integral role in the coal operators' handling of the strike. Within days of his signing on, a shipment of rifles arrived at Northcutt's newspaper office, a two-story brick building a block from where Lippiatt was killed in downtown Trinidad. The guns were quickly ferried north to Ludlow and turned over to deputized mine guards.[6] Northcutt denied knowing anything about the shipment, but there was no doubt he was an active agent for the coal operators. In early October, Northcutt used his personal and political connections to ask the chief justice of the New Mexico Supreme Court for help in hiring gunfighters for the coalfield.[7] Northcutt sent along a check to cover the hiring and transportation costs. The chief justice called in the head of the New Mexico state rangers, who lined up fifteen men and led them north to Trinidad, arriving by train on the morning of October 14. Northcutt had a man meet the New Mexicans at the train station and escort them to the *Trinidad Chronicle-News* office, where Northcutt and Sheriff Grisham were waiting.

Grisham quickly swore in the men as sheriff's deputies, despite state laws that limited such commissions to Colorado residents, and doled out a .30–30 rifle and a revolver to each man. The new deputy sheriffs were then sent back to the station to catch a train to one of the mine camps. Shortly after leaving the newspaper office, though, they encountered a throng of striking miners, which seems to have been the first time the gunmen were made aware that the security detail for which they were hired was actually protecting mines under strike. The picketers persuaded them to go to the UMWA office, where strike leaders talked the new deputies into refusing to report to the mines. Grisham, meanwhile, heard that instead of following his order to go to the train station, his new deputies were on the second floor of the Packer Block. Grisham demanded the men return their weapons and commissions. The gunmen complied, boarded a train, and went home.

In what can only be seen as an egregious conflict of interest, Northcutt also became a voluntary "special prosecutor" in criminal cases against strikers, assisting John J. Hendrick, district attorney for the Colorado Third Judicial District covering Las Animas and Huerfano counties.[8] About the only role Hendrick did not allow Northcutt to perform was delivering the opening and closing statements in trials; he reserved that job for himself. Northcutt handled interviews with witnesses, investigations of crimes, decisions on what charges to file, and some courtroom appearances. "I generally put as much work on him as I can," Hendrick said. The net effect was the overt co-option of local legal authority by the mine operators, which, combined with the deputizing of Baldwin-Felts gunmen and mine guards, cemented the miners' hard-to-refute belief that the local political structure had been corrupted against them.

Any doubts were removed by mid-October, when the line between the sheriff's deputies and the mine guards dissolved completely. On October 14, a throng of about thirty-five strikers, half of them armed, gathered on a roadway leading to a Santa Fe Coal Co. mine, about three miles south of Trinidad. The company was owned by J. E. McLaughlin, the governor's brother-in-law, and his mine, known as the McLaughlin mine, had continued to work with its own miners despite the strike. The working mine attracted the attention of striking picketers from the nearby Starkville mine, owned by CF&I and all but shut down in the walkout. As the McLaughlin miners showed up for work that morning, picketers met them with curses and guns, and warned them against going in.[9] About twenty of the strikebreakers turned back. Sheriff's deputies arrived a short time later by car, and after a tense confrontation—Undersheriff Zeke Martin fired a warning shot in the air—about twenty strikers were arrested, enraging union leaders, who argued that the strikers were doing nothing illegal. The strikers were marched at gunpoint the three miles to the county jail in Trinidad.

The next morning, the strikebreakers arrived at the McLaughlin mine without incident but around 10:00 A.M. a group of sixty strikers walked over the hills from Starkville and gathered on the county road, shouting for the scabs to come out. Sheriff Grisham dispatched about fifteen deputies. Some of the strikers managed to disappear over the hill before the deputies, armed with Winchester rifles and a gatling gun, could corral them. But the deputies rounded up forty-nine strikers and again marched them to the Trinidad jail. The parade attracted a jeering crowd of strikers and their supporters, some of whom seemed prepared to try to use the mob scene to free the arrested strikers, but they fell back as the sheriff's deputies were augmented by the newest weapon in the mine operators' arsenal: an armored car with a mounted machine gun rigged out a few days before by A. C. Felts.[10]

It was an odd-looking machine, with waist-high sides fashioned from thick steel and a bug-eyed single spotlight mounted on what should have been the dashboard. Felts had the machine built out of a car the Rocky Mountain Fuel Co. had sent from Denver to transport the Baldwin-Felts men around the coalfields. One of the first times they used it, the detectives encountered some armed strikers and the car was shot up. So Felts ordered plates of three-quarter-inch steel from CF&I's Pueblo steel plant and had them sent to a CF&I garage at Jansen, near the Sopris mine outside Trinidad. Under Felts's personal supervision, the original open back of the vehicle was replaced by one cobbled together from wood and some of the steel plates, and other plates were emplaced as three-foot-high sides out almost over the wheels. The front and back were formed in a V-shape, like a land-bound dinghy.[11]

Purely functional, the car looked like a metal open-topped box perched on spoked wheels, a kid's outsized Soap Box Derby entry. If not for the Colt machine gun, mounted where the backseat should have been and with its muzzle just clearing the edge of the steel walls, it would have been a comical sight. But the gun, which Felts had shipped in from West Virginia, was serious business, capable of firing up to four hundred shots a minute with a killing range of two miles, mounted on a tripod that let it swing from side to side and up and down while the gunman was nearly completely hidden by the high steel walls.[12] Northcutt's *Trinidad Chronicle-News* described Felts's ersatz armored car as a "battleship,"[13] while strikers quickly named it the Death Special. Just as a gun introduced in the first act of a play usually gets fired by the end, the Death Special was not long silent.

About 1:20 P.M. on October 17, a rain-soaked Friday, strikers ensconced on the high canyon sides above the Forbes mine began taking potshots at the tipple, the mine apparatus that transfers coal from mine cars to rail cars. Mine guards returned fire, and as the shots echoed out of the high, narrow canyon, women and children in the Forbes tent colony scurried to a nearby stone ranch house for safety. Most of the men grabbed their own guns and headed for cover on the hillside and in arroyos.[14] Forbes mine officials called Sheriff Grisham in Trinidad and the Hastings mine in Del Agua Canyon, the next canyon to the north, for reinforcements. Within a half hour, ten mounted deputies left Chicaso Station and, passing the Forbes

The "Death Special," converted at detective A. C. Felts's direction into an armored gun car. The machine gun was turned on striking miners and used to riddle the Forbes tent colony. *Credit: Denver Public Library, Western History Collection, Call No. X-60380.*

tent colony, arrived at the mine camp. The shooting from the hillsides died away. The Death Special was at the Hastings mine when the call for help went out, and strikers at the Ludlow tent colony watched as it rolled past holding eight mine guards, including Belk and Belcher. Other cars bearing Zeke Martin, the undersheriff, and another force of ten deputies then arrived from Trinidad, all getting there within a few minutes of each other.

A clear view of how the shooting resumed is unavailable. One of Martin's deputies, C. W. Kennedy, who was also a mine guard,[15] approached the Forbes tent colony waving a large white handkerchief. Kennedy said later the strikers shot at him as he approached; the union version was that when Kennedy neared the strikers, he tossed the white cloth and dropped to the ground, rolling out of the way as his fellow deputies and gunmen opened fire. Each side accused the other of planning the attack under the ruse of a cease-fire, but neither version seems entirely true. Regardless, the exposed deputies scurried for cover behind the rail embankment. R. B. Bradley, a CF&I guard who had arrived with Martin, was critically wounded in the groin by a shot fired from the hillside. The men in the back of the Death Special bailed out—all except the gun operator, Baldwin-Felts detective C. B. Cunningham—as the driver swerved the car into position about a hundred yards from the tent colony. Cunningham opened fire, a protracted spurt that sent some six hundred bullets tearing through the thin tents. One of the shots struck miner Luka Vahernik, fifty, in the head, killing him instantly. Another striker, Marco Zamboni, eighteen—he often is erroneously described as much younger and as the son of a miner—suffered nine bullet wounds to his legs, five in the right and four in the left (he spent six weeks in a hospital recovering).[16] Just after the guards and Baldwin-Felts men opened fire, "there came up a fearful storm, and about that time the firing ceased and the men withdrew."[17] One tent was later found to have about 150 bullet holes in it; strike supporters made it part of a touring show mounted to spread word about the strike and to raise funds.[18]

After the machine-gunning of the Forbes tents, union leaders sought help from Washington and supported nascent efforts by a local congressman and supporter, U.S. Rep. Edward Keating, to introduce legislation Stewart had recommended creating a special commission to investigate the causes of the strike and its conduct.[19] But the leaders also hinted at violence to come, drawing direct parallels between the strike under way in Colorado and the earlier battles in West Virginia. It is clear that union leaders saw a war in gestation. "There are about seven hundred gunmen in this field, a great many of them being imported from West Virginia and the bad lands of the big cities. They are desperate characters and will not hesitate at anything in order to accomplish their ends. Handicapped as we are, we do not propose to let the operators shoot us into submission."[20] Brake, too, lobbied for a federal investigation. In a letter to U.S. Sen. Charles S. Thomas, he warned that "there are no less than eight hundred to one thousand gunmen in these two counties, most all of whom have deputy sheriff commissions. It looks like a civil war, the streets of Trinidad and Walsenburg are infested with Baldwin & Felts detectives, all armed, aggrative and abusive."[21]

The night the machine gun was turned on the Forbes colony, Ammons summoned Doyle, the union's Denver-based secretary-treasurer, to his office.[22] According to Doyle, Ammons was upset by violence in the coalfields and warned him that the union "ought to control our men." Doyle told Ammons that much of the violence was provoked by the Baldwin-Felts gunmen, who were repeating what he saw as the West Virginia game plan: draw the strikers into violence, then use that as an argument for declaring martial law. Ammons ignored Doyle's point and said that both Farr and Grisham had asked for help and "there seemed to be nothing else left for him to do but to send troops down there." Doyle urged caution, mentioning the disastrous effects of Governor Peabody's sending the militia into Cripple Creek during the 1903 strike. That strike ended, Doyle argued, but the conditions did not change, leading to the current crisis and demand for union recognition. Doyle asked Ammons if "he intended to deport one-half of the miners and shoot the other half, by way of settlement, and if this was done it would only be another ten years" before the same battles were fought again. Doyle suggested the governor throw the principals into jail together until they agreed to "a gentleman's conference."

Ammons brushed past the suggestion, and the two men argued about the proper role for the militia. Doyle asked pointedly whether Ammons would help Lawson out if he called and said he was having trouble controlling the strikers. "Oh, no," Ammons said. "I would not give him assistance while he had armed murderers shooting at innocent people on the road."

"Why, Governor," Doyle said, "you have offered to give assistance to the Baldwin-Felts detectives—to the deputies—knowing as you do that you have no control over them because they are county officers, yet you refuse a citizen of the state of Colorado, Mr. Lawson, assistance."

Ammons bristled and told Doyle what he would expect the state militia to accomplish. "I want peace; the armed guards will be taken away and these people will be disarmed and we must have peace." Doyle said the miners wanted peace, too, but also the right to picket. Again Ammons bristled. "There will be no picketing, there will be no picketing—that is positive—that is where the trouble will start." Ammons ended the meeting, and Doyle left feeling the governor was in over his head. "He never seemed to know what to do and when to do it."

What Doyle didn't know was that the coal operators were pressuring the governor heavily on the other side, trying to get him to restore what they saw as normalcy in the coalfields—men going into the mines and coal coming out. Ammons was slow to bend. Some time in mid-October, the operators rented a suite of rooms in a Denver hotel and arranged to meet Ammons there, a secret gathering on neutral turf. Reporter Gene Fowler was in the newsroom of the *Denver Republican* when a source, a Colonel Jamieson, wandered in to tell Fowler that "he had overheard in court chambers that the coal operators soon were to hold a secret meeting with Governor Ammons."[23] Fowler, with an introduction from his editor, went to see Brown at the Rocky Mountain Fuel Co. to check out the report. Brown told Fowler that he was on his way and "to my pleasant amazement" invited Fowler to tag along. They were the first to arrive, and Brown put Fowler in a bedroom of the suite, where he listened as the operators arrived—eight men in all, including Osgood and Welborn. "They exchanged pleasant greetings while waiting for the governor to appear, and spoke of golf and fishing and the Supreme Court." They also settled on a strategy: Welborn and Osgood would do the talking—CF&I and Victor-American teaming up to lobby the governor.

Ammons finally arrived, and after a brief cordial exchange of greetings "Welborn got down to business. He bluntly requested that troops be sent to subdue the striking miners." Ammons told the operators he couldn't do it; he'd been elected on the strength of labor's support and could not turn his back on those voters. "At this, Mr. Osgood began not only to threaten the Governor's political future but also to call him names." It went on for an hour, the operators haranguing, Ammons defending, until, like water on a stone, they wore him down. "The governor wearily surrendered to his browbeaters. He promised to dispatch members of the National Guard to the Trinidad fields on October 28." The specificity of Fowler's anecdote, published in 1946, is suspect. Ammons's recollections closer to the events, corroborated by others, indicate he had not made the decision at that point, or at least had not offered a date, since he was still trying to negotiate a settlement between the two sides. It seems more likely that Fowler's recollection conflates the episode in the hotel suite with Ammons's eventual decision. In any event, the flavor of the scene and the ferocity of the operators' lobbying seem both reasonable and in keeping with the men's hard-driving personalities.

At the end of the meeting, a lawyer for one of the coal operators entered the bedroom en route to the bathroom and spotted Fowler, whom he knew. "How the hell did you get in here?" he asked. The noise brought the other men into the room. Ammons stayed at the doorway "more wrinkled than I had ever seen him before, and he worriedly plucked at his cuffs." Fowler and Osgood argued—in Fowler's convenient memory, he got the better of the coal operator—and the reporter left with his notes as Brown admitted nervously to the others that he had invited Fowler along.

By the time Fowler returned to the newsroom to begin writing his scoop, the operators had already been on the phone to the paper's editor. The story was killed.

The strike was not all violence. Conditions in the tent colonies were harsh, but for many of the strikers this did not mark much of a change from their lives in the canyons. As winter pressed in, strikers had less success hunting rabbits and other small game, and it became harder for strike leaders to find fresh supplies for the Ludlow camp commissary.[24] But the sense of shared purpose buoyed those who did not drift off to return to work, or to take nonmining jobs in Trinidad or other places. Each morning someone would raise the American flag outside Ludlow's community tent in the colony's main square, which also held an elevated wooden platform, like a low stage. In good weather, union meetings were held outside. When it rained or snowed, the men gathered inside the big tent, warmed by a large potbellied stove in the middle. Workmen had cobbled together large picnic tables outside some of the tents, and clotheslines stitched the air.

The strikers also tried to create a sense of normalcy inside their assigned tents. "Many used their old linoleums to cover cracks in the floor boards to prepare for colder weather," Mary Thomas recalled years later. She had two cots for her girls to sleep on. "The store gave me three empty wooden orange crates with dividers in them which, when put on end, made fine stands with a shelf underneath for food or dishes. I covered them with the tablecloths I'd been given for a wedding present. I put my bright bedspreads on the cots, with curtains to match which I hung over the two small windows. These, too, I had brought from Wales. I got three chairs and a table from the commissary to round out our furnishings, and took great pride in hanging my trinkets on the four-foot-high sidewalls. One thing which especially pleased me was that each tent had a door which could be locked."

Thomas painted a picture of a strikers' utopia, a commune born of need and always filled with good cheer—a rather burnished accounting. The reality can be read in small moments. Thomas and her friends Cedi Costa and Margo Gorci would meet for morning coffee at the Gorcis' tent, sitting outside in the sun on nice days. "What a bleak view. For miles and miles there was uneven prairie, with small hills scattered all about. Half a mile back of the colony was the deep arroyo which took the waters from the melting snow to the valley below." It also was the route followed by caravans of scabs protected by armed guards, who would draw jeers from the tent colony. Threats and insults were hurled back and forth, and occasionally fights broke out. At the start of the strike, Tony Gorci, Margo's husband, had been set upon by mine guards as the family was leaving the mine camp and had to be carried out of the canyon like one of the family's possessions, strapped on top of the wagon of household goods. "When I saw his face I got sick to my stomach. I couldn't see his eyes. His face looked like a blubber of blue and black jelly mixed with red blood."[25]

The violence cut both ways. Lawson was in charge of the tent colony but during his protracted absences Louis Tikas, the Greek organizer, took over. The standing order from the union was to avoid violence, on the theory that the mine guards were provoking confrontations to create disturbances that would lead Ammons to send in the militia. But controlling hundreds of idle, armed men was a hopeless task. "Lawson had ordered time and time again that there should be no violence, but when he wasn't around the men who picketed each of the passing vehicles shouted 'scabs,' and beat the hell out of them whenever they encountered those who had thumbed their noses rudely at the women and children."[26]

From Bowers's standpoint, the strike was an inconvenience to the bottom line. CF&I held its annual meeting in Denver on October 20, and the next day Bowers repeated in a report to Twenty-six Broadway his earlier view that "net earnings would have been the largest in the history of the company" had it not been for the wage hike meant to buy labor peace. "With everything running so smoothly and with an excellent outlook for 1914, it is mightily discouraging to have this vicious gang come into our state and not only destroy our profit but eat into that which has heretofore been saved. There are a few more miners working today than at any time since the strike, and if the miners who were forced out on account of fear had the protection of the militia, a large percentage of them would return to work at once."[27]

Bowers may have truly believed that—there is no evidence indicating he had any doubts about this misreading of the strikers' intents—but the stress was having a physical effect. His son Clement arrived in Denver on October 20, traveling from Binghamton. Bowers met him at the train depot, and they went to a restaurant for breakfast. "I didn't think that he looked well and he was complaining somewhat of an attack of lumbago. But what worried me was his worn-out look, and upon inquiry I learned that he had been pretty well tied down with this strike stuff." Clement noted that his father had earlier written him that "the coal operators have installed six gattling guns, so I guess that the situation is becoming serious. . . . I feel some slight concern over my father's safety."[28]

The union organizers were just as concerned about their own safety. On October 20, Germer and Neelley, the Walsenburg hardware store co-owner, made a return trip to Holmes's hardware store in Pueblo, where they had bought revolvers on the eve of the strike. This time they came for heavier arms. Neelley told Holmes that Germer wanted to pick out some guns, and that Holmes should charge them to Neelley's store account. Germer said he was interested in .30–30 rifles. He picked one up, looked at it, then turned to Neelley. "I believe that ought to be about the right caliber to go through the armor on that automobile," Germer said. "I'll take it." Holmes showed Germer a smaller .30 caliber rifle, and "he made the remark that that would be a very good gun to pull down those searchlights with." Germer bought twenty rifles and one revolver that day and sent Neelley back over the next few days to buy one hundred more rifles. But stocks were low and Neelley only managed to find twenty-one at Holmes's store and another seventeen rifles and revolvers at another Pueblo gun shop.[29]

The union found weapons to the south, too. Claude Shy ran a hardware store in Trinidad in the Packer Block—downstairs from the union headquarters—and sold as many guns as he could order, often in small quantities to men he didn't know, and always for cash.[30] Some he did know—Charles Snyder and John Barulich, who first came into the district to spy for the union. But both men were too well known by the other miners in the coalfields, so instead they became bodyguards for Lawson, McLennan, Germer, and other union officials. And, apparently, they became gun runners.[31] Over the course of a few weeks, Shy sold about two thousand mostly modern high-powered rifles, at around seventeen dollars apiece, to Snyder, Barulich, and other men he presumed to be part of the miners' union. Men would just show up at his shop, ask how many guns he had in stock and how much they were, and then leave and return a few minutes later with the cash. Often the weapons were set aside in the back of the store and Snyder and Barulich would pick them up.

After the violence at the Forbes tent colony, Ammons decided that he needed a personal view of the strike district. On October 21, he left Denver for Trinidad, putting up in the Cardenas Hotel, a two-story, mission-style building next to the Atchison, Topeka & Santa Fe depot on the north bank of the Purgatoire River, a short walk over a bridge and then along Commercial Street to downtown Trinidad. But most of the people he needed to see—and many more he didn't—beat a path to the Cardenas. Mother Jones led a demonstration outside the hotel the afternoon Ammons arrived, and the hotel lobby swarmed with union officials, agents for the operators, and local businesspeople hoping to bend the governor's ear as, between scheduled meetings, Ammons came and went on driving forays to some of the mines. Among the milling lobby crowd was a moon-faced man about five feet, nine inches inches tall and stocky with blue eyes, brown hair, and a light complexion. His name was Karl E. Linderfelt, a name that would come to be inextricably linked with the killings to come.

Linderfelt, a National Guard volunteer, had arrived in Trinidad some-time during the four days between the Forbes battle and the governor's arrival. When the strike began, he had been working as a contractor sinking and timbering a shaft in a Cripple Creek gold mine. Shortly afterward, he traveled to Denver for "a rifle match or a school of instruction," and saw General Chase, with whom he had served during the 1903 strike. Chase asked Linderfelt to stay over an extra day, because he wanted him to travel to Trinidad for early reconnaissance in case the militia was called out. But the next day Chase sent Linderfelt back to Cripple Creek and dispatched to Trinidad two other experienced guardsmen, Lt. Morris Bigelow and Lt. Al Chase, the general's nephew. As the violence continued in the strike district, Linderfelt, the eager volunteer, kept calling Chase from Cripple Creek. "It is about time to go now, isn't it? I would go—my affairs are all straightened out up here." Chase finally gave the word. "I had all my stuff ready to move, and when I left I took my wife with me as far as Pueblo, and she went on to Denver, and I went on down there."[32]

Linderfelt had spent his working life as a miner—usually gold—or as a military man. In his own self-descriptions, Linderfelt was a reasonable professional soldier; to others, he was a brutal braggart; and the historical record suggests he was a liar as well.

Linderfelt was born November 7, 1876, in Janesville, Wisconsin, a farm town of about eight thousand people some ten miles north of the Illinois state line. His mother, Maggie Cooper, was born in Vermont.[33] His father, Klas August Linderfelt, was born in 1847 in Sweden, where he overcame the early deaths of his parents—he was five when his mother died; eleven when his father died—to earn a doctorate at Uppsala University before emigrating to Milwaukee around 1870.[34] Klas Linderfelt taught the classics for several years at Milwaukee College, but when the city opened its first library in 1880 he landed the job as chief administrator—the city's first librarian. By then he was married, and his wife had given birth to Karl and a sister (two brothers would follow). The family was living at 278 Pleasant Street, where their neighbors were railroad clerks, a builder, and a piano tuner.[35]

The elder Linderfelt immersed himself in library science, writing extensively on library management and financing. He also co-wrote *Volapük: Easy Method of Acquiring the Universal Language* with Johann Martin Schleyer and Alfred Kirchhoff in 1886, touting an early planned language along the lines of Esperanto. And he rose through the ranks of the American Library Association (ALA) until, during an 1891 convention in San Francisco, he was elected president of the group. By then, the Linderfelts

Lieutenant Karl E. Linderfelt, center, a miner and soldier whose aggressive and profane encounters with strikers made him one of the most hated figures in the strike district. He personally recruited mercenaries to join his Colorado National Guard unit and was one of the officers in charge of the troops involved in the Ludlow Massacre. *Credit: Denver Public Library, Western History Collection, Call No. X-60536.*

had moved into the upper circles of Milwaukee's elite, living in a house at 408 Grand Avenue, a wide boulevard that in nice weather was an irresistible promenade for people out for a stroll or a carriage ride. His son, Karl, was active in several youth cadet and zouave (marching and drilling) clubs, displaying an early affinity for at least the pageantry and trappings of military life.[36]

If the neighborhood seemed expensive for a city librarian's budget, it was. In 1888 Klas Linderfelt was investigated over $2,000 (the equivalent of $40,000 in 2005) that had been found missing from the library's fines collection, dating back over the previous three years. The probe ended when two directors reimbursed the amount. In April 1892, as Linderfelt, the national ALA president, led the city's drive to build a magnificent limestone library in the French and Italian Renaissance style, he was arrested on embezzlement charges after another $4,000 (the equivalent of $80,000) was found missing from the library funds. Linderfelt was dismissed, but again

directors rode to his rescue, urging he be shown leniency—fearing, perhaps, that without him the new library project might stall. But even his
friends fell away when a deeper audit discovered that since 1883 a total of
$14,000 had disappeared—the equivalent of nearly $300,000. A sympathetic judge who accepted Linderfelt's nolo contendere plea in July 1893
decided that the shame had been sufficient punishment and suspended his
sentence,[37] outraging the city as Linderfelt moved immediately to Boston
and a promised job there. Over the next few weeks, political pressure in
Milwaukee increased until the mayor ordered Linderfelt arrested on any
charges that might not have been cleared away by the nolo contendere
plea. By then, though, Linderfelt was long gone, first to Sweden and by the
end of the year to Paris, where he studied medicine and then worked at *La
Semaine Médicale,* a French journal. He died in Paris in 1900.

Klas Linderfelt's very public fall began when Karl was twelve and
reached its nadir when he was sixteen. In 1892, after his father's arrest, Karl
entered the Beloit College Academy in Beloit, Wisconsin, seventy-five
miles southwest of Milwaukee on the Illinois state line—and less than ten
miles from Janesville, where he had been born. The academy was a private
feeder prep school for Beloit College, an attempt to replicate the elite private East Coast colleges, and Linderfelt entered as part of the "junior
preparatory class."[38] He finished the year and resumed classes in the fall of
1893, after his father had moved to Boston, but then dropped out around
the time his father left the country.

While the father ran east, the son ran west, and the privileged life of
Milwaukee and private prep school was replaced in early 1894 by the
rugged mining town of Cripple Creek, where the young Linderfelt—then
seventeen—moved in with some uncles who worked as gold miners.[39] Linderfelt joined the trade and eventually enlisted in the Colorado National
Guard on April 29, 1898, five days after President William McKinley issued
a call for 125,000 volunteers as he ordered a blockade of Cuba on the eve
of the Spanish-American War.[40] Linderfelt's Guard unit was quickly transferred into the U.S. Cavalry, and he was stationed in Florida and then the
Presidio in San Francisco before being deployed to the Philippines in 1899.
By the time Linderfelt arrived, the Spanish-American War had ended and
the U.S. fight against Filipino insurgents had begun, a bloody and brutal
campaign that was more repression than warfare. Linderfelt took part in
more than two dozen battles before being mustered out October 12, 1900,
when his father died. He then traveled to China and joined the quartermaster corps in the northeast city of Taku during the Boxer Rebellion be-

fore returning to the States.[41] He was called up for service during the 1903 strike, serving in Cripple Creek and near his home in Telluride, and in 1912 he went south as a mercenary to fight with Madero, spending six months in Sonora and Chihuahua.[42] If Linderfelt wasn't a soldier of fortune, he was close to it.

Most of Linderfelt's military record—except the Boxer Rebellion service—is documented in federal records, but some of his claims seem to be contradicted by records and circumstance. For instance, Linderfelt claimed that he had studied medicine for two years at the Sorbonne, where, he said, his father, the librarian and language inventor, was a "professor of anatomy," and that he spent two years at Beloit College but "didn't finish my sophomore year," skipping over the fact that he had attended as a prep student and was in fact a high school dropout.[43] Except for military service, Linderfelt said he had lived in Colorado since joining his uncles in 1894, leaving no time for study at the Sorbonne—where it is not clear that his father ever worked. They were similar to the embellishments, half-truths, and outright falsehoods that would mark Linderfelt's later renditions of what transpired during coalfield battles, where he took every opportunity to install a halo over his own head in defiance of credible witnesses who offered sharply contradictory versions.

When Linderfelt arrived in Trinidad in October 1913, he contacted Sheriff Grisham and told him that he had been sent south to be General Chase's eyes and ears. "My mission was to give the absolute truth to the adjutant general [Chase] and the governor of this state."[44] After confirming Linderfelt's contention in a phone call to Chase, Grisham swore Linderfelt in as a deputy sheriff on October 23.[45] Chase told Linderfelt to stay in Trinidad until Ammons arrived to consult with a Colonel Lee, who was in the governor's entourage. Linderfelt hung out in the Cardenas lobby, within sight of Lawson and other union officials, and the operators and their representatives, but none of them knew the rather nondescript man, and he passed unnoticed.[46] During Ammons's stay, it was decided that Linderfelt would take command of the deputies encamped at Ludlow, working for Grisham—he was paid by Las Animas County—since the National Guard had not been authorized to work in the southern field. But his prime responsibility was to report daily, and first, to Chase. Linderfelt headed to Ludlow immediately and took command, directing his deputies as they escorted strikebreakers from the train station to the mine camps in Berwind and Del Agua canyons.[47]

Ammons's visit to the strike district was largely uneventful, but it seemed to have cemented a decision: He would have to send in the troops to maintain the peace. Yet Ammons did not give up on trying to forge an agreement under which the miners would return to work. The operators had earlier agreed to abide by state laws and said they had no outstanding issues with the strikers other than the UMWA's demand for recognition. The union, for its part, believed—probably correctly—that any agreement without union protections was worthless and that the working environment in the coalfields would shortly revert to prestrike conditions unless the union was there.

Once back in Denver, Ammons summoned the strike leaders to his office. Before the meeting, Lawson, Hayes, McLennan, Doyle, and Germer were in the UMWA offices at the German-American Trust Company Building reviewing scenarios they might anticipate. The telephone rang, and a mysterious man said he had an urgent need to talk with McLennan out on the street, at the corner of First Avenue and Broadway. McLennan begged off, telling the caller he was preparing for a meeting with the governor. "I want to see you before you meet the governor," the caller told him. His curiosity piqued, McLennan, with Doyle at his elbow, went down to meet the man, who warned them that the operators "were making to import men . . . and he said that the operators were preparing for a fight." The man offered to play double agent, working for both sides, an offer McLennan turned down. The meeting with the governor ultimately was fruitless. Ammons told the union men that the operators had agreed to obey state laws governing mining but held firmly against recognizing or negotiating with the UMWA. Doyle and the others decided later that the mysterious man was part of the operators' ruse to threaten the union into calling off the strike, and the details about importing men and preparing for a fight were meant to be intimidating.[48]

The mining work itself remained as dangerous for the scabs as it had been for the now idle miners. On October 10, rock falls at the Delagua and Morley mines killed two strikebreakers, Giuseppi Nicalotto, thirty-eight, and Patrick Moore, fifty-three.[49] But the mining world was stunned a few days after the Forbes battle when, a little after 3:00 P.M. Wednesday, October 22, coal dust in the Stag Canyon Mine No. 2 in Dawson, New Mexico, ignited in a flash explosion. Rock ceilings crumbled, and more than two hundred men were feared trapped. Rescuers from across New Mexico, Colorado, and Kansas hurried to the scene, and five would-be rescuers died in a fog of poisonous gas within the shambles.[50] Each passing hour heightened fears over the extent of the catastrophe, as bodies were pulled singly and in groups from below ground.

Doyle was dispatched to take money to the widows of the dead men but had barely arrived before he was arrested and deported from Dawson by the mayor at the request of mine officials who did not want "agitators" on the scene while rescuers were working, even though the mine was not affected by the Colorado strike. "When I got off of the train I was taken by armed men bodily and told to get off the company's property," Doyle recalled. He demanded to be taken to the local post office—federal property—but was ignored. "Two men were on either side of me, and they walked me out and said, 'The closest border line to this property is six miles,' and they walked me out at night. I was picked up by an automobile, and went that night to Trinidad, over the mountains, and at every turn we made . . . searchlights were thrown into our faces. It was a wonder they did not kill men who were not concerned with the strike at all."[51]

Deep below Dawson, there were few miners to rescue. Five men managed to escape the blast relatively unharmed. The death toll reached 263, the worst mining disaster in the western coalfields. But the rescuers did not give up easily, and they were still working frantically when violence returned to the Colorado field.

SIX

Deadly Encounters

For the first few weeks of the strike, the small city of Walsenburg, about forty miles north of Trinidad, had settled into tense idleness. Despite being Sheriff Farr's seat of power, Walsenburg was an open city, and most of the striking miners were not forced from their homes. The few that had been living on company property moved into a small tent colony at the western end of Fifth Street, partway between the mines and Walsenburg's Main Street. The UMWA set up its headquarters not in a tent but in a suite at the Oxford Hotel on Sixth Street, a block west of Main. Striking miners had the run of the town, which brought them into steady contact with strike-breakers and their families, who were routinely harassed and threatened. A few were beaten; the worst of the violence was the dynamiting of the La-gresto home on September 28. In response, many of the miners who did not join the strike and many of the newly hired strikebreakers moved into the protection of the mine complexes.

One coal digger at the Walsen mine by the name of Wahlmeier, known locally as "Dutch,"[1] cast his lot with the company and refused to join the walkout. The mine was only a short walk from his house at 627 West Seventh Street, near Ysidro Street a few blocks from Main, but constant threats led Wahlmeier to move into the mine camp. His wife stayed behind in the house, but on October 24, with reports circulating of the gun battle near Ludlow, she decided to seek protection in the camp, too. The final prod: a note she found attached to her door that morning. "Warning to Mrs. Dutch, if you don't move out of this neighborhood within forty-eight hours, we will blow you out. Scabs can't live with white people. Your husband is scabbing. Signed by the committee. We mean business."[2] Mrs. Wahlmeier summoned Farr's deputies and sent word to her husband in the mine, and by early afternoon three wagons pulled by teams of horses and protected by about fifteen armed mine guards arrived in the alley behind her house to begin loading the family's belongings.[3]

Few things go unnoticed in a small town, and it wasn't long before the packing of the wagons attracted a small crowd, at first mostly women, some of whom shouted taunts and jeers. A nearby elementary school let out about 3:30 P.M., adding scores of excited youngsters to the growing throng, which by now had attracted a number of striking miners as well. Alexander Osvirk, twenty-one, an Austrian, was standing in a pool hall on Main Street when he noticed people hurrying toward Seventh Street, so he joined in. "I thought there was fighting up there and I went to see." Moses Nelson, twenty-two, fell in with the crowd, too, arriving just as passions began to boil over. "When I got there they were loading wagons up and ladies were throwing rocks and tin cans and they were hollering, 'scabs!'" The mine guards tried to push the women back by turning on a hose, but the pressure wasn't strong enough to reach them.

By the time the wagons were loaded, around 4:00 P.M., the crowd had grown to more than 250 people, spilling out onto Seventh Street itself. Frederick Henney quit working in his butcher shop across the street and stepped outside for a look. "When the wagons came out of the side street onto Seventh Street there was a lot of children there, and they began to cheer and holler 'scab' and throw bits of dirt at the wagons." As the wagons moved, so did the crowd, trailing out of the alley and onto the street like a swarm of bees. The wagons and the guards, about half on horseback, the others walking, moved a hundred yards down the street before the crowd gave up the chase in a crescendo of insults, catcalls, and the occasional thrown rock and dirt clod. Despite the distance, one of the clods of dirt knocked a guard off balance, and he tumbled from his horse.

Guards later claimed that the first shot came from a man in the yard of "a negro's house" on West Seventh Street and that the guards returned fire to defend themselves.[4] Ana Atencio, watching from a window in her family's house next to the Wahlmeiers', reported seeing a striker crouching behind a fence take aim with a rifle and fire, clipping one of the guards in the ear.[5] A striking miner in the crowd, Eugene Thorne, who described himself as a friend of Germer's, saw a man with a revolver squeeze off several shots from around the corner of a house.[6] That lent some credibility to Atencio's story, as did the fact that mine guard H. C. Wetmore had a chunk of his ear carried off by a bullet,[7] even though no one in the striker crowd reported anyone from their side firing a gun.

But the bulk of the crowd—both strikers and townspeople—said that the first shot they saw or heard came as the wagons reached the next cross street and Jesse Russell, a captain of the mine guards, suddenly raised his rifle to his shoulder and fired into the crowd. "[H]e ran down the street and yelled, 'line up, boys,' and the guards ran around and down by him, leaving him at the rear of the line." At least two other guards on foot and three more on horseback joined in. "Then he raised his gun again and shot a man who was standing in front of Fred Richard's house." A striking miner named Romarovski dove to the ground as he spotted Russell raising his rifle; a bullet clipped his cap as a volley passed overhead and struck miner Andy Auvinen, thirty-six, just above the heart and in the groin. Auvinen, clutching his abdomen, staggered to a nearby fence, then fell to the ground; he died about seven hours later at the Oxford Hotel.

The crowd panicked. Children and women and men scurried for cover, ducking into side yards and fleeing eastward along Seventh Street. Samuel Huarez was watching from his front porch and saw the first man fall before "a bunch of women rushed up on our porch and pushed me in with them." The fusillade was brief but effective. Auvinen was on the ground, blood spilling from his abdomen. Cristo Croci, twenty-nine, had been caught in midword, a bullet entering his mouth and smashing through the lower part of his skull, stopping in the brain and killing him instantly. A third miner, Kris Kokich, twenty-four, was hit in the neck, the bullet passing between his windpipe and spine. He died the next day.

The strikers moved to high ground north of the Walsen mine and over the next several hours set up a steady assault. Some sought but failed to shoot out the powerful searchlight. Rumors swirled of another charge by the mine guards, then of a counterattack by enraged strikers. Germer, the UMWA organizer, went to the Neelley-Caldwell hardware store and bought some thirty rifles for the UMWA office in the hotel about a block south of the Huerfano County Courthouse,[8] which Sheriff Farr had ringed with armed deputies and called for reinforcements. A detachment of mine guards and deputies stationed at the mines near Ludlow arrived after dark. Another crew of twenty-four mine guards rode in from the Rouse Mine, a dozen miles to the south. Sporadic gunfire continued through the night, mostly potshots into and out of the mine camps seemingly aimed more at intimidation than targeted attacks. Near midnight, a squad of twenty-five deputies under the command of Las Animas County undersheriff Zeke

Martin arrived from Trinidad bearing two of the coal operators' machine guns, which had been assigned to Ludlow,[9] and cementing the strikers' perceptions that the sheriff's departments and the mining companies were the same enemy. Germer wired from Walsenburg to U.S. Rep. Edward Keating urging a federal investigation into the local collusion.[10]

Farr and others presumed the miners were planning another assault, but rumors, rather than action, ruled the streets of Walsenburg. "If the miners are congregating, they are doing it quietly. Hardly anyone has been on the street since dark. The [tent] colony at the head of Fifth Street is quiet. The people who live near the courthouse are making preparations to protect themselves in case of attack. Lights are seen in the cellars of many houses and people are preparing to sleep there."[11]

The next morning, the detachment of twenty-five guards returned to Rouse. But tensions continued in Walsenburg. Mine guards and sheriff's deputies raided the Neelley-Caldwell store, operating from a rumor that the miners had had a machine gun shipped there. Striking miners carried their own weapons in the open. Around 3:00 P.M., a detachment of deputies moved toward the Oxford Hotel with a purpose they never got to state. Germer presumed the deputies had come to seize the miners' weapons, something he was not about to let happen. Before the deputies arrived, the miners—armed to a man—arrayed themselves on the hotel roof, and after a brief standoff, the deputies retreated.[12] The feared second wave of attacks did not come to Walsenburg.

But by then, a battle was under way in Ludlow.

The C&S rail line from Denver ran along the prairie edge, and from the cars travelers looking east could see the countryside spreading flatly to the horizon, an unending table of emptiness save for low grass, flecks of scrub brush, and the occasional ranch. The view to the west, though, was spectacular—a slow-changing vista of peaks and canyons and intermittent coal camps. Travelers looking down West Seventh Street in Walsenburg, as the train pulled out of the station, could see in the distance the twin Spanish Peaks lurching some thirteen thousand feet into the sky, snow-capped for much of the year.

A southbound C&S train neared the Ludlow station around 2:30 P.M. on October 25, a Saturday afternoon, slowing to cross the narrow steel bridge over the Del Agua Arroyo and then on past the geometrically arrayed Ludlow tent colony, its square-sided white tents a bright spot of color against the sere brown of the prairie edge. Usually, at least a few kids from the camp could be counted on to wave at the passengers on the slowing train, but by midafternoon that day the camp was empty of children and women. They had moved in the morning to Trinidad and other tent colonies at Forbes and Aguilar. The mine guards and sheriff's deputies concluded that the strikers were planning trouble, but it is just as likely, given the killings at Walsenburg the day before, that the strikers moved the women and children to safety in case the next attack came at Ludlow, the de facto field headquarters for Lawson and other strike leaders.

As the train neared the station, a detachment of four deputies made their way from their encampment at a railroad section house just south of Ludlow, planning to greet and protect arriving passengers—who often included a strikebreaker or two who needed protection to reach the mine camps.[13] While the deputies were still out in the open, near Water Tank Hill, strikers hidden behind a steel rail bridge opened fire, sending the deputies skittering for cover. Other strikers who had tucked themselves into a nearby arroyo began firing, too, as more deputies, roused by the sound of gunfire, spilled out of the section house. Ralph Tafoya, twenty-eight, who was helping cook dinner, ran out with the others, returning gunfire as they looked for places to take cover.[14] They moved slowly toward the bridge, and after a while Tafoya hooked up with John Nimmo, thirty-one, a National Guardsman from Denver whom he had befriended when Nimmo signed on two days earlier as a deputized mine guard.[15]

These were some of the men Linderfelt had been dispatched to lead, but he had spent the bulk of that day meeting with other deputies at Chicosa, some twelve miles west of Trinidad, getting them organized and "having the horses shod in shape." Linderfelt was on his way back to the section house when he heard the first gunshots. "I immediately spurred up my horse and started over to the section house, but before I had gone very far, heavy firing broke out from Water Tank Hill toward the section house." Linderfelt also heard guns firing on the hillside. He jumped down from his horse "and got behind the railroad bank with two men and returned the fire. I worked around this railroad cut, on the opposite side of the road [from the hillside gunmen], which gave me protection." The strikers' gunfire had dislodged most of his men. "I found the deputies that were there were driven back from all points except a few around the station house. Then a lot of men [about sixty, including storemen, strikebreakers and guards] came down from Berwind Canyon and joined in with us and we drove them from Water Tank Hill."[16]

The battle lasted for about three hours, mostly a desultory exchange with gunmen from each side sending "several hundred" bullets over hundreds of yards, neither group making much gain, content to shoot and duck. A couple of hours into the battle, Nimmo moved ahead of his fellow mine guards and scrambled up a small rise leading up to the rail line, drawing the strikers' fire. "He turned and ran back quite a distance and fell."[17] Thad Sowder ran to him, using the berm as protection, and asked Nimmo, bleeding heavily from a gunshot wound to the abdomen, if he wanted his coat for extra warmth. "Never mind," Nimmo said, "let me die." Sowder left him, returning to a more protected position. Around dusk, snow flurries increased to a heavy snowfall, and the shooting died away as the targets became harder to see. In the dark, guards recovered Nimmo's body, facedown under a dusting of snow.

Word spread quickly through the strikers' colonies about the Walsenburg killings and the Ludlow battle, and armed miners began arriving in both places in groups. About fifty men came in from Aguilar to the north, and dozens of others worked their way over the hills from other colonies. Some eight hundred men convened in the Ludlow colony itself; countless others were out on the plains and in the hills. Linderfelt, fearing another attack would overrun the guards in the section house, abandoned the position. "There was no other place I could go—no place I could defend myself at all." The men slipped deep into the canyon, arriving at Berwind around 2:00 A.M. and bedding down in the coal mine's small power plant.

An hour or so later, another group of guards from the Berwind camp moved out of the canyon to take up positions at the same C&S steel bridge from which the strikers had attacked the Ludlow guards. It was a key piece of turf, commanding a high-ground view of the canyon mouth and offering the strikers a vantage point from which they could stop scab-bearing trains. The guards wanted to make sure they controlled the bridge as the sun rose. But they were too late. As the guards arrived in the snowy darkness, strikers unleashed a volley from the bridge that sent them scurrying back the way they had come. This signaled something of a military turning point as the strikers, clearly organized, and with the killings at Walsenburg fresh in their minds, began a siege of Berwind Canyon.

With the break of dawn, mine guards near the mouth of the canyon and the Tabasco mine camp could make out the silhouettes of strikers advancing down the hillsides and in view of witnesses like Harvey Deuell, a reporter for the *Rocky Mountain News*. "The guards opened fire and their bullets flicked the dust about their antagonists' feet but the advance of

the latter continued while the brief and frequent whiffs of smoke from before each figure and the sharp pop of exploding cartridges indicated that
the fire of the guards was being returned." The guards retreated farther
into the canyon as the strikers pressed on, slipping from boulder to tree for
protection "and pouring into the base of the canyon a harassing stream
of lead."[18]

The mine guards retreated to Berwind, where Linderfelt was on his way
to breakfast when a deputy intercepted him to say that armed strikers were
moving in. "I gathered, I think, about 20 men and started up the left-
handed [north] side of the canyon, because of the military importance of
the crest of those hills." The hillsides were covered with large boulders,
many larger than the men themselves, which offered key protection for an
attack on Berwind—or for its defense against attackers creeping up the
canyon mouth. As with the steel bridge near Ludlow, the strikers had
beaten the guards to the high ground and opened fire. "Just as I arrived at
the crest I think there was, from the volume of fire, about twenty-five or
thirty men." Linderfelt, who had brought a leashed dog with him, and a
few of the other guards and deputies dove for cover behind boulders. But
most fled, sending a cascade of men tumbling down the hillside on the
fine-grain slag from the washer of a nearby hillside mine. "They could
jump off the cliff ten feet high and strike this slide and go right down into
the canyon," Linderfelt said. One of the men, Thomas Whitney, fifty, an
Ohio native who had been working in gold mines near Telluride before
signing up as a mine guard, was shot dead before he could make the leap.[19]

The battle carried on for about an hour. Linderfelt huddled between
two boulders about twenty feet from the strikers. "I could see these men
and hear them talking and firing. . . . Every time one of us would show a
head or anything we would be fired at, so it was almost suicide to raise my
head, and so I could not notice what was going on" up above. Linderfelt
could see down below into the canyon, though. "They were firing all along
the ridge into the entire canyon." After about an hour, guards from the
pump house managed to climb the hill deeper in the canyon and "came
across the nose of the canyon toward the position I was in and flanked
those people out of there and they left." The guards continued their push
and dislodged the strikers from the canyon, pressing them back out past
Tabasco to the prairie edge.

But the guards found themselves isolated, with ready communication
cut off after strikers took over the railroad section house Linderfelt and his
men had abandoned the previous day. The small wooden building held the

telephone connection for the line into Berwind Canyon. Whenever Linderfelt or one of his subordinates sought to call out, strikers monitoring
the line "would holler and make a noise or something, so that we could not
get telephone messages out, and finally burned the section house that Sunday afternoon." The telegraph wires were carried along poles on a different path, and Linderfelt was able to send and receive wired messages. The
next day, Linderfelt telegraphed his superior, General Chase: "There has
been a continuous battle for 40 hours. We have no expectation of ever receiving any help from Sheriff Gresham [sic]. Too damned much politics to
do anything from Trinidad. We must have ammunition and high-power
rifles to hold this place and protect women and children." Chase telegraphed
back that Grisham had in fact agreed to send reinforcements, but Linderfelt reported they never arrived. "Mounted man from Tabasco reports special [train] with deputies and soldiers driven back. I don't question report.
Large body of men leaving Aguilar to reinforce. Rebels at Ludlow openly
make statements they are going to clean up Berwind and Hastings. Situation looks hopeless. No hope can be expected only from troops, as there is
nothing left to hope for."[20]

Though the governor had not ordered out the National Guard, Chase
telegraphed Linderfelt that a squad of about fifteen members of B Company, Second Infantry, which had been formed of Trinidad-area men several years earlier, was being readied for service. They were joined by Felts,
who had just arrived from Denver, where he was interviewing potential
mine guards, and another fifty or so of Grisham's instant deputies. Carrying one of the machine guns, the reinforcements boarded a C&S "special"
train in Trinidad, but the regular train crews—union men—refused to
work. Strike supporters milled around the train station jeering and cursing the guards, and phone calls flew between sympathizers and the
UMWA office at the Ludlow tent colony. After a several-hour delay, former
railroad man George E. Hunt—now a Baldwin-Felts detective—was
pressed into service as the engineer and the train began moving north, an
engine pulling five open-topped coal cars filled with deputies.[21]

The train traveled the main line as far as Forbes, then veered off west-
ward on a spur to the Ramey mine at the southern edge of the entrance to
Berwind Canyon, where the track continued on to the Tabasco and Berwind mine camps. As the train neared Ramey, strikers on the hillside and
lying prone on the open prairie opened fire, the bullets first kicking up the
dirt around the tracks and then, as the riflemen found their range, pinging off the steel sides of the rail cars. "The popping of their guns became

continuous." The train slowed. Hunt, the temporary engineer, ducked below the protective walls of the locomotive; the gunmen in the cars also kept their heads below the steel wall. In a show of either extreme bravery or stupidity, a lone figure stood erect amid strikers fanned out on their bellies in the prairie. He was Victor Miller of Cleveland, a cameraman for the new Pathé Weekly newsreel company, and he held his ground against the flying bullets as he caught the battle on a thousand feet of film.

When the train was about a half mile from the strikers' positions on the hillside, the deputies began a counterattack, scouring the hillside with the machine gun. "Simultaneously heads appeared over the edges of the cars and guns popped in a steady series of concussions," the *Rocky Mountain News* reported. Rather than driving the strikers back, or forcing them to cease fire and seek protection, the fusillade increased return fire from the hillsides. "Reinforcements from the Ludlow camp pressed rapidly forward and spreading fanlike as they neared the canyon's mouth and threw themselves into action. The Colorado & Southern water tanks, near the bridge, sheltered five who fired with clocklike regularity. . . . Several stood out in the open and apparently oblivious of danger, fired round after round." Another group of strikers huddled behind the steel walls of a rail overpass, which provided a head-on point of attack.[22]

About thirty-five bullets struck the open-top coal car carrying Felts and the other reinforcements.[23] Hunt threw the train into reverse and hurriedly backed it up first to safety, then another four miles to a siding, where it swung off the Berwind spur and braked, the last car somehow striking a telephone pole before the train stopped. Under Felts's direction, the men alit and, lugging the forty-pound 7mm Colt machine gun, skirted the strikers and made their way over the hills until they reached Berwind around dusk, an arduous trek "through snow and mud" over rough terrain.

Felts, Linderfelt, and the National Guard officers—three full-time sergeants who lived in the Trinidad armory—held a "war council" at Berwind. By 3:00 A.M. Linderfelt and the National Guardsmen were carrying the machine gun and seventeen Springfield rifles to a high hillside overlooking the mine. Dawn was ushered in by blinding snow squalls sweeping in from the Sangre de Cristo Mountains, but still the armed strikers moved up the canyon past Tabasco toward Berwind. Linderfelt and his men waited quietly on the high ground, biding their time. Felts's assignment was to move down the canyon and try to flush the strikers back to the prairie. But the strikers began firing first, pinning Felts's men down and raining bullets into the Berwind camp, where other mine guards, strikebreakers, and their wives and children huddled in root cellars to hide from the bullets. Two children were wounded, the thin walls of the company shacks offering as little protection from bullets as they did from the winter cold. The trapped guards fired back from the mine buildings and from behind boulders and dirt berms. Linderfelt, atop the canyon's highest wall, watched and waited as the miners rained bullets into the camp and slowly advanced up the canyon. Still he did not give the command to shoot, afraid that if he fired too early the strikers would scatter to safety. Linderfelt seemed less interested in defending Berwind from attack than in drawing the attacking strikers into a murderous trap.

Finally, a half hour after the strikers' first shots, Linderfelt gave the order. Each man fired two clips—about twenty bullets—and the machine gun ripped loose with up to two hundred bullets. It was a brief and deafening assault, and when it ended the strikers had ceased their fire, too, plunging the canyon into an eerie, snowy silence. Linderfelt sent some men to look over the now empty battlefield. "We found a great many pools of blood up there, and I think thousands of empty shells."[24] But no bodies.

It is hard to imagine that Linderfelt's men killed none of the strikers, which exposes one of the recurring problems in the historical record. The Las Animas County coroner's log details scores of killings during the strike, but it does not back up many contemporary news accounts, which routinely refer to one or two strikers killed, never identified, and never revisited in later articles. The body counts are usually attributed to unidentified local officials based on reports from the mine guards involved in the battles, and while it is hard to believe there were no deaths in some of these exchanges, it is also hard to imagine that the strikers were secretly burying their dead out in the prairie somewhere, or deep in the canyons. Each body carried propaganda value, which both sides were more than happy to tap. What seems more likely is that the contemporary accounts of some of these battles were embellished, either through company lies or by the confused excitement of the breaking news. For example, as speculation ran wild about whether and when Ammons would send in the militia, an October 28, 1913, information box in Denver's *Rocky Mountain News* tallied the dead at eighteen. Yet local records and verifiable killings put the total at that point at eleven, beginning with Lippiatt. Five of the dead were strikers, three of them from the Seventh Street shootings in Walsenburg; five were mine guards or sheriff's deputies. The eleventh was Mack Powell, the striker-turned-cowpuncher shot dead on his horse.

The last on that list of deputies killed was Angus Alexander, twenty-four, a Scottish immigrant who before the strike had lived in a Hastings boardinghouse while working in the nearby mine.[25] The morning of the Berwind battle, a separate group of strikers had moved up Del Agua Canyon to positions on the hillsides above the Hastings mine camp, where Alexander had recently been pressed into service as a guard.[26] A group of four mine guards led by Marshal Clinton A. Robertson was out trying to spot the strikers' positions and became cut off near the canyon mouth. Fellow guards from the mine camp, including Alexander, moved out to provide cover for Robertson and his colleagues. They emerged from the camp firing shots up the hillside as they ran. Alexander shot one of the strikers in the foot; another striker immediately returned fire, hitting Alexander in the forehead and killing him instantly.

Though he did not tip his hand during his brief visit to the strike district, Governor Ammons had already determined that local authorities were overwhelmed and unable to keep the peace. On Friday morning, after returning from Trinidad, Ammons dropped in at the law office of Thomas M. Patterson, a former U.S. senator and congressman, and onetime publisher of the *Rocky Mountain News* and the *Denver Times*. Ammons "told me that he was compelled to call out the troops" but wanted to "make another strong and great effort to bring about a settlement" even as he met with rail officials to arrange for the Guardsmen's transport.[27] Patterson agreed to go to Ammons's office the next morning to help with the negotiations.

It was a busy few days for the "cowboy governor" as he conferred with Patterson, the union leaders, and the coal operators, the latter even more insistent that Ammons call out the militia.[28] Ammons still clung to the hope that he could bring the standoff to an end. Ammons and Patterson decided to try a ruse using Ammons as a go-between. In a series of meetings that took place in the governor's offices, at his home, and through couriers bearing copies of memos and letters, by Sunday Ammons had elicited an agreement from the UMWA that it would accept a promise from the operators to obey state mining and wage laws, and in return for an informal meeting would be willing to call off the strike.

Welborn was at the private Denver Club Sunday evening when he was summoned to receive a phone call from the governor. "He said he thought the strikers would waive recognition and increase of wages, and if the operators could see their way clear to do some small thing it might help him out." Ammons sought to appeal to Welborn's sense of humanity, telling the businessman that "he was tired and sick and ought to be in bed." Ammons offered to draft a letter that would detail the positions of each side; through the use of that "stalking horse" and bit of "subterfuge" he would in effect have the two sides negotiate—though he did not reveal the ulterior motive to Welborn. Welborn told Ammons he could see no concession the operators could make that would lead the UMWA to "cease its murderous attack on our people." But he also told Ammons that if the governor were to send the operators a letter setting out what laws they were to promise to agree to obey, the operators would likely sign it.[29]

Ammons and Patterson wrote the letter, and the two sides converged on the governor's office at 8:00 A.M. Monday. After some back-and-forth, the tactic stalled over the union's insistence that strikers be rehired without penalty and the operators' refusal to do so, as well as their refusal to meet even informally with the strikers. The obstinacy bordered on the absurd: The two sides were in neighboring rooms in Ammons's office suite. "They knew they were in the adjoining room all the time ready to confer." Patterson thought the moment was the closest the two sides came to an agreement. "If they [the operators] had but granted a conference . . . they would have reached a settlement of the strike."[30]

Yet neither would yield. Ammons also felt a deal was at hand—a woeful misreading of the situation. "I thought I was very close to a settlement the night the troops had to go out," he said later. "I had, in fact, a feeling that there was such a fair prospect of settlement I had delayed sending the troops probably a couple of days longer than I should have. Finally things got so bad I could not postpone that any longer."[31]

In between sessions with the two warring sides, the governor was working out his plan to deploy the militia. First, though, he had to figure out how to pay for it. The state budget had no extra money, and Ammons wanted to pay for the troops using "absolutely independent sources," presumably meaning he did not want the mine operators to underwrite the costs as in earlier strikes, which had led to "considerable criticism." So he decided to borrow the cash. On Monday, as the bullets were flying at Ludlow and operators and miners were refusing to budge, Ammons summoned to his office about two dozen Denver bankers, the state treasurer, and the state auditor, Roady Kenehan, an iconoclastic labor supporter. Ammons had been talking with some of the bankers individually about buying state "certificates of indebtedness," and on Monday night he pressed his case that the state needed to borrow $150,000 immediately. "I explained to these bankers that I wanted to be absolutely independent of these contending forces, and that they would probably have to carry these certificates for about a year; that the rate of interest was small and times hard, but it was absolutely the only way I knew of to control the situation."[32] Kenehan, arguing against the bonds, said that he did not think the troops were necessary—following the union line on the issue—and that he would not promise to sign the certificates when they came to him for approval.[33]

The bankers asked Ammons to leave his own meeting room while they talked the matter over. "At the end of this meeting they told me they would give me the amount of money I wanted for the first thirty days. I was still hoping that in thirty days' time I might get this thing settled and would not need any further money."[34] The bankers agreed to buy the certificates at 4 percent interest. Kenehan, to no one's surprise, refused to sign the certificates, but his stance was not enough to derail the deployment of the troops. (The state Supreme Court ruled on November 20 that he lacked the authority to refuse to sign.)

A little before midnight on October 27, a Monday, Ammons summoned General Chase, who must have been "in waiting, because he came almost immediately." In fact, Chase was in the statehouse receiving updates from Linderfelt and others on the battles at Berwind and Hastings. Patterson suggested to Ammons that he make it clear that the National Guard was entering the fray to establish peace. The final order reflected this, directing the troops to protect anyone who wanted to return to work but not to help import strikebreakers, in effect freezing the strike in time. The scabs who were already there and the mine works would be protected; the strikers would be protected; no new strikebreakers would be imported.

Around 1:30 A.M. on Tuesday, October 28, Ammons signed the order.

SEVEN

Enter the Militia

Chase had been planning for the call-up since mid-September, when Ammons warned him to be ready to move in case the strike got out of hand.[1] A large man with a generous belly and a wide curling mustache, Chase, fifty-six, cut a comical figure in his military uniform, like a grandfather playing dress-up soldier with the grandkids. But Chase saw himself as the real thing. A Michigan native who, like so many others, moved west to make his fortune, Chase joined the Guard for a few months in 1887, then resigned, but reenlisted in 1895.[2] His first confrontation with labor came in Leadville in 1897, and he played a crucial role in quelling the 1903 strike.

Although Governor Ammons issued his order in the middle of the night, by the middle of the next day, October 28, Chase had about eleven hundred National Guardsmen and equipment loaded onto trains for Las Animas and Huerfano counties, most leaving from Denver. Chase kept specific plans of what he was going to do close to his vest. Even Governor Ammons, the general's new commander in chief, didn't know how Chase planned to stop the violence.[3] Chase ordered his troops to establish two main camps, one at Trinidad under Col. W. A. Davis, and the other at Walsenburg under Col. Edward Verdeckberg, another veteran of the 1903–1904 Cripple Creek strike. Eventually, Chase would further divide the troops into twelve camps, then thirty-four.[4] Ultimately, sixteen hundred militiamen would be deployed to keep the peace in a region nearly the size of Connecticut.

Chase rode south with the first troops and a handful of Denver journalists. The general was edgy as the train traveled with its lights dimmed, led by a single engine sent on ahead as a scout car. Early in the trip, the engineer of Chase's train braked to a stop when he spotted a red warning flare dropped ahead by the scout engine. "The General ordered everyone to stay calm, but he himself began issuing loud and conflicting commands." Chase told his men that if a battle were to break out they were to fire from a prone position, yet he ordered them to stay on the train, which meant they would be shooting into the side walls of their own cars. After a few minutes the report came through that the lead engine had hit a cow on the tracks. Gene Fowler, the reporter for the *Rocky Mountain News*, recalled that he laughed out loud and "the general dressed me down." Fowler sketched out a story on the first casualty of the troop deployment—the unlucky cow—and sent it to his office by telegraph at the next station. "When the General learned that I had sent this story without first seeking his approval, he denounced me and threatened to place me in military custody."[5]

Verdeckberg and his four hundred soldiers left Denver about 7:30 P.M. and set up camp in Walsenburg between the C&S tracks and the D&RG rail yard and station, within two hundred yards of the scene of the Seventh Street shootings a few days before.[6] "Guns and cartridge belts disappeared from the rooms of the union where they had been openly displayed for weeks, and word is given out by union leaders that there will be no trouble disarming the men, providing no preference is shown and company guards lay down their weapons at the same time."[7]

But there was trouble. "Scarcely had the camp been established when on the evening of our first day a report reached these headquarters of an outbreak at Aguilar." Verdeckberg ordered Maj. Patrick J. Hamrock to take five companies totaling 105 men and a three-man medical squad to quell the disturbance. As they assembled, "another hurried [call] for assistance came to this office. It was reported that a group of alleged deputies would arrive on the evening train all heavily armed for service in guarding the mines in this vicinity." Verdeckberg ordered Hamrock to the Walsenburg depot instead to intercept the train and "to arrest these men and confiscate their arms and ammunition." The gunmen were taken to the militia camp, where they identified themselves as Texas Rangers "imported for duty as mine guards." Verdeckberg detained the men then deported them. But the incident delayed Hamrock's departure for Aguilar, and the troops did not arrive until the next day.[8] By then, the Rocky Mountain Fuel Co. had lost two office buildings at the Southwestern mine; they were attacked and burned to the ground by armed men early on October 29—likely strikers returning to Aguilar from the Ludlow, Hastings, and Berwind battles.[9]

General John Chase, left, and Frank E. Grove, a lawyer for the coal operators. Chase, a Denver ophthalmologist and grandfather, saw his Colorado National Guard troops as an occupying force and assumed military control of the strike district even though martial law was undeclared. Under his command, strikers and sympathizers were rounded up and held without charge, and in some cases tortured, and homes and businesses were searched without warrants. *Credit: Denver Public Library, Western History Collection, Call No. X-60525.*

Yet for the most part, the arrival of the troops in the district defused the immediate tension. Lawson traveled from Denver to Ludlow on October 29 to tell his strikers that the militia had pledged to be impartial, and would not help the companies import scabs. He urged them to give the militia the benefit of the doubt. Gunfire at the mine camps died out as the attacking strikers melted away into the hills. Chase reported that an uncounted number of rifles and handguns were confiscated as troops encountered armed strikers and mine guards.[10]

Earlier accounts of these days stressed that the strikers welcomed the militia as potential guardians, but that seems fanciful, based on a few welcoming words by some strikers and later testimony by General Chase and other militia officers about conditions when they arrived. "I found in a territory 100 miles long a condition of turmoil and terror, each side of the controversy being in mortal fear of the other and each side welcoming the arrival of the troops and recognizing the absolute failure of the civil authorities to preserve peace," Chase said.[11] Captain Philip S. Van Cise, a Denver lawyer who led Company K of the First Infantry, was assigned for the first couple of days to Trinidad, arriving in the middle of the night and setting up camp in the rail yard. "The next morning we found a large number of strikers in the depot grounds, who seemed to be favorable; there was no unfriendly demonstration by any of them, nor was there any unfriendly demonstration while we were in Trinidad."[12]

Company K was redeployed to Ludlow a couple of days later and built its own tent colony a few hundred yards southwest of the strikers, an encampment the National Guard maintained until the end. Van Cise reported that the militiamen received a warm welcome. "[We] reached there about noon of November 1. All the troops that were in Trinidad district went up together—the artillery, cavalry, and the infantry—and we marched past the Ludlow tent colony. The entire colony turned out to receive us. They lined both sides of the road with their band; the women and children had flags and were singing their union songs and gave us a very fine demonstration of good feeling. . . . Our relations with the strikers were very friendly for some little time. We played football with them and seemed to be getting along all right."[13]

The embrace was not universally warm. In Trinidad, some openly jeered Van Cise and his troops.[14] Chase described the attitude of the strikers as "suspicious at all times." Yet relations with the coal operators were chilly, too. The day Chase arrived in Trinidad, Northcutt, CF&I's lawyer, and Weitzel, the general manager, paid a courtesy call at the military camp at the edge of town, Weitzel bearing maps of the coal district that the men thought Chase might find useful. Later that night, Northcutt returned with two other men, this time with an agenda: "To inform him of the terror-stricken condition that had been reported from Aguilar, with a request that he send a detachment of troops there. He declined to do so. The interview was very brief."[15]

The next night, Chase summoned Weitzel and two other men "to advise them of his program or policy which he intended to pursue." They asked Northcutt and a local politician named Hayden to tag along. "Gen. Chase explained to us that it was his intention to go the next morning up into Berwind and Delagua canyons and disarm the sheriffs deputies and guards and send them down the canyon. . . . [F]rom there he was going to some other place—I think up the [Purgatoire] river—and disarm the guards and deputy sheriffs and send them down the river." Only then, Chase told the men, would his troops disarm the strikers in the tent colonies. North-cutt, appalled, argued against the plan but could not sway the general, whom he described as "pettish and whimsical." Though Chase later said, under oath, that Northcutt consulted him regularly during the militia's presence in the district, Northcutt said the three meetings were his only contacts with Chase. "I did not have anything more to do with him. . . . He knows the statement is not true, and his departure from the facts is deliberate."[16]

Over the next few days, Chase's troops, true to the general's plan, sought to establish their presence in the field. After disarming the mine guards, which apparently went without notable incident, the soldiers began visiting the tent colonies to track down who had what weapons, but found the strikers cagey and elusive. "In some cases we disarmed both the mine guards and the strikers—in some places some of each, and in other places none of each," Chase said. "In Starkville, 200 guns were in the hands of strikers."[17] The militia registered the Starkville weapons but let the strikers keep them. "When we thought that the men were not telling the truth their houses were searched and the guns taken." Around 9:00 A.M. on October 30, Verdeckberg ordered Maj. C. C. Townsend to take some men into Walsenburg to patrol and disarm any "unauthorized persons who carry firearms."[18] When word filtered into the militia headquarters about the locations of supposed strikers' weapons caches, including at the Sample Ranch half a mile north of Walsenburg, Verdeckberg sent out detachments. They returned from several trips with confiscated weapons in hand, though Verdeckberg's reports do not tally them.

On the day Van Cise and his troops arrived at Ludlow, the militia issued an order for all guns within the tent colony to be handed over. With soldiers standing guard outside the colony, a Captain Dorn entered with some men to gather the arms. They received "about fifteen or sixteen guns" from a colony that previously held hundreds. Over the next few days more guns were collected, a total of about sixty—a fraction of the weapons that had been on hand just days before. It was clear the strikers were hoarding weapons.[19]

When the militia swept Berwind Canyon on November 1, they encountered Linderfelt and his men, disarming them and sending them down the canyon despite Linderfelt's contention that he was a National Guardsman, an act of self-mobilization he had claimed once the bullets had begun flying at Berwind. "I understood at that time that martial law had been declared by the governor,"[20] though in fact it had not. But Linderfelt quickly established his bona fides, went to Trinidad to get his uniform, and the next day was back at Berwind in charge of some fifty men—B Company, Second Infantry.

Linderfelt augmented his assigned troops with about ten conscripts from among the mine guards and sheriff's deputies with whom he had fought at Berwind, the first blurring of lines between the presumed independence of the National Guard and the partisanship of the mine guards and coal operators. Linderfelt stressed later that the men he signed up for his B Company were military veterans "and were very desirable men and soldiers." They were also sheriff's deputies; Linderfelt implied that the distinction meant they were law enforcement officials, but the deputies who had been sworn in around the time of the strike were simply mine guards empowered to make arrests, and their backgrounds had not been vetted. Early in the strike, the blurring of the line between mine guards and local law enforcement cemented the strikers' distrust. Now, blurring the line between mine guards and state troops would prove to be just as vexing, and problematic. And Linderfelt's effectiveness in rooting out cached weapons from the tent colonies quickly established his reputation for ruthlessness. Relations between B Company and the strikers at Forbes and Ludlow, "particularly friendly" at first, quickly became strained under Linderfelt's heavy-handedness.[21]

The militia's searches extended beyond tent colonies and the mine camps. Soldiers, without warrants, rummaged through private homes and stores in Ludlow itself. An unidentified Italian storekeeper told the soldiers he had no weapons; soldiers found a Colt .45 hidden among some "dress goods. . . . We searched, and in a refrigerator we found about a thousand rounds of ammunition and a Winchester rifle and one or two revolvers." The take was even richer at a nearby Greek bakery, whose owner, a strike supporter, was out when the troops arrived. An assistant said there were no weapons in the building. The troops searched, as always without a warrant. "Under the floor, after taking up some boards, we found about a thousand rounds of ammunition. And then we went upstairs into the loft and we found three or four guns hidden there, and we also found four or five revolvers, mostly new and high class."[22]

Whatever positive relations existed crumbled quickly. On November 2, the day after the troops arrived at Ludlow, soldiers and strikers from the tent colony played a good-natured game of baseball, which the soldiers won 19–6.[23] Some thirty-six hours later, mine guards at Forbes reported about thirty shots fired around 1:00 A.M. into the camp from the hillsides. General Chase was awakened with the report at his tent at Camp Rafael, at the edge of Trinidad. In the excitement, the flue from his stove was dislodged, filling the tent with smoke and forcing Chase, wrapped in a blanket, to wait outside in the cold night air until the pipe was repositioned and the smoke cleared.[24] The general ordered troops to take up positions in Forbes, and on November 6 more troops began patrolling the streets of Trinidad. Others returned to Berwind Canyon and moved from house to house, confiscating some two hundred hidden rifles as the militia made the transition from peacekeepers to occupiers.

A day later, strikers burned out five rail bridges over which scab-dug coal was being shipped from mines in the Cuchara Valley through La Veta. On Saturday morning, November 8, strikebreaker Pedro Armijo, fifty, decided to walk into Aguilar from the mine north of town where he had been working and living with his family. He quickly attracted a crowd of mostly idle strikers who surrounded him and began shouting curses and threats. As some of the strikers attacked Armijo, Marshal J. T. Davis swept in and, with the help of two strikers who acted as bodyguards, escorted Armijo to safety. Word spread quickly through the streets, attracting an even larger crowd of the jeering and the curious. "We went to see, me and another person, who this scab was," said Michele Guerriero, an Italian striker. "When we arrived, we saw there were already forty to fifty people who had put themselves all around the poor guy who wasn't even worth five cents." He described Armijo, whom he didn't know, as "a small, disabled Mexican. He looked like a fourteen-year-old, he was so small." As the marshal and his two union supporters ushered Armijo out of town, someone fired a shot from a nearby stand of brush. "Pum!! The bullet went through his head and hit me in the eye." Armijo died instantly. Guerriero, who lost his eye, was arrested and held for three months "because the militia said I knew who had shot this person."[25]

The same morning Armijo was killed, Billy Gamblin, a miner at Oakview who had not heeded the strike call, felt confident enough to venture into nearby La Veta to see a dentist "with the intention of getting an old stump drawn."[26] The decision would prove to be a bad one, and what followed came to have as much impact on the operators, mine guards, and soldiers as the killing of Gerald Lippiatt on the eve of the strike had on the union miners.

The dentist's chair was occupied when Gamblin arrived, so the strike-breaker walked over to the telephone office to make a long-distance call to Trinidad, then returned to the dentist's office to wait. Frank Krupa, a thirty-year-old striking miner who had immigrated from Poland in 1902 and had worked at the Berwind mine, wandered in and sat down next to Gamblin but left when it was Gamblin's turn in the chair. While the dentist was working, a messenger came in and told Gamblin he had a long-distance call; as Gamblin walked to the telephone office he saw Krupa, whom he knew by name, and a few other strikers gathered at the edge of the road. After tending to the call, Gamblin went to the nearby Springer Hotel to wait for the mail wagon, which he hoped to ride back to La Veta.

Krupa entered the hotel, walked up to Gamblin, and struck up a conversation, inviting him to join the strike. Gamblin declined, and the exchange became testy. Gamblin told Krupa, "I don't wish to have anything to do with you," and said he wanted to remain independent. Krupa walked out. The mail hack arrived about 12:30 P.M., and Gamblin climbed aboard. Krupa and two other strikers, Pete Bioni and Ed Richards, were waiting for it at the edge of town with another unidentified man. They hailed the rig and ordered Gamblin out. When Gamblin balked, the unidentified man drew a handgun and pointed it at his face. Gamblin dismounted and headed back to town, walking on the railroad tracks rather than the road, the men following close behind. Near the middle of town he encountered another group of about a dozen men. After again refusing to sign a union card, he began walking toward the Springer Hotel, where yet another man intercepted him and invited him to have a drink. Gamblin, now a rabbit for union wolves, veered away and made for the telephone office, where he called the Oakview mine and asked the mine guards to send a car and some men to pick him up at the hotel.

It took a half hour or so for the car to arrive, and when it did the driver of the open-topped motor wagon, Luke Terry, barely stopped. Capt. Harry F. Bryan, a twenty-three-year-old Denver man who had worked as a mine guard for two years,[27] jumped out of the car and rushed into the hotel and retrieved Gamblin. They both jumped into the backseat, Gamblin taking the middle and Bryan the outside. The car turned in the street and roared off; Gamblin spotted Bioni standing in front of a store as the car turned, but the other men were gone. After the car cleared the edge of town, two boys flagged down Terry and told him they had seen some men building a "fort" with railroad ties on the far side of the Rio Grande Reservoir, just up the road. Bryan and Terry lit cigarettes as they talked about whether what the boys saw was something they should be concerned about. After a few minutes, the men decided to press on.

The car reached the top of a hill at the edge of the reservoir. Terry slowed to turn north, and as he accelerated and shifted into a higher gear, "the first shot hit the automobile." The second shot hit Gamblin, wounding him slightly. Terry slammed on the brakes to the sound of more gunshots. One of them hit him, and he slumped over the wheel with a groan. The other men scrambled from the car amid a storm of bullets, as many as a hundred in a span of a few minutes. Terry died behind the wheel, shot through the heart. Bryan, the first to jump free of the car, was killed after scurrying back down the road seeking a low spot behind a berm from which to return fire. Walter Whitten, a fellow guard from Denver, followed Bryan for a few feet, then squeezed off a couple of shots before diving back behind the car with another guard, R. G. Adams, and Gamblin. The machine, set high above the ground on open-spoked wheels, offered little protection. Adams caught a bullet in the arm, which spun him around, and then another in the foot. Whitten fired off a couple of shots before he was hit in the chest and toppled face forward into the dusty road. The car was riddled with bullets; others kicked up dust all around the men. "The firing kept up for some time afterwards, until they was practically sure that everybody was killed."

Once silence settled in, Gamblin tried to help Adams, the only other survivor, whose wounded arm was shattered and bleeding profusely. "I was getting cold and I told the miner [Gamblin] to get two overcoats out of the back seat to cover me up. He did, but at first he brought only one coat, and I told him I wanted two, and he brought the other, and I told him to cut away my shirt." Gamblin made a tourniquet out of Adams's sleeve and undershirt and tied off the wound. He helped Adams into the backseat, covering him with the coats. Then Gamblin, dripping his own blood, went for help. Adams died the next day in a Pueblo hospital after making a statement. Gamblin's wound was minor and he returned to Oakview.

Word of the ambush spread through the district in a "feeling of horror,"[28] as militiamen scoured La Veta for the culprits. They eventually arrested eight men, all strikers: Bioni, Krupa, Thomas Santarilli, Pete Rich, and four brothers, Charles, George, Dan, and Edward Richards. Three of the men were captured awaiting a train to take them out of the district. Most of the others were found at the home of Charles Richards in Walsenburg, where the soldiers also found four high-powered rifles clipped to the underside of the dining table, capable of firing the kinds of bullets that matched casings left at the railroad-tie fort at the reservoir.[29] Ammunition was found stashed under Mr. and Mrs. Richards's mattress.

Not all of the attacks were deadly. Around the time of the La Veta ambush, other strikers burned five bridges connecting mines near Rouse with the D&RG main line.[30] Other strikers blew up the main water pipe between CF&I's Segundo and Primero mine camps, effectively cutting off the water supply to Primero. A funeral in Walsenburg for a scab who died in a mine accident was disrupted by protesters. A clerk at the McLaughlin mine south of Trinidad was beaten senseless and left at the side of a road. Hendrick, the district attorney, swore out arrest warrants for four Mexican strikers believed to have beaten the man, but no deputies were available to go find the suspects. McLaughlin tipped off some of General Chase's men, who tracked down the strikers, arrested them, and turned them over to the sheriff's office in Trinidad.[31] The four suspects were arraigned by a justice of the peace who set bail at $500 per man, which was posted (apparently by the UMWA), and the men were released pending further court appearances. "Gen. Chase heard of this and it seems, immediately, and it made him very angry."[32] Chase ordered the four men rearrested and thrown back in jail. Then Chase called Hendrick's house; the district attorney was out of town, but his son, a deputy district attorney, answered the phone. Chase "cursed and damned him a while" and threatened to "throw the whole damn bunch in jail." Chase sent two detachments to arrest Hendrick's son and another assistant district attorney named Ralston, but members of Chase's staff who had served with Ralston in the Spanish-American War persuaded the irate general to call off the arrest before the squads could round up the lawyers.

The steady pace of violence, acts both large and small, led Chase to move some of his troops from their encampments into the mine camps themselves, an act that quickly ended the middle-of-the-night potshots that had been raining down from the hills. On November 15 Chase clamped down even further, issuing an edict that in effect trumped the civil authorities, decreeing that "all persons arrested, incarcerated and held as military prisoners in the counties of Las Animas and Huerfano" were under his charge.[33] Although it was never established that Ammons had declared martial law in the district, Chase acted as though he had, and the militia's presence became a full military occupation, down to Chase's stationery, which read "Military District of Colorado." And he created by fiat a military commission as something of a legal triage unit to review detentions to determine whether the person should be held without charge for the sake of the public good—scores were held that way in blatant violation of the U.S. Constitution—whether the person should be released, or whether the person should be turned over to civil authorities for criminal prosecution.[34] Ultimately, the military commission handled 172 cases.[35]

Over the last two weeks of November, armed with Chase's orders to ferret out troublemakers and cached weapons, the soldiers again swept through towns, tents, and camps confiscating guns and summarily arresting strikers. They patrolled city streets from Walsenburg to Trinidad. Soldiers even raided the Hall and McMahon funeral home in Trinidad, used by strikers to bury their dead, and searched coffins and storage areas for cached weapons (none were found). Victor Miller, who in October had filmed the battle at Ludlow in which Nimmo, the Guardsman, was killed, was screening the silent picture at a Walsenburg cinema on November 16. Soldiers swooped in and confiscated the film.[36]

Nearly everyone the troops encountered was a suspected union radical. Under the weight of the military presence, tensions among people not involved in the strike intensified. "The attitude of the citizens was to keep quiet and not say much, because they were liable to be thrown in jail. And the prisoners that were thrown in jail down there were held incommunicado. No one wished to enjoy that distinction. They did not say much. . . . There was an intensely bitter feeling down there. . . . People expected any minute something to happen. There was a tenseness about the situation that was appalling."[37]

The occupation had the intended effect—the killing was effectively stopped. But not before one last act of vengeance was exacted.

George Belcher, one of the two Baldwin-Felts detectives who killed Gerald Lippiatt on August 16, maintained a high profile in Trinidad, despite being out on bail awaiting whatever court action might come.[38] The local belief was that Belcher was untouchable because he had encased himself in steel plates beneath his shirt—a primitive flak jacket—to foil would-be assassins. Around 7:30 P.M. on November 20, a cool and cloudy Thursday evening, Belcher and fellow Baldwin-Felts detective H. L. DeWeese stopped in at the Hausman Drugstore on West Main Street across from the Columbian Hotel.[39] About a hundred people were out on the dimly lit street, popping in and out of stores, bars, and the hotel itself, where Chase was meeting with several of his subordinates. Louis Zancanelli, a striking miner, had been watching Belcher for three or four days, and he was watching again that night as Belcher and DeWeese drank sodas under bright lights at the fountain inside the drugstore. They may have been celebrating payday: Belcher had twenty-two dollars in his pocket,[40] a hefty amount at a time when four dollars was a good daily wage. When the men finished, they arose and walked out the door into the night, passing Zancanelli as they stepped from the sidewalk down into the street in the direction of the Columbian. Zancanelli fell in behind the two men, drew a gun, and, placing the barrel inches from the base of Belcher's skull, pulled the trigger. Belcher collapsed dead in the street; DeWeese whirled around, then ran off into the shouts and screams of the startled crowd. Zancanelli dropped the gun and began walking away, trying to get lost in the confusion, but a Trinidad city policeman grabbed him before he could leave the scene.

Zancanelli confessed to the crime two days later, claiming he had been offered $1,025 by union officials to kill Belcher. He identified UMWA organizers Anthony B. McGarry and Sam Carter as the men who offered him the money—paying a retainer of twenty-five dollars in gold pieces—and who provided the gun. Germer was involved in drawing the men together. Arrest warrants were issued, and a $1,000 reward was offered for McGarry, who was seen as the key link.[41] But McGarry and Carter had already been spirited out of the strike zone, and were never arrested. Although union officials claimed that Zancanelli was coerced into confessing, his guilt seems certain.[42]

State and federal officials were still trying to find a way to get the two sides together. On October 30, President Wilson had inserted himself into the fray with a letter to Welborn in which he described Stewart's assignment to try "to bring about conferences between the operators and the miners that would lay the basis for a settlement. His efforts were not welcomed or responded to in the spirit in which they were made, and he reports that he has met with complete failure." Wilson's two-paragraph letter had the disciplinary tone of a schoolmaster dissatisfied with one of his charges. The fledgling Department of Labor's "efforts . . . are of so much importance to the country in matters of this kind, and I am personally so deeply disappointed that the Department's suggestions should have been rejected." He demanded that Welborn, in essence, explain himself. "I now take the liberty of asking from the responsible officers of the Colorado Fuel and Iron Company a full and frank statement of the reasons which have led them to reject counsels of peace and accommodation in a matter now grown so critical."[43]

If the president thought that a letter from his office might intimidate the operators into negotiating, he was wrong. Both Welborn and Bowers wrote lengthy, detailed responses laying out the company's now-familiar position: The miners had been happy and well paid; the strike was a power play by a group of brutal anarchists hoisting a union banner; Labor Secretary Wilson and Stewart were in the union's camp; and the operators had no intention of taking part in any negotiations that could be construed as recognizing the UMWA as the bargaining agent for its miners.

President Wilson sent a copy of Bowers's letter, which included Bowers's detailed rendition of his meeting with Stewart, to Louis Freeland Post, the deputy labor secretary, with a request: "I would like to know whether Mr. Stewart corroborates the statements contained in that letter."[44] He also asked Post for his own reaction to Bowers and the prognosis for any sort of peaceful end to the strike less than three weeks after the National Guard had been called out and a week after the killing of the four mine guards in the La Veta ambush.

Post, a writer and social reformer, defended Secretary Wilson and Stewart as impartial advocates for labor peace. Stewart particularly, he said, had developed a reputation for evenhandedness during some thirty years of work in Chicago before joining the Department of Labor. "He is not a leader in labor union circles, as Mr. Bowers implies, although he does command great confidence in those circles. . . . And he has earned this confidence by fair-mindedness, industry and competency in the performance of official duties."[45] Bowers had condemned Mother Jones as a woman of loose morals based on the 1904 "Polly Pry" report that she had been a brothel madam, but Post defended the legendary organizer as a dedicated champion of workers and said her past, shady or sunlit, was irrelevant. Post also disassembled Bowers's main argument that southern Colorado miners had been happy with prestrike conditions, that less than 10 percent of the miners had been union men, and that wages exceeded four dollars a day. Were all of that true, Post argued, there wouldn't have been a strike in the first place—"there would have been a stampede of miners to that field."

Post also succinctly drew the line from Twenty-six Broadway to Bowers's office in Denver and his power over CF&I and, by extension, the Colorado coal operators. "Mr. Bowers himself is the one man whose simple word could at once bring that strike to an end. His extraordinary business abilities have made him absolute, so I am informed, as manager of the Colorado Fuel and Iron Company, even its president [Welborn] deferring to him in vital matters of administration, and the principal owner (Mr. Rockefeller) trusting him implicitly."

President Wilson, after receiving the operators' letters and his subordinates' reports, returned the ball to Bowers's court while refusing to involve himself in the nuts-and-bolts of the dispute, ironically echoing JDR Jr.'s position that he was too far removed. "I do not feel that I can at this distance enter into any discussion of the questions involved in the strike," the president wrote to Bowers. "I can only say this, that a word from you would bring the strike to an end, as all that is asked is that you agree to arbitration by an unbiased board." The president described arbitration as "a reasonable request, conceived in the spirit of the times," whose rejection "would be universally censured by public opinion."[46]

Bowers was unmoved. "We would invite arbitration in the present disturbance in this state, if there were any differences between the company and its employees," he wrote, somewhat truculently, to the president. He added that the state's powerful business leaders supported the operators' stance against "recognition of their union and the abandonment of the open shop policy. To this demand, we will never consent, if every mine is closed, the equipment destroyed and the investment made worthless." He saw the battle in Colorado as an early skirmish in a nationwide fight over the open shop, a fight he claimed Secretary Wilson had already joined on the side of labor during a speech in Seattle in which the secretary equated labor peace with collective bargaining. Bowers warned that a government-supported union movement would spur "employers who run open shops together with their millions of employes, to make the rights of the open shop a national issue without delay, as the liberty loving American people will not submit to any organization forcing men to quit earning a living whether they belong to a union or not."[47]

Bowers was sending copies of all the correspondence to Twenty-six Broadway, along with regular updates on the strike itself, though not in much detail. The tone of the letters bordered on arrogance even as Bowers confirmed that the operators were importing strikebreakers from out of state. "You will be interested to know that we have been able to secure the cooperation of all the bankers in the city, who have had three or four interviews with our little cowboy governor, agreeing to back the state and lend it all the funds necessary to maintain the militia and afford ample protection so that our miners could return to work, or give protection to men who are anxious to come up here from Texas, New Mexico and Kansas, together with some from states farther east." Bowers said that leaders of Denver's business community were pressuring Ammons and that regional editors had backed the operators with a resolution demanding the mine workers end their strike. "There probably has never been such pressure brought to bear upon any governor of this state by the strongest men in it as has been brought to bear upon Governor Ammons." Yet Bowers complained that Ammons still "hobnobs" with the union men.[48]

The letters received close readings by JDR Jr., Gates, and Murphy. JDR Jr. personally commended Bowers on his handling of the struggle, from the conduct of the strike itself (JDR Jr. would later say he was unaware of the details) to his rebuff of President Wilson, which encapsulated "the recent history of the strike in a way which brings home to us with fearful clearness the sorrow and horror of it all." JDR Jr. wrote that Bowers and Welborn "are frequently in our minds, and we have none but words of the highest commendation for the energetic, fair, and firm way in which you have handled this very trying matter." The magnate's son also extended sympathies to the strikebreaking workers, "who are suffering so severely." He concluded the letter with simple words of support that were music to Bowers's ears: "We are with you to the end."[49]

Ammons was proving to be incapable of gauging the depths of anti-union sentiment among Bowers, Welborn, Osgood, and the other operators. He stubbornly clung to the belief that if he could somehow get them all in a room with the mine workers, he could end the stalemate. On November 19, less than a week after the La Veta ambush, Ammons telegraphed both the White House and Secretary Wilson, then traveling in the West, hoping to jump-start the nonexistent negotiations. "Strike situation critical and growing worse hourly, on behalf of people of Colorado I appeal to you to come to Denver immediately and lend your efforts toward settlement," Ammons wired to Secretary Wilson.[50]

The telegram caught up with Wilson in Wells, Nevada. His first response the next day was to the White House; presidential aide Joseph Tumulty, Wilson's secretary and longtime friend and confidant, gave him the go-ahead. Secretary Wilson wired to Ammons: "Will take pleasure in lending my efforts toward Settlement of strike situation in Colorado. Will arrive in Denver Friday noon and stop at Albany Hotel." Then Secretary Wilson wired UMWA president John White in Indianapolis about his plans, and White agreed to meet him in Denver. The operators, he knew, would be a tougher sell, and he wired JDR Jr. seeking his help. "The governor of

Colorado has asked me to lend my efforts toward settlement of coal strike there. He says the situation is critical and growing worse hourly. Can you help by using your influence to have representatives of coal companies in Colorado meet representatives of miners with view to finding a mutual basis for settlement? I will be at Albany Hotel Denver Nov. 21st, remaining indefinitely." He contacted the White House again, too, asking the president "if you can bring your influence to bear on the New York end." Secretary Wilson also wired a rather unromantic message to his wife at 1600 T Street NW that he would be late. "The President has asked me to stop in Denver in an effort to settle the coal strike in Colorado. Consequently will not be home as originally scheduled." He signed it "W.B. Wilson, Secretary."

Wilson's hopes that JDR Jr. would direct his people in Colorado to meet with him went nowhere. "So far as the Colorado Fuel and Iron Company is concerned the matter is entirely in the hands of its executive officers in Colorado." And JDR Jr. repeated the company line that the strike was launched by outside agitators who did not represent CF&I's miners. "The action of our officers in refusing to meet the strike leaders is quite as much in the interest of our employes as of any other element in the company. Their position meets with our cordial approval and we shall support them to the end. The failure of our men to remain at work is due simply to their fear of assault and assassination. The governor of Colorado has only to protect the lives of the bona fide miners to bring the strike to a speedy termination."

Once in Denver, Wilson and Ammons concocted a scheme that they hoped would sidestep the recognition issue. They persuaded the operators to meet on November 26 in Ammons's offices with three striking miners, none of whom was a UMWA official, selected by Ammons, and with the caveat that the two sides would not discuss union recognition. It would simply be a meeting between the coal operators and, from the operators' standpoint, some of their former workers: T. X. Evans, Archie Allison, and David Hammon.[51] The UMWA leaders, meanwhile, told Secretary Wilson they would step back from insisting on union recognition if a system for handling grievances was devised and were willing to send all of the other strike issues to arbitration. Secretary Wilson and Ammons clung to a sliver of optimism that the operators' acceptance of an invitation to talk with three strikers constituted a thaw.

It didn't. "We reached no direct understanding," Welborn said later in a letter to a CF&I investor. "In fact, we wanted none, as we were almost sure that had an understanding between the miners and ourselves been reached it would have received the stamp of approval of the officers of the organization and in that way been twisted into an arrangement between us and the organization."[52] The meeting lasted all day and evening and into the early morning. The operators held fast to their stance that they would agree only to obey the law. The UMWA similarly refused to agree to anything that did not include a mechanism for arbitrating grievances, within or outside union recognition. UMWA officials put the mine operators' proposal to the strikers for a vote a few days later, at the operators' insistence, and it was soundly rejected.

Secretary Wilson reported to the president that failure was at hand and that strikebreakers were being ferried into the strike zone from elsewhere in Colorado, and from other states. "The situation is serious. A condition of guerrilla warfare exists and many people have been killed. Each side places the responsibility upon the other." The secretary's summary was bleak: Armed laborers were fighting a militarized feudal system. The secretary's solution, in the face of the dire circumstances, was mild. "It seems to me that the situation is so grave that it ought to be investigated by a special committee of Congress, which will have full authority to send for persons or papers, administer oaths, and take such other action as may be necessary to get to the facts and give them to the public."[53] Such an investigation, of course, would do nothing to defuse the violent showdown.

That Bowers was in charge of CF&I and its strike policy is undeniable in a close reading of the letters. Most seem constructed under the concept of "plausible deniability," carefully omitting any details outside of the company line that the union men were brigands and vagabonds and the mine operators the victims of a conspiracy among radicals. For instance, while Bowers informed his son about the buying of machine guns, similar references do not show up in the existing correspondence between Denver and New York. There is no written discussion about the operators hiring Baldwin-Felts, or about their desire for the militia to be called out, unless those letters were destroyed, which while possible seems unlikely. Letters between Bowers, JDR Jr., Gates, Murphy, and Welborn are scattered among three archives, drawn from at least three sources: Bowers's personal correspondence, the Rockefeller offices, and Welborn's personal files. Had there been a purge, chances are good that somewhere one of the letters would have slipped through. But none did.

If New York was consulted directly, it likely happened during Bowers's regular trips east, which included brief vacations with Gates at New York's Lake George, in the Adirondacks. But given the Rockefellers' management approach of giving loyal and trusted managers autonomy, it seems most likely that Bowers was the Rockefellers' autonomous general in the field. Some of the exchanges bear that out. In early December, Starr Murphy wrote to Bowers suggesting Bowers consider President Wilson's proposal for arbitration. Murphy suggested a committee of three judges be used, "thus guaranteeing that the investigation would be made by men whose positions were not dependent upon the votes of the labor unions." Bowers wrote back a few days later rejecting the idea out of hand. "On the surface, the president's suggestion looks plausible, but we are too well advised to believe that it would be possible to secure an impartial committee named by him. . . . We know that the president will not ignore the head of the department of labor, but will let his secretary of labor name the committee, if such an agreement were entered into, or else he would direct him to demand an end to the strike instantly." Then Bowers excoriated Secretary Wilson as a labor tool "regarded as one of the most determined fighters for unionism in this country" and accused him of supporting the strike and being part of a national labor conspiracy to achieve closed shops. "He is a cunning schemer and has tried, during his stay here, to trap the operators into some corner, that the labor leaders can claim that they have won recognition through him." Murphy backpedaled quickly, deferring to Denver. "As we have said many times before, we leave this matter entirely in your hands, having the utmost confidence in your judgment and the way you are handling the matter."[54]

Bowers enjoyed the full and sometimes solicitous support of JDR Jr. himself. "I am sorry to learn, from your penciled note of the 3rd, that you are under the weather. It is hardly strange, however, in view of the severe strain which has been upon you these many weeks. You are fighting a good fight, which is not only in the interests of the company, but of the other companies of Colorado and of the business interests of the entire country and of the laboring classes quite as much. I feel hopeful that the worst is over and that the situation will improve daily. Take care of yourself, and as soon as it is possible, get a little let-up and rest."[55] On December 15, as CF&I was hemorrhaging money, Twenty-six Broadway rewarded Bowers and Welborn with 20 percent pay raises, from $25,000 to $30,000 a year.[56]

It's hard to mount guerrilla attacks from a jail cell, and General Chase's troops were quickly filling the jails with striking miners and union organizers. Scores of men were held for as much as two months, often incommunicado, on grounds no better than that General Chase and his subordinates considered them to be troublemakers. Chase's troops were indiscriminate in who they rounded up, though they targeted organizers and activists. Doyle, Livoda, Tikas, Germer, and Robert Uhlich—who, like Germer, was an openly Socialist UMWA organizer—were arrested. Doyle was hauled in on November 24 because the militia believed he knew the hiding place of McGarry, suspected of arranging for Zancanelli to kill Belcher.[57] Uhlich, a German immigrant and head of the UMWA office in Trinidad, was jailed on November 25 simply because Chase considered him a "dangerous agitator." Chase's military commission, to no one's surprise, agreed and ordered Uhlich held indefinitely without criminal charge. Northcutt's *Trinidad Chronicle-News*, by then in full propaganda mode, made Uhlich's arrest the top story of the day, describing him as "a wanderer of many lands, yet a man without a country" who was "an avowed anarchist, not in sympathy with the laws and constitution of the state or nation."[58] Northcutt's portrayal of Uhlich as an outside agitator with no vested interest in southern Colorado was part of the operators' strategy to paint the strike as a battle of "us v. them," with the "us" being the reasonable people of Colorado and the "them" being radical foreigners and men of dangerous inclinations. That Uhlich was a former Western Federation of Miners organizer yet had never worked in the coal mines himself (he was a foundry man) was held up as evidence that he was an interloper. Yet Uhlich, who immigrated in 1905, had been living in southern Colorado since 1907—the same year Bowers moved to Denver—and took out papers to become a naturalized U.S. citizen in 1910, though he apparently never filed them.[59]

Germer was arrested a few minutes before midnight on December 5 as he stepped off a train at the Walsenburg station. The arrest was no surprise. He had taken the northbound train on December 1, and "a friend of mine called me aside and told me that I was going to be arrested on my return to Walsenburg."[60] Northcutt's newspaper made much of the fact that Germer, a reputed ladies' man, was in the company of another man's wife, with whom the paper said he had spent several days in Denver. After Germer was arrested, Major Townsend summoned Germer's wife, Mabel, through twenty-six inches of fresh-fallen snow to the militia headquarters to show her both her husband's valise and that of the other woman. He told her that they found the clothing intermingled, that the couple had been "caught dead to rights in the Adams Hotel" in Denver, and that Germer had told the other woman, a baker's wife by the name of Klein, that he was not married and that Mabel Germer was a traveling secretary.[61] Mabel, whom Germer had introduced to Mrs. Klein a week before at the Kleins' shop, called Townsend's bluff. "I told him it was a company trick . . . I told him that it was their intention to humiliate us and force us to leave the strike territory." But Germer's alleged offense was more serious than an illicit dalliance. He was suspected of helping McGarry and Carter solicit Zancanelli to assassinate Belcher in Trinidad and of helping the other two conspirators escape.

The searches and arrests were clear attempts at intimidation, and some of the detainees were tortured. Andrew Colnar, a striking Serbian immigrant camping at the Pryor tent colony, heard that a friend of his, Billy Antoniovitch, was scabbing nearby at the Pryor mine in southern Huerfano County. Antoniovitch had decided to leave the mine but feared union reprisals. Colnar wrote him a letter, delivered through an intermediary, urging him to move into the tent colony. "I guaranteed him there would be no trouble if he wanted to come down."[62] Antoniovitch eventually left the camp and the strike district entirely, but a few days after Colnar wrote the letter he was arrested and held overnight under armed guard in the militia's washroom. The next day, Captain Drake of the Colorado militia interrogated Colnar, asking him if he had written the letter, which Colnar acknowledged—he had signed it, he pointed out. "He raising hell with me, and I thought he going to lick me with the gun. He was pretty cranky and mean."[63] For some reason, Drake asked Colnar to write the letter again, which Colnar attempted. "I could not remember just what I said, but I wrote what I remembered." Drake became enraged, calling Colnar names before storming out. Colnar was taken to the nearby jail, a filthy, cold cell, but begged his guard to return him to the soldiers' washroom. "He then took me back to the room where I was in the first night. He tied my hands and kept them tied all night and had a soldier with a bayonet watch me."

On the morning of November 30, Colnar was taken under guard from the room and handed a pick and shovel and ordered to dig a trench about forty feet from the back of the house. The hole to be dug was marked out on the ground, measuring about two and a half feet wide and six feet long. As Colnar began, two soldiers approached and asked him why he was digging. Colnar told them he didn't know. He worked a little more before two more soldiers wandered by and asked the soldier guarding Colnar what the striking miner was doing. "What is that going to be? It looks like they are going to bury someone in there." It was going to be a grave, the guard said—Colnar's. A steady stream of soldiers continued to stop by the hole, the conversations getting more detailed as the morning passed and as Colnar dug deeper into the hard-packed earth, softened slightly by autumn rains. "They were talking about what they were going to use—blankets or a coffin." The hole was half dug when Colnar was ordered to stop and fall in with a nearby line of soldiers doing drills. "I thought they were going to shoot me." But after a few minutes, Colnar was brought back to the hole, handed the shovel, and ordered to keep digging, though he was nearly senseless with fear. "Hurry up, this must be done by noon," the guard yelled at him.

The stream of observers continued, including the mine camp doctor, who signed off on the dimensions of the grave-in-progress. "After a while another soldier came without a gun or a bayonet" under orders, he said, to speak with Colnar in Polish, Colnar's native tongue. Colnar asked whether it was true that he was preparing his own burial ground. "Yes, that is what I came over here to tell you. You are digging your own grave, and you are going to be shot tomorrow morning."

Colnar collapsed into the hole, crying and unable to keep digging as the guard yelled at him to get back to work. Colnar asked for a telephone so he could call the colony and talk with his wife but was refused. He was also denied paper and pencil to write his wife a note. "A little before noon I was taken back to the dirty jail," where he couldn't stomach the lunch he was offered. Colnar curled up on the floor and was left alone for a couple of hours. Eventually, two guards opened the door and looked in at him. "Is that fellow going crazy?" one of them asked. "It looks like it," the other said.

Colnar was left with his fears for a while longer, then rousted and dragged into the jail office, where Drake was waiting for him. The militia commander lectured Colnar on the letter he wrote to Antoniovitch, warned him not to write any more, then told Colnar he was free to "go home now, with your wife and children, and don't go out at all" or he'd be arrested again. Grateful to be alive, Colnar went home.

Over the last few days of November and into early December, rain and occasional snow drifted across much of Colorado, the edge of a slow-moving storm that had stalled over Arizona and New Mexico. While October had been unusually cool and wet, most of November seemed like a protracted end of summer, with dry skies and warm days.[64] On December 4, after the storm had strengthened considerably, as though recharged from several days' rest, it began moving north and east into Colorado and Texas, ending the late summer.

The storm grew huge, and it was relentless. In Texas, where the air was warmer, rains turned into floods that killed more than a hundred people. In Colorado, the precipitation was nearly all snow. Denver was buried by 45.7 inches—nearly four feet. In the Front Range mountain village of Georgetown, sixty-three inches, or more than five feet, fell in one day. With daytime temperatures hovering around the freezing mark, the snow was heavy and springlike, dangerous to flat roofs, hard to shovel and even harder to forge through. More than twenty trains were stranded by drifts of eight feet and more in and around Denver. In the early days of the auto age, cars quickly became nonfunctional; with their open sides, many filled with snow (one photograph shows a snowman positioned in a driver's seat). Some owners resorted to a hybrid of old and new, hitching up horses to the fronts of their cars and temporarily converting them into carriages. Trams were not much better off as thick drifts blocked urban rail lines. Telephone and telegraph wires snapped under the weight of the snow, disrupting communications. Two men living in a Platte Canyon cabin while cutting mine props were buried in their temporary shelter. They had to tunnel out through deep drifts and fashioned snowshoes, then skis, to make the seventy-mile trek out of the mountains and into Denver.

A tally of the dead from that storm seems never to have been compiled, but there were scattered reports of dead miners and farmers. Seventy-seven-year-old George Buzbee froze to death when the mail stage he was driving became mired. A Golden dairyman's wagon overturned. He began following a fence toward his home but, like Buzbee, never made it. For three weeks, search parties looked in vain. In January, his frozen body was finally found buried in a drift 150 feet from home. Remote farm and mountain families, accustomed to isolation and the laying in of weeks' worth of stocks, weathered the storm better than their more urbanized cousins, who kept relatively few provisions around, relying instead on ready access to stores they now could not reach.

The snow was not as deep in Walsenburg and Trinidad, but it was still impressive, and heavy. Two brothers, Aniceto Garcia, thirty-five, and Benancio Garcia, twenty-two, were out in Mesa de Maya, a mining and hunting region about sixty miles east into the prairie from Trinidad, when the storm blew in. Their frozen bodies were not found until February 12.[65] Pictures of the Ludlow tent colony show drifts and mounds of snow shoveled higher than ten feet by strikers trying to clear paths among the tents, and to clear the tops of the tents themselves. Beatrice Nogare's family was living in one of the tent colonies near the Suffield mine, just north of Trinidad, when the storm hit, the snow falling so fast and deep they were unable to reach the coal they had stored outside to feed their camp stove. "There was so much snow on the coal, we couldn't find where the coal was."[66] The family scrounged through the ashes in the stove to find unburned bits. The snow collected on the angled roof of the tent, bowing it inward. "My daddy had to go out because the tent was coming down." He told his wife to hold a screen door up to support the tent roof while he went outside to reach up with a shovel and clear the snow. The mother, who was short, climbed up on a chair to reach. "He didn't know she was on the chair," and, through the canvas wall, "he hit my mother on the head with the shovel, almost killing her."

In Farr's jail in Walsenburg, Guerriero was still recovering from having his eye shot out when Armijo was killed at Aguilar. He and the other prisoners slept on the cement floor of the unheated cell, suffering in the cold. "There were four or five feet of snow [outside]. All of the windows of the jail were broken. The bastard companies had broken all of the windows to make the prisoners freeze."[67]

The snowstorm, combined with the military occupation and the roundup of activists, dampened the strikers' passions. The killings ebbed as the strike—a proxy war between the classes—moved into a new phase.

EIGHT

The Battle at Ludlow

When Governor Ammons ordered the militia into the strike district, he saw the part-time soldiers as peacekeepers—a mechanism for dampening the growing violence. At former senator Patterson's insistence, he ordered General Chase to direct his troops to freeze the conditions in place. The mines that had been operating with strikebreakers could continue to operate; the strikebreakers who were already there could continue to work; the strikers themselves were to be protected from mine guards, and mine guards and scabs were to be protected from strikers.

Most important, Ammons took Patterson's advice that he bar the militia from escorting fresh scabs—red capes to the union bulls—into the district, an edict that stood on a shaky legal foundation but that Ammons thought important. Despite intransigence on both sides, Ammons felt that by limiting the flow of strikebreakers he could build credibility with the union leaders and add pressure on the operators to start negotiating with the UMWA, either formally or informally. The decision aggravated the mine operators, who had assumed that the mobilization would give them a state-sanctioned military force to protect their new workers—their main reason for wanting the militia called out in the first place.

Except for such noted outbreaks as the La Veta ambush, the worst of the violence did fade away. But in late November, after Ammons failed to draw the two sides together with his version of shuttle diplomacy, he acceded to the operators' demands to let them import strikebreakers openly under the militia's protection. The strikers interpreted Ammons's new orders to Chase as proof that the governor had picked a side and was now against them.

They did not respond warmly. Even Welborn, the CF&I president, noticed. Once the militia started protecting fresh strikebreakers, "the feeling by the strikers toward the militia immediately changed."[1] Senator Patterson viewed Ammons's decision as a crucial mistake. "From that time things went from bad to worse, crimination and recrimination, the operators insisting that all violence was committed by the miners, and the miners insisting that there was ample provocation for whatever violence they resorted to. . . . It seemed to me that the absolute management of the strike territory had been turned over to Adjt. Gen. Chase."[2] And that, he felt, was a critical error. "It is a tremendously grave mistake [for] any governor to turn over the government of any section of any of the state of this nation to a military officer."

The operators had already been recruiting scabs in the East through employment offices.[3] Colorado law barred importing workers into a strike without informing them that a strike was under way. The operators' hiring agents often ignored that law, much to the surprise and deep consternation of workers who signed on in ignorance. Scores, if not hundreds, of workers were duped into taking free train tickets from the East to promised jobs in Colorado, not realizing they were signing up for indentured servitude in strike-bound coal mines. James Adams was one such miner, and his experience is interchangeable with that of countless others.

Adams, then twenty-three, was a Denver native who had left school at age fourteen and spent most of his life bumbling around the country from one job to another. He washed up in Joplin, Missouri, in August 1913 and signed on to work a nonunion lead mine. The mines, though, closed a few weeks later for the winter season, and he could find no other work.[4] In mid-December Adams heard rumors of a "land proposition" in Colorado being organized through the O'Neil & Price offices in downtown Joplin.[5] Adams went down, listened to the spiel, and signed on. He would get twenty acres of alfalfa and wheat lands, already planted, for sixty dollars an acre, no money down. To pay for it, Adams would do unspecified work on dams or irrigation systems near the new land in Alamosa in Conejos County, eighty-five miles west of Trinidad along the New Mexico border.

On the morning of December 19, Adams and some thirty other men who had signed on for the "land proposition" boarded a train for Colorado, some bringing their families with them, for a total of fifty-three passengers. They had company: two uniformed militiamen, one stationed at each end of the car, and an unidentified private detective. When the train reached Trinidad around 3:15 A.M. on December 20, a Saturday, twelve more militiamen boarded, and the passenger car was uncoupled and added to a string of freight cars that took the expectant farm-owners to the Victor-American mine at Delagua, where the men were shunted off to the Japanese boardinghouse and the women and children to the "American," or white, boardinghouse. Adams and several of the other men asked the superintendent where they would find their land. "You have got no land," the superintendent told them. The new job had nothing to do with farms, dams, or irrigation. Adams and the others were strikebreaking coal miners, kept under near-constant armed guard. The superintendent gave them a written order for tools—for which the new miners' pay would be docked—to be picked up at one of the mine buildings.

Adams worked for the first few days. The mines were closed Christmas Day, and he and three other men decided they would to try slip out of the camp. They made it about three miles before they were caught by mounted uniformed militiamen. "They pointed their guns at us and asked us where we were going," Adams said. "They marched us back to the coal mine." Adams worked a few more days, until December 29, which was payday for the mine guards and militiamen. The bulk of the gunmen got drunk, and Adams and a few other men saw their chance, slipping off into the night. "We walked twenty miles to get three and a half miles, through hills of snow up to the hips, and when we got to Ludlow we got the first train out." Adams's total pay: a twenty-five-cent piece of company scrip the superintendent had advanced him for tobacco.

As angry as the strikers were over watching nonunion miners traipse past their tent villages and into the mine camps, they became even more enraged when they started noticing familiar faces among the militiamen. By the end of November, many of the first wave of state soldiers had begun drifting back to their civilian lives, mostly in Denver. Some had tired of the assignment; many became frustrated with the state's failure to pay them. (On November 28, soldiers in Trinidad circulated a petition to be sent to Ammons demanding their back pay. The signatures covered eight pages. Ammons responded in a telegram: "I am exceedingly sorry that circumstances over which I have no control have delayed this matter so long. Indications at the present time are that you will be paid next Tuesday.")[6] With the militia's ranks thinning, commanding officers scrambled to find replacements among a willing pool of men who, until the militia arrived, had served as the protectors of the camps: the mine guards.

Captain Harold G. Garwood, a Denver surgeon, was in charge of a detachment of cavalrymen who, after spending a few days in Trinidad, were redeployed briefly to Delagua and then Aguilar. By early December, he reported to General Chase that he needed more men. Chase ordered one of Garwood's subordinates, Lt. Garry Lawrence, to go to the Sopris mine camp and round up new enlistees "who had been employed about the mines in different capacities, probably as mine guards."[7] Lawrence came back with as many as twenty-five men, converting Garwood's detachment of Denver-area professionals, college boys, and working-class soldiers into a state-sanctioned battalion of company thugs. The process was repeated up and down the strike district as more and more of the initially deployed men returned home.

In some cases, mine guards were ordered to join the militia. Joseph V. Kimsey, a meat cutter from Magdalena and Gallup, New Mexico, hired on as a CF&I mine guard at the Sopris mine on September 26, earning $4.50 per shift. On November 7, his boss told him that to keep his job he would have to sign on with the National Guard. "He said this was only a temporary enlistment . . . and any time we wanted to get loose, it was just like giving up our jobs. The reason they wanted us to enlist was to give us more authority, and more protection as well." The National Guard wasn't very picky. One of the CF&I guards was missing three fingers on one hand, the legacy of a sawmill accident, which one of the other guards pointed out. "The enlisting officer turned his head the other way, and says, 'I can not see anything wrong with it,' and he was enlisted."[8] In all, eighteen Sopris mine guards joined the militia, collecting pay from both CF&I and the state of Colorado.

In fact, there was some indication that mine guards had been slipping into the militia from the first few days the troops were in the district. Gene Fowler, the *Rocky Mountain News* reporter, found "clear-cut evidence" in Trinidad that "a number of gunmen strikebreakers had put on a militiamen's uniform. These professional sluggers and snipers were members of the notorious Baldwin-Felts organization, specialists in strike breaking, imported without the Colorado Governor's knowledge from the West Virginia coal fields."[9] When Fowler tried to wire the story past Chase's censors to his editor in Denver, the general "flew into a rage," calling Fowler a "damnable socialist." Fowler offered to supply proof. Chase replied that as general he was in a position to know everything about his troops. Fowler insulted Chase, suggesting the eye doctor get his own eyes checked. A short time later, Fowler was recalled by his paper, at Chase's insistence, and replaced by "a more diplomatic young man."

By early December there was no pretense, other than to insist that the new recruits be upstanding men. Yet there was no indication anyone's background was ever checked, which opened the ranks to all manner of unsavory characters. The new troops had a much more aggressive attitude than the original occupying force, employing extralegal tactics that played out in dramas large and small. On December 12, five of the new militiamen broke into a saloon in Rameyville and stole "about forty-two dollars worth of liquor, cigars and cigarettes." Three of the men, it turned out, had come in from out of state. One had been dishonorably discharged from the U.S. Army and had "served time in Leavenworth." Another of the men had forged his army discharge papers, though it was unclear whether he was a deserter or had simply never been in the service. All five were court-martialed; two were sentenced to serve time in the Las Animas County jail while the other three were fined—and returned to duty.[10]

Linderfelt was also recruiting new soldiers for his Company B, Second Battalion, assigned to Cedar Hill, near the mouth of Berwind Canyon just out of sight of Ludlow. But he cast a wider net, sending letters and telegrams to men with whom he had served in the Philippines and Mexico. Slowly, he built up a body of veteran soldiers and mine guards who, because of their close proximity to the Ludlow tent colony, had regular confrontations with strikers as they conducted warrantless searches for weapons and engaged in other acts of harassment. To Linderfelt, the role his troops played was a function of their soldierly expertise and a lack of guts among the part-timers who made up most of the National Guard's officer ranks. "Any work that . . . Maj. Kennedy or Capt. Van Cise did not care to do was forced on me," Linderfelt said.[11]

But some of his fellow officers were appalled at the relish with which Linderfelt approached his run-ins with the strikers. To Van Cise, Linderfelt was "a typical soldier of fortune" and "the worst man that could have been put in command of troops charged with preserving the peace." Linderfelt's Company B initially was composed of mostly Mexican Americans from Trinidad, the detachment formed by Sheriff Grisham to defend Berwind Canyon in the days before Ammons called out the National Guard. After Linderfelt replaced the original soldiers, the company "was always in trouble with the colonists. This group and the strikers constantly sought opportunities for assaults on each other." Linderfelt's men, with superior weapons, usually "had the best of it." But as a consequence, Linderfelt and his men were constantly in fear of attack, while—for a few weeks anyway—other militia companies got along well with the strikers. Soldiers assigned to the

First Company, for instance, often entered the Ludlow tent colony in small numbers, and unarmed. "Lt. Linderfelt and his men went in parties armed to the teeth, in constant danger of being wiped out if caught unaware."[12]

One incident displayed Linderfelt at his most arrogant. Around December 28, Linderfelt and his men found a piece of barbed wire left loose on a snowy roadway and tossed it aside. That evening, after darkness had settled in, another militiaman, Corporal Cuthbertson, was riding along the same stretch of road when the horse was tripped up by a length of barbed wire. Cuthbertson fell, and in its scramble to regain footing his horse stepped on his chest, injuring him severely. Linderfelt returned from his own sojourn to Aguilar a short time later, stopping in at the Ludlow depot, where the injured soldier had been taken. When he learned the details he flew into a rage, "just like a mad lion turned loose," assuming sabotage by the strikers. "He began charging around there and wanted to know who had stretched that wire." Tikas, the Greek Ludlow colony leader, was in the depot, and Linderfelt threatened to kill him. He also slugged an uninvolved teen-aged boy in front of a handful of witnesses, then denied to his superior officers and investigating committees that he had touched the youth. His arrogance knew no bounds. Linderfelt repeatedly told the strikers that he was "Jesus Christ," that his was the word of God and he must be obeyed—a stance rooted in hubris and the desire for intimidation. Linderfelt had an utter disregard for the immigrants among the strikers, calling them "wops" and "rednecks" and cursing at men and women alike.[13]

That bully's ethos, though, was instilled from the top. Chase, who first sent Linderfelt into the strike district, and many of his top aides acted as though they were the supreme law in the district—which, in fact, they were, since no one was able to mount a serious legal challenge to their authority. Governor Ammons's silence on reports of abuses could be read as tacit approval, or an abdication of authority. And the legal system, where not trumped by Chase, focused not on the marauding militiamen but on the strikers.

On December 1, a federal grand jury that had been convened in Pueblo handed down indictments and a report that, to someone not familiar with the political structure of the region, could be read as a damning assessment of the UMWA and its organizers. The jury had some criticism of the operators' political control, their use of marshals to rule the closed mine camps, and their practice of delegating moral decisions governing the care of workers to "minor company employees, whose efforts are often directed more particularly to accruing large mine production at low cost, in many instances to the real detriment of the miners, than to furthering welfare of employees."[14]

But the indictments only targeted strike leaders. The grand jury accused President White, Vice President Hayes, and Treasurer William P. Green of "maintaining a monopoly on labor," and charged Lawson, McLennan, Mc-Garry, Germer, Edgar Wallace, who was the editor of the *UMW Journal* and former editor of the union's strike paper in Trinidad, and other strike leaders and union organizers with conspiracy to restrain trade, and interference with interstate coal shipments.[15] "They have brought experienced strike agitators and have armed hundreds of irresponsible aliens who have become a menace to the peace and prosperity and even the lives of our citizens," the jury wrote. "They created open insurrection in Southern Colorado and have resorted to measures which all fair-minded labor organizations repudiate. The officers in charge of many of the tent colonies confess their inability to control the men whom they have armed and aroused."[16] The union leaders shrugged off the indictments, saying they had expected them as soon as the grand jury was announced. "If I am one of those indicted," said Wallace, "then at least I'm in good company."[17]

No matter how deplorable conditions might be, it takes a spark to start a fire, and Chase and Ammons concluded that their lives—and the strike district—would be a lot more peaceful without one particular flashpoint: Mother Jones. As early as September 25, Ammons was complaining about the rabble-rouser, telling Charles A. Newell, editor of the *Denver Express,* "that he thought the entire trouble to date in the strike zone was due to the incendiary teachings of Mother Jones."[18] How did Ammons know what Jones had been saying? Company spies had been taking down her speeches in shorthand, and the operators sent copies to the governor.

The general and the governor decided that Jones in the district was likely to cause nothing but trouble, so they worked hard to keep her out. Chase's troops were waiting for Jones when she stepped off the train from El Paso at the Trinidad station on the morning of January 4, 1914. They detained her for a few hours, then put her on another train, sending her on to Denver, drawing a flurry of telegrammed complaints from union officials to Secretary Wilson: "Mother Jones deported from Trinidad Colorado by State Militia, in violation of all law of the land. We ask you to intervene and protect Constitutional rights of American citizens."[19] Jones took the deportation in stride; getting bounced from a strike zone was not exactly a new indignity for her. She wired Secretary Wilson that she was heading for Washington, D.C., and would like to meet with him, and he agreed to see her.[20]

By the time Wilson responded, however, Jones's plans had changed. She had read a newspaper report quoting Governor Ammons as saying that she had been kicked out of the strike zone and wouldn't be allowed back in. Jones apparently took this as a personal challenge and immediately bought a ticket for the January 11 night train from Denver to Trinidad.[21] A supporter warned her that detectives had staked out her Denver hotel and the train station, so Jones sneaked out of the hotel more than an hour early. Bypassing the train station, she went directly to the rail yard and persuaded the porter to let her board before the train went to the station for the other passengers. She sent the porter with two dollars to ask the conductor to stop the train short of Trinidad and let her off. The next morning, Jones was in her room at Trinidad's Toltec Hotel for some three hours before Chase's troops learned she was there, rousted her, and took her to the San Rafael Hospital, run by the Sisters of Charity, a mile northeast of Trinidad, where she was ordered held indefinitely under guard as "dangerous to the peace of the community."[22] The arrest prompted another telegram of howling protest by UMWA president White in Indianapolis to Secretary Wilson: "How long will the federal government tolerate such outrages? Prompt action is necessary to safeguard Constitutional liberty."[23]

Neither Ammons nor Chase foresaw the inevitable: Mother Jones in a de facto prison cell was a flag around which the miners and the entire national labor movement could and would rally.[24] Scores of letters and telegrams landed at the White House and at the Department of Labor, many from local unions or labor committees urging federal intervention to free Jones.[25] On January 16, some nine hundred miners gathered in Rockvale, in Fremont County, and issued an ultimatum to Ammons: Free Mother Jones or the coal miners would march to the San Rafael Hospital and do it themselves.[26] Strikers' wives were particularly vocal, and organized a protest march through the streets of Trinidad for 2:00 P.M. January 22. Chase approved the protest with the caveat that the marchers not try to reach the hospital, and he ordered saloons in the district closed.

The organizers envisioned an orderly affair, and by the time the parade started some thousand women had filtered in from the tent colonies and as far away as Denver. Led by a woman carrying a large American flag, the protesters—with a smaller throng of men bringing up the rear—moved from the train station southward along Commercial Street, coincidentally retracing the steps Gerald Lippiatt took five months earlier. At Main Street, they turned east for two blocks until they reached the U.S. Post Office, where General Chase personally led a detachment of mounted troops barring the way. Chase ordered the women to end their march, and the crowd slowed but continued to press forward until they reached the cordon of men and horses, where a small group of protesters led by Bernardo Verna tried to force their way through.[27]

Not surprisingly, no two accounts agree on the first act of violence, but a brief fracas broke out. One young woman later claimed that Chase, mounted on his horse, started it by kicking her in the breast. If so, he displayed an unenviable lack of horsemanship. Frank Gatz, a photographer, had climbed on top of a fence for a better vantage point from which to take pictures and watched as the portly Chase fell, remounted, and then began swinging his revolver like a club through the crowd.[28] Others closer at hand heard the general, enraged at the indignity of falling from his horse, issue the order: "Ride the women down!"

His troops responded instantly, racing their horses through the crowd and swinging gun butts and the flat sides of their swords at anyone they could reach. The crowd responded in a riot, heaving rocks and epithets as they scattered, long dresses billowing as women ran from the rearing, twisting horses. The riders made three passes, leaving blood and bruises in their wake. Maggie Hammons was slashed deeply across the forehead. One of Mrs. George Gibson's ears was torn partway from her head. A saber cut deeply into Mrs. Thomas Bradley's hands as she tried to ward off a blow. Even children were attacked; Robbie Arguello, ten, was punched in the face by a passing militiaman. One soldier suffered a broken rib when he fell from his horse. Another, standing a couple of feet from Chase, stumbled and dropped his rifle, accidentally firing a shot that splintered the stone curb and sent shards of both bullet and stone whizzing among the troops' legs, though no one was hurt.[29]

The melee only lasted a few minutes, and when it was over the militia had arrested six women and twelve men. Northcutt's newspaper took its usual tack and painted the confrontation as the loyal troops protecting the city from marauding strikers' wives bent on freeing Mother Jones. But even that article confirms the use of military weapons against unarmed women: "[T]he cavalry plunged through crowds of mingled men and women and upon the sidewalks where spectators were forced to run and keep moving on out of the way of prodding bayonet or saber point."[30]

At a time when women nationwide were fighting for the right to vote (they gained suffrage in Colorado in 1893) and society clung to the concept that the "fairer sex" lived on a plane above the baser lives of men, the clash became an emblem of the strike. If the militia was willing to ride down unarmed women and children on a public street, then what else were they capable of?

The fall was a season of violence in southern Colorado; winter was a season of investigations. After the Pueblo grand jury indictments, state labor leaders induced Ammons to appoint a small commission to investigate the strike. Ammons named five men, mostly pro-union, including Lawson. General Chase refused to let his men testify, despite a letter from Ammons giving the panel the authority to question them—yet another instance of Ammons's inability to control his general. The resulting report was predictably one-sided, filled with details of undeniably bad behavior by some of the militia and virtually none by the strikers, though the testimony offers stark insight into both the abuses committed by the militia and the deep frustration felt by strikers and uninvolved citizens. The panel interviewed 163 witnesses, "about one third [of whom] are not connected with the strike, nor are they members of the union."[31]

In January, the federal government began its own fact-finding. After weeks of lobbying, and with the support of Secretary Wilson and his mediator, Stewart, Representative Keating persuaded his colleagues in the House of Representatives to direct its Committee on Mines and Mining to look into both the Colorado strike and a simultaneous but unrelated strike of copper mines in Michigan's Upper Peninsula to determine whether "any system of peonage" existed in either place, whether postal services had been interrupted, immigration laws flouted, or arrests made unconstitutionally, whether federal laws had been violated in getting the coal and copper out to market, and whether weapons had been imported to interfere with that process—any of which would make the strikes a federal rather than local concern.[32]

The Mines and Mining Committee appointed a five-member subcommittee chaired by Rep. Martin D. Foster, an Illinois physician, which held hearings in Denver, Trinidad, and Walsenburg over a four-week period between February 9 and March 7. The subcommittee, aided by questioners drawn from both sides of the strikes, took more than two thousand pages of testimony. Most of the key players appeared, as well as scores of rank-

and-file strikers and strikebreakers and uninvolved local residents. A prime absentee: General Chase, who refused to testify unless the committee promised that he would not have to answer questions posed by the striking miners. By not testifying, he avoided a likely scorching. The overwhelming tone of the witnesses, including some of the militia members, was a searing indictment of Chase's command. "Defenseless women and children did not escape the brutality of some of the members of this military organization," the subcommittee found. "Many people were thrown into foul and miserable cells and kept there for days without any opportunity to prove their innocence, and were then released. It is to be regretted that the governor and those directly in control . . . did not succeed better in maintaining stricter discipline and a clearer conception of their duty than was exhibited by many of these militiamen." The subcommittee pointed out that accepting mine guards as militia members was indefensible and that the militia undoubtedly would have outraged the operators had it done the inverse and let striking miners don the National Guard's colors and authority. "It seemed the militia was on the side of the operators in this controversy, and the evidence seems conclusively to prove such to have been the case."[33]

The subcommittee found fault with the strikers as well, describing the siege of the Berwind mine camp as "inexcusable," but the weight of its conclusions fell on the militia and mine guards. The machine-gunning of the Forbes tent colony "seems to us to have been equally unjustifiable from any standpoint." Oddly, it found inconclusive evidence "that a system of peonage" existed despite deciding that strikebreakers had been kept in the mine camps against their will. Similarly, it found that some access to post offices had been interfered with but saw no conspiracies to interfere with free trade. That there were plenty of weapons around was undisputed, and the subcommittee found it "strange" that the state took no steps toward gun control. "If it was necessary, to prevent violence and to preserve order in this strike, that men should be deprived of their liberty and put in prison, it was of equal importance" to ban the importation of guns. Instead, the opposite happened. Some local businessmen—including one city council member—saw the strike as a business boon, "that it was right and proper for a good citizen to sell firearms to anyone who had the money to pay for them."[34]

But what propelled the strike was the conditions in the mine camps themselves, and the subcommittee condemned the operators for allowing something "like a system of feudalism" to reign and for refusing to meet with the UMWA to try to talk their way out of the showdown. It criticized the operators for clinging to what it described as an outmoded style of capitalism. "The method of fighting out industrial disputes by force on either side should be a thing of the past. Society in general cannot tolerate such conduct on either side. The statement that a man or company of men who put their money in a business have a right to operate it as they see fit, without regard to the public interest, belongs to days long since passed away."[35] The subcommittee found that ultimate responsibility for the strike belonged to such absentee owners as the Rockefellers, who reaped the rewards of a system based on exploitation while claiming to be oblivious to the human toll it exacted.

It is telling that a similar postmortem conducted by the state militia reached a similar conclusion, at least in part. While, not surprisingly, clearing itself of wrongdoing, the military commission blamed the violence on the mine owners who had created a system that so easily spun out of control—but in terms that displayed crass ethnic intolerance and classism. "We find that the remote cause . . . lies with the coal operators, who established in an American industrial community a numerous class of ignorant, lawless, and savage south-European peasants."[36]

The day after the subcommittee's adjourning hammer fell in Denver, the body of a forty-five-year-old strikebreaker named Neil Smith was found lying on the C&S tracks near the Suffield mine, close to the Forbes tent colony. The coroner determined that Smith, who had worked in the Bowen mine before the strike and crossed the line to work the Forbes mine, had been beaten to death and his body left where a train would dismember it, an attempt to obliterate evidence of the murder. "A stout club was found on the track near where there was a pool of blood," and a tracking dog supposedly led investigators to the Forbes tent colony.[37]

The next day, Chase ordered sixteen men from Forbes arrested, effectively depopulating the colony of its male inhabitants. Once the men were out, the soldiers tore down most of the tents. In ways hard to measure over the distance of time, the miners' outrage over the loss of their temporary homes marked a small but critical change in outlook. Until Forbes, the strikers were engaged in a struggle against the operators, militia, and scabs to gain recognition for their union. Even though the strikers had attacked the strikebreakers and mine guards in their own homes, in some cases destroying them, that the militia would systematically destroy an entire village, however small it was, crossed a line of a different sort. Lawson fired off a telegram to the international headquarters in Indianapolis. "Yesterday twenty-three mounted militia-men tore down tents at Forbes. Mrs. Zanatell who gave birth to twins Saturday being thrown out with others into storm sleet and snow. Colonel stated he had received orders from Gen Chase to clean out camp." President White, Vice President Hayes, and Treasurer Green forwarded the telegram to Ammons and added their own voices. "It seems scarcely possible that such outrages can be permitted upon American soil. These tents are our property located upon our land and occupied by striking miners who had been thrown out of company houses. We protest against such inhuman methods and call upon you to stop perpetration of such outrages by military authorities."[38]

Between the winter snows and the focus on the congressional hearings, the strike district remained relatively calm. After ten weeks imprisoned in the San Rafael hospital, Mother Jones was released just before a scheduled March 16 hearing on her legal challenge to the militia's authority to arrest her, a tactic that, for Ammons and Chase, meant a delay in a legal ruling on their actions. Jones was taken to Denver but within days of being freed was again aboard a southbound train. She was arrested and removed from the train at Walsenburg, where she was turned over to Farr and jailed. Union leaders once again registered their objections, but the strikers themselves did not rise to the provocation.

Despite the quiet in the fields, Ammons was under increasing pressure. The soldiers had not been paid in months, bills were mounting, and the state's financiers were balking at lending any more money for the occupation, which had already run up a $600,000 debt. Ammons, looking at the balance sheet, mistook the lull for peace and in early April began withdrawing the troops from southern Colorado, believing that Chase and his troops had managed to disarm most of the strikers. "I did not believe along the 1st of April that there would be any serious further trouble, and so I had reduced the troops considerably at that time and I ordered the balance of them out. I was taking them out gradually."[39]

Ammons was still convinced that although the strike was being waged in Colorado, it was not a Colorado strike. He began lobbying Washington for a law that would allow the federal government to force both sides in a strike into mediation or binding arbitration. Ammons was scheduled to be in Washington, D.C., on April 20 with several other western governors to discuss irrigation rights with Interior Secretary Franklin Lane. He thought that would also be a good time to push for a national mediation law, and arranged to meet with Representative Foster, who chaired the congressional investigating subcommittee, and other federal officials. Ammons wanted the troops withdrawn from the strike district before he left on the evening of April 17, a Friday, getting him to Washington, D.C., around 8:30 A.M. Monday, April 20. But under pressure from local officials in the strike district, he agreed at the last minute to leave a small squad of thirty-eight men "including a cook and a doctor and his assistant" divided between Ludlow and nearby Cedar Hill.[40]

The militia began pulling out in the first few days of April; by April 17 nearly all had been withdrawn, leaving the remnants of Linderfelt's B Company in place. A new Troop A was being assembled in Trinidad from local ranchers, businessmen, and former mine guards and deputies recently "enlisted among employees of the operators,"[41] for eventual deployment to replace B Company, which Ammons had ordered out of the district by April 22 or April 23.[42] Bowers, in a letter to JDR Jr., saw peace in the offing as well and all but declared the UMWA beaten.[43] He crowed about the formation of the new Troop A and "another squad . . . being organized at Walsenburg. These independent militiamen will be subject to the orders of the sheriff of the county." Bowers did not point out that in Las Animas and Huerfano counties, that meant the troops would be under the de facto control of the mining companies. "On the whole, the strike we believe is wearing itself out, though we are likely to be assaulted here and there by gangs of the vicious element that are always hanging around the coal mining camps."

As if to prove him right, after sunrise on Monday morning, April 20, Albino Vigil and a friend, Librado Moro, a Walsenburg barber, took two wagonloads of Moro's family belongings to the strikebound Pryor mine camp, where Moro was moving—and, in effect, crossing the picket line. On their way back, with Vigil in the lead in a wagon and Moro following in a buggy, they encountered a group of men Vigil didn't know, who demanded a ride. Vigil and Moro refused and continued on. Moments later Vigil heard a gunshot from behind, and "the ball lifted up the dirt 10 or 15 feet in front of my horses. Right after that they came down shot after shot in succession. Moro told me, 'You better whip up your horses and let's run.' And so I seen that the bullets was whizzing right close to me." Vigil ducked down on the floorboard of the wagon as his horse took off, then looked back and saw Moro motionless on the side of the road, his riderless buggy overtaking Vigil's wagon. Moro quickly bled to death from a single bullet wound to the back.[44]

The step-down by the militia also affected Linderfelt, who had been in the field since before the troops were sent in. He was relieved of his primary duties and was staying at the Columbian Hotel in Trinidad, where his wife had joined him from Denver. His orders changed from protecting scabs and arresting strikers to checking on militia storehouses in Segundo and Tercio, west along the Purgatoire River from Trinidad, and in Hastings.[45] On Sunday night, Linderfelt was in Hastings, where a letter caught up to him from a woman complaining that her husband, Carindo Tuttolimando, was being kept against his will in the Ludlow tent colony. Simultaneously, rumors were reaching the soldiers about a possible new arms cache for the strikers in Aguilar.

Monday morning dawned bright and breezy but full of suspicion. Word of the Aguilar guns meshed with the militia's fears that their reduced ranks would be too inviting a target for the strikers to resist. On the other side, the strikers were buffeted by their own fears and beliefs. After months of harassments and arrests, and the machine-gunning and eventual destruction of the Forbes tent colony, even a small detachment of former mine guards was, to the union men, a breathing threat. The day before, April 19, had been Easter Sunday for the Greek Orthodox Church, and the Ludlow tent colony, with its large Greek population, had held traditional and nontraditional celebrations, from a feast to a baseball game. Some of the soldiers "had always come over and would watch the games, but Sunday they brought their rifles over with them, and they stood there and held their rifles up, some got right on the diamond, and one of the fellows asked him to move out of the way of the runners." There were four soldiers in all, and the one who strolled out onto the field—about thirty years old, tall, with light skin and wearing a militia uniform—began swearing at the players, then yelled to his comrades to raise their rifles, an act of intimidation that merely drew jeers from the onlookers. "One of the women made a remark, and said if she should go near them with a BB-gun that they would drop their guns and run, and she laughed . . . and he said, 'That's right, girlie, you have your big Sunday today and tomorrow we will have the roast. . . . It would take me and four other men to wipe that bunch off the earth.'"[46]

When he awoke Monday morning, Linderfelt handed off the letter about Tuttolimando to an underling with orders to deliver it to Major Hamrock at Ludlow.[47] The letter reached Lt. Ray Benedict, who had just finished filling out the morning report and, accompanying the four-man "train detail" that still watched over trains stopping at Ludlow station, had dropped it off for the morning mail run to Denver. Corporal Patton, Linderfelt's man, showed Benedict the woman's letter, and Benedict ordered the train detail—the same militiamen who had interrupted the ball game the day before[48]—to swing through the tent colony to find Tuttolimando.

The soldiers stopped outside the colony's "office tent," where the business of the strike—from strategy sessions to doling out the weekly support checks—took place. Several strikers were on hand. Joe Dominiski was going over the books with James Fyler, the union's paymaster; the weekly relief had been handed out on Saturday.[49] Others were drawn by the approaching soldiers. After a brief conversation, one of the strikers went off in search of Louis Tikas, the camp leader, who was sitting with Dominiski's wife, Maggie, and Pearl Jolly, another striker's wife, looking over some Easter Sunday photograph postcards in Jolly's tent. Tikas went to the office tent, followed by Dominiski and Jolly, and talked briefly and tersely with the soldiers on the roadway. One of them handed Tikas a piece of paper with Tuttolimando's name on it. "Tikas asked him who gave the authority to get this man," military officials or civil. The lead soldier said they were acting under military authority. Tikas rejected the troops' right to make the demand because he "understood that the military authorities in Las Animas County was out of commission" once Ammons had withdrawn the bulk of the troops. Besides, Tikas told the soldiers, the man wasn't there.[50]

The soldiers were not persuaded. They ordered Tikas to turn Tuttolimando over by noon or they would be back to search the colony tent by tent.[51] The soldiers then returned to the military camp and reported to Benedict, who relayed the information to Hamrock. From the early days of the occupation, Tikas had been an energetic intermediary between the militia and his fellow strikers, so in moments of friction between the troops and strikers, Hamrock usually turned to him to try to smooth the way. Hamrock called the colony. Tikas was back looking at photos with Dominiski and Jolly but returned to the office tent to talk with Hamrock, who asked him to walk up to the military camp.[52] Tikas refused, having already made it clear that with the troops formally withdrawn from the district, the strikers did not recognize the militia's authority to issue edicts or make demands. Hamrock, suspicious, called the encampment at Cedar Hill and ordered the troops to head for Water Tank Hill, the low rise that had figured prominently in earlier battles because of the commanding sweep it offered.[53] By then Linderfelt was at Cedar Hill, as was Lieutenant Lawrence, and as they mounted up and issued orders Hamrock called back and told Lawrence: "Lieutenant, you had better put that baby"—the machine

Colorado National Guard troops manning a machine gun at Water Tank Hill overlooking Ludlow. The high point gave them a commanding view of the rail line and Ludlow, in the background, and the open plains leading to coal camps in Del Agua and Berwind canyons. *Credit: Courtesy Colorado Historical Society, ID No. 10029000. All rights reserved.*

gun—"in your buggy and bring it along with you." Linderfelt took charge. "So I had the machine gun put in the wagon we had, and the mules hitched up . . . and we started down" the canyon.[54]

As with the gun battle at Berwind in October, Linderfelt was concerned that if violence did break out, whoever held the high ground would win. "That hill controlled the road. . . . If that hill had been occupied at any time by the enemy they could have wiped us out as soon as we got out into the open." Linderfelt's choice of words is telling: The union men were "the enemy," indicating that even though the strike district had settled down and most of the militia had been removed, he still saw a battlefield. Linderfelt ordered some of his men, under Lieutenant Lawrence, to ride on ahead at a gallop to reach the hill quickly in case the strikers decided to try to get there first, even though he had no indication beyond Hamrock's call that a fight might be at hand. Linderfelt "followed with the machine gun and the balance of men."

Benedict, back at the military camp, watched the tent colony turn into a beehive of activity as word of—and outrage at—the soldiers' ultimatum and noon deadline spread. "We noticed a large crowd of men, several groups, standing around the tent colony, and wondered what it was," Benedict said. Some shrugged off the threat; a small group of Greek strikers picked up their instruments and began running through traditional tunes, singing along and dancing. Other knots of men continued to talk over what they should do. The demolition of the Forbes colony a few weeks earlier was still fresh in their minds, and as rumors swirled around the camp that trouble was brewing, some of the men went to their tents and emerged with rifles. From his vantage point, Benedict spotted two coal wagons suddenly emerge from the colony, still partly loaded, and take off at a fast clip, as though fleeing in mid-delivery. He saw the men with rifles and some women with children also drifting to the protection of the arroyo. "At once we thought something was up," Benedict said.

Tikas urged the armed strikers to stay in the colony and said he would go talk to Hamrock. He called the military commander and agreed to meet at the Ludlow train station, where Hamrock was joined by Tuttolimando's wife and daughter.[55] Tikas recognized her and told Hamrock that her husband had been in the colony but had left the previous day.[56] While Tikas and Hamrock talked, the bulk of Linderfelt's troops under Lawrence's command, riding hard, reached Water Tank Hill. Lawrence and a few other men continued on into Ludlow itself to report to Hamrock. Linderfelt and the last of the men arrived with the machine gun and began to set it up as Lawrence and his men turned to gallop back to Water Tank Hill, a flurry of mounted activity that the strikers watched unfold from the tent colony. To them, the racing horses and the arrival of the machine gun were ominous. It looked like the militia was preparing an attack. With Tikas at the train depot, more strikers grabbed their rifles and began filtering out of the tent colony.

Lawrence looked back from his horse and, seeing armed strikers emerge from the colony, galloped back to the train station, calling out, "Major, my God, look at those men on the hill with their guns."[57] Hamrock and Tikas watched the rifle-toting miners scurry from the colony, and Tikas told Hamrock he would try to rein the men in. Waving a white handkerchief, he hurried back down to the colony as the usually quiet hamlet stirred like a flock of birds ahead of a storm. "Everybody was in a hurry flurry, getting their children out of the way," said Susan Hallearine, the Ludlow postmistress.[58]

Hamrock, meanwhile, had dispatched Lawrence back to Water Tank Hill with orders to bar anyone from moving up the line and into Berwind Canyon. Hamrock then returned to the military tent colony to call General Chase in Denver.[59] At that point, the militia men were settling into positions along the C&S rail line and Water Tank Hill south of the hamlet of Ludlow; the armed strikers were falling into place along a parallel D&RG railroad cut a few hundred yards to the east, in the arroyo north of the tent colony and in "rifle pits"—low spots dug out of the grounds—to the north and west of their tent colony itself.[60]

The militia had agreed early on in the strike to a set of signals warning of danger: three blasts of explosives, which would echo through the canyons and immediately let any militiamen within miles know that trouble was brewing. As activity picked up both in the tent colony and among the militia, Lieutenant Benedict, at the military camp west of the Ludlow depot, ordered the three signals to be fitted with fuses. No one has been able to conclude with certainty what set off the battle that morning. Strikers insisted afterward that the militia began firing first. The militia insisted it was the miners. Lieutenant Julian Lamme, a La Veta physician whom Benedict ordered to send the signals, testified that strikers' bullets were kicking up the dust around him as he touched flame to fuse.[61]

Relatively nonaligned witnesses suggest the battle began in confusion, fueled by distrust and fear. A Mr. Farber, a Ludlow train station manager, was at work inside the depot and heard two loud blasts, one quickly followed by the other, from the direction of the military camp, but no gunshots before those blasts. "The firing opened up, it appeared to me from the sound . . . just about instantaneously from both sides, although I couldn't say as to which fired the first shot after the two bombs were fired."[62] Farber did not mention the third signal blast, which suggests that by the time Lamme lit the final signal the gun battle was under way, the explosion lost in the cacophony of rifle fire.

Major Boughton, the former hard-metal mine company lawyer and National Guard officer who oversaw the militia's internal investigation into the events at Ludlow, concluded that the line into battle was crossed with the firing of the dynamite signal, which drew a volley of gunfire from the strikers.[63] Even with Boughton's partiality, this version seems to corroborate that Benedict, nervous and anxious to sound the alert, ordered the signal to be fired, which either by design on the part of the militia or misinterpretation on the part of the strikers—or both—led to the battle. Boughton's military panel concluded that the strikers had been slipping weapons into the camp for weeks and that the bulk of the combatants were unmarried Greek men who had planned to attack the militia at a moment of weakness.[64] But when the strikers had mounted previous attacks, they had done so at dawn after making their way to attack positions in the dark hours of night. It makes little sense that they would suddenly, in bright daylight, as they saw the machine gun emplaced, decide that would be the best time to attack. In the end, it seems most likely that the gunfire began through a misreading of signals on both sides—and one has to wonder about the sagacity of using loud explosives as a signal in an environment in which a sudden sharp explosion could be interpreted by jumpy combatants as the onset of an attack.

Within minutes, bullets crisscrossed the plains from arroyo to hillside, flatland to rail embankment. Lead punched through walls and shredded canvas tent sides, kicked up puffs of dirt and pinged off steel rails. Women and children fled for cover in a dramatic and deadly scramble. The dominoes had begun to fall.

Frank Bayes, a deliveryman for the Continental Oil Co., lived on a small ranch about a half mile northeast of the tent colony. He was up and out early that morning, before 7:00 A.M., making a delivery to Tabasco, and started on his return trip about 9:00 A.M. He was taking a shortcut through the tents when a young boy, one of Winnie Lowe's sons, hailed him and told him his mother wanted to see him. Bayes changed course and pulled up outside the Lowes' tent, where the mother asked him to take her children to his ranch. She had seen the soldiers set up the machine gun on Water Tank Hill. "I believe we're going to have trouble, the way everything looks," she said. Bayes loaded several kids on the back of his tank wagon, "and she threw a suit of clothes up on the wagon, that belonged to her husband," and they moved out.[65]

Marian Derr, wife of a railroad man, was washing her hair at their home near the depot in the middle of the small village. Her husband came in and told her to look outside as a couple of mounted soldiers galloped past, then stopped to talk briefly with more soldiers near the station—Lawrence reporting to Hamrock, who was meeting with Tikas—then turn their horses and gallop back down the tracks. "Good, we're off," one of the soldiers said to the other as they rode by. The Derrs then watched as the militiamen fell into position down the railroad tracks and set up the machine gun on Water Tank Hill. Alarmed, Derr scurried across the dirt road to warn her neighbors.

In the strikers' colony, Maggie Dominiski had returned to her own tent and, after tucking the Easter pictures into envelopes to mail out to relatives, was rousting her children from their beds. A shout came from the outside: "Look out! The militia is coming!"[66] Dominiski hurried out the tent door and ran into Mary Thomas, who had emerged from her own tent, the shouts interrupting her oatmeal breakfast with her children.[67] They talked briefly about what the militia might be up to. "We had better take our children and go to the pump station—I think there is going to be trouble," Thomas said.[68] Dominiski was less certain, but to be safe she asked Thomas to take her children, too, while she went to find her husband, who was part of a throng gathered near the office tent waiting for Tikas to return. As Dominiski joined the group, Tikas came running down the road from the train station waving his white handkerchief. "When he was near the tent colony, one bomb was fired. Before the second was fired he was in the tent colony," and the gunfire began.

Thomas was already hurrying to the arroyo. "The prairie was covered with human beings running in all directions like ants. . . . We all ran as we were, some with babies on their backs, in whatever clothes we were wearing, . . . not even thinking through the clouds of panic. We were terrified."[69] Thomas, dragging her and Dominiski's children with her, caught up with her friend Margo Gorci, who had only slippers to protect her feet against the prickly pear and other hard vegetation of the prairie and who was slowed by her three young children. "I took the baby and she carried the other, her boy pulling at her skirt and my two girls hanging onto mine." They had covered half of the distance to the arroyo when the bullets began to fly. "The guards couldn't help but see us out there in the brush, going as fast as we could, and they kept shooting at our heels, I suppose to hurry us on." Frank Rubino was one of several striking miners running with the women and children for the arroyo. A bullet blasted away a large piece of his skull, and he fell dead among the scrub grasses.[70] Thomas lost a shoe, and as she stooped to slip it back on a bullet or ricochet shard clipped her wrist. Bleeding and in pain, she continued on, and the women finally collapsed over the edge of the arroyo. "There were eight dazed women and fifteen children . . . huddling together against damp clay walls." Thomas pulled the cactus spines from Gorci's feet, and Gorci returned the favor by shredding a bit of her petticoat to bind Thomas's bleeding wrist.

In the tent colony, the blasts propelled the remaining strikers. Dominiski's husband told her to flee; gathering up her skirts, Dominiski ran to the pump house, north along the tracks. Helen Korich, a young girl of seven, was still wearing her lace Easter dress when the gunfire began. "My dad got his gun out, and the shells were flying all around our heads. I wanted to go with my father. We were out of the tent, and I wouldn't let him go. I hung onto him. My mother had to send my sister out to get me, and she pulled me by the hair until I let go of him. I was so mad! I knew my dad was going to get killed. They were going to murder all of us."[71]

As bullets flew through tents, some families headed below ground into the deep pits strikers had dug in the early days of the strike, makeshift foxholes against the machine guns and sniper fire. William Snyder, who with a partner ran a small store in the tent colony, locked up the shop and trotted to his family's sixteen-by-twenty-four-foot tent and led his wife and their five children into the pit beneath the floorboards. Mary Petrucci, who was born and raised in southern Colorado's mine camps, huddled in her pit with her three children. One extra-large pit—a man-made cave with steps carved into the earth—had been dug under a tent in the southwest of the colony, behind the Petruccis' tent, and used primarily as a maternity ward. Alcarita Pedregone headed there, slipping into the cave with her two children.

Dozens of women and children found sanctuary down a deep and wide water well near the pump house just north of the colony, an elaborate pit nearly twenty feet across with three levels of wooden landings and connecting ladders to the lowest platform, some eighty feet below ground. Korich and her mother, two sisters, and infant brother fled their tent for the water well, bullets chasing them. "I had a little puppy behind the kitchen stove, and we had our other dog, Princess. She started running with us, and they shot her. . . . They killed the puppy, too. We ran as fast as we could. . . . I remember how quiet everything was, except for the shooting." The family huddled together on one plank, the mother nursing Korich's six-month-old brother to quiet him as the rest of the children shared a loaf of bread. "My mother didn't eat anything. She was trying to be brave. . . . You could hear all the shooting, but nobody yelled."[72]

The fighting grew in intensity and confusion. Linderfelt's men made three attempts to move from Water Tank Hill northward, hoping to dislodge the strikers taking cover in the railroad cut. Lieutenant Lawrence led one of the first forays but made little progress before a bullet struck Pvt. Alfred Martin, thirty, of Denver. Blood gushed from his neck; Lawrence used his thumb to try to stop the flow, then fellow soldiers bandaged the wound. As they retreated they tried to carry Martin with them, but the gunfire was too intense, so they hid him beneath a bush as the strikers pushed them back toward Water Tank Hill. When they regained that land near dusk, they found Martin dead, and word spread among the soldiers that he had been badly mutilated—shot a second time through the mouth at close range, and his face crushed in as though struck with a rifle butt.[73] Sometime in the morning a bullet also hit a striker in the temple, and he either crawled or was dragged into the water well, where he lay, delirious with pain, on the top platform as more than twenty women and children huddled below, listening to the echoes of gunfire above.[74] "He was hurt so bad," Korich said, "he cried and cried."[75] On the road outside, Primo Larese, eighteen, the son of a Trinidad brewery worker, stopped to watch the fighting while en route to visit a friend in Hastings. A bullet ripped off the top of his head, killing him instantly.[76]

The battle was not being fought in a vacuum. Around ten in the morning, Ora Linderfelt, the lieutenant's wife, made a panicky call to the Trinidad National Guard armory, where the new Company A was being put together. "She said the troops at Cedar Hill were being killed and that they wanted to have help."[77] The soldiers rounded up their gear, including a machine gun, and headed for the train station. In what by now had become a common occurrence, the union crew refused to work the train, and the soldiers were delayed an hour until a less recalcitrant crew could be found.[78] The troop train arrived in Rameyville, on the southern side of the hill overlooking the Cedar Hill military outpost, around 1:00 P.M. With no wagon to move the heavy machine gun closer to the battle, the troops commandeered a car near the station driven by William J. Hall, who was out for a drive with a friend, the friend's daughter and another man. "I was under the impression that it was of no use trying to resist letting them have the car."[79] Hall knew a few of the soldiers, but not all. One named Jack Cold placed the gun in the back of the car while another handled the tripod. Still others slid heavy long boxes of ammunition—about six inches high, a foot wide, and eighteen inches long—in beneath the gun. Hall slowly drove up the hill to a crest overlooking a steel bridge, where the soldiers unloaded the weapon and ammunition. While Hall was there, a commander he didn't recognize gave the order of the day: "For those men to go in and clean out the colony. For them to drive everyone out and burn the colony."[80] As Hall drove back down the hill, the machine gun opened fire, adding to the constant chatter from Water Tank Hill.[81]

Reinforcements chased in from all directions. Mine guards and scabs emerged out of the Del Agua and Berwind canyons to join the militia, and armed strikers headed south from Aguilar. Two doctors, Aca Harvey and Joseph Davis, arrived in a horse-drawn buggy after being summoned by union officials to tend to wounded strikers,[82] but their buggy was stopped by several men who had gathered near Bayes' ranch, northeast of the colony. "They told us we couldn't go any further, that it wouldn't be safe." Harvey could see some of the strikers and militiamen jockeying for position in the distance, guns cracking. He decided to press ahead alone, figuring one doctor stood a better chance of slipping into the battlefield than two. Davis climbed back in the buggy and left for Aguilar. After he was gone, Harvey realized he would need help toting his medical bags; Bayes volunteered, and the two men, moving low, headed for the arroyo.

One striker was reported lying wounded near the pump house off the C&S tracks just north of the colony, next to the well hiding the women and children. The two men had followed the arroyo to within a hundred yards of the spot when shots rang out from around Dominic Ray's stone farmhouse about three hundred yards west of the water well. One of the bullets whizzed past Bayes's head, and he dove into a low spot for cover. Other bullets narrowly missed Harvey, who was trailing behind and even more exposed. The doctor scurried across a barren section before diving into a cutout. He unfurled a small white flag he had ripped from a cotton sheet and tried to signal that he was not part of the battle. "Every time I stuck it out, it would be shot at."

Bayes waited more than a half hour for Harvey to catch up with him. When the doctor didn't move—"I think it was cold feet," Bayes said— Bayes dropped back with the bags, left them with Harvey, and headed home. A handful of strikers, meanwhile, made their way to Harvey and began returning fire on the stone house, offering cover for the doctor to sprint across the open space to the rail bridge. "I found a man there who was shot through the head. He was not dead, but he was dying." The strikers told Harvey of another wounded man further north, by the pump house. His pockets stuffed with supplies, Harvey crawled along the rail line until he reached the water well and slipped over the edge. He saw the Korich family, the Gorcis, Thomas, and others, huddled with fear and damp, and two wounded men on the upper level, just out of reach of flying bullets. "One of the men that was shot crawled away," Harvey said. The other man, the one Korich heard crying, stayed where he was as Harvey tried to treat his wounds.

Word of the gunfight spread quickly by telephone and telegraph. Joe Dominiski was pinned inside the union's office tent, bullets shredding the canvas around him as he hid in a low spot beneath a desk with the phone at his ear, calling union offices in Trinidad with updates and pleas for help.[83] Lawson, in Trinidad, grabbed a car and rode with two other men—John Barulich and Peter Corman—as fast as the roads would allow, arriving near the battlefield about 11:00 A.M. He halted about 150 yards east of the colony. "The bullets were flying pretty thick and we got out of the machine and laid down on the ground."[84] Lawson and the others spent a few minutes watching as bullets exploded around them, then retreated to the main county road and north to Bayes's ranch. From there Lawson moved along the arroyo to the rear of the colony, encountering the sheltered women and children and a few armed men.

The militia was calling out, too. The afternoon edition of Northcutt's *Trinidad Chronicle-News* hit the street while the battle raged. It led with a story on President Wilson's showdown with Mexico, but the top right third of the front page was devoted to hastily gathered, typo-laden, and inaccurate details from Ludlow under a story with a two-line headline followed by an eight-line subheadline: "Force Under Lieut. Linderfelt Surrounded. Militia and Deputies Rushed from all Parts of County to Reinforce Troops. Strikers Carry Out Plan to Exterminate States Armed Force. People Run Panic-Stricken to Places of Safety. Bullets Rain Like Hailstones Upon Houses. Reports Indicate Loss of Life Great." The story's opening sentence made the battle sound like a struggle between good and evil: "The enemies of law and order are truly making a desperate attempt to make good on their repeated threats to exterminate the state militia left in the strike zone." Citing reports of another attack in Huerfano County, the paper said the battle seemed to be part of a conspiracy by the strikers to seize the coalfields.

The reality was much different. The militia might have been outnumbered, but they were not outgunned. By the time the paper hit the streets, about forty men from Troop A—recent mine guards, mostly—had arrived from Trinidad with some 7,000 rounds of additional ammunition,[85] augmenting the troops stationed at Cedar Hill and Ludlow, who had already been reinforced by mine guards and scabs from the Hastings, Delagua,

Berwind, and Tabasco mine camps. Slowly, over the course of the afternoon, the relentless fire of the machine guns and Springfield rifles dislodged the strikers from the area near the tent colonies.[86] Just before 5:00 P.M. Hamrock, on Water Tank Hill, "told the operator of the first machine gun to direct the fire towards the pump house, arroyo and steel bridge. . . . He directed the other gun to fire on the rifle pits in the rear of the tent colony and on the arroyo, and to keep a hot fire while these men of Capt. Carson's went along the track."[87] With that protection, Carson and his men, numbering twenty-two, slowly worked their way from Water Tank Hill along the railroad cut to the steel overpass and then to the Ludlow station itself.[88] Hundreds of bullets sliced through the tent colony even though it had been abandoned by the combatants—but not by unarmed strikers and their families. Pearl Jolly, one of the women looking at Easter pictures with Tikas, huddled in the back of her tent as bullet after bullet whipped through, tearing holes in the walls, some smashing into her furniture. Two or three bullets shattered the mirror on her dresser. Outside, "there was one Irish family that was shooting at the scabs from a toilet."[89]

In the Snyders' tent nearby, the family huddled in the pit beneath the floorboards for most of the day.[90] As it seemed the gunfire was dying down just ahead of the militia's final push, William Snyder and two of his sons ventured forth. Young Frank Snyder, a month short of his twelfth birthday, sat down in a rocking chair near his younger brother, George, as the father stepped outside to see what he could see. "I heard the bullet pass by me," Snyder said. "I heard it strike something." George cried out that Frank had been shot, and Snyder, alarmed, hurried back into the tent "and caught the boy before he fell out of the chair." A bullet had torn off a large piece of the boy's skull and brain, killing him instantly. Snyder, in shock, laid down on the floor with his dead son, yelling into the pit to his wife, "Frank is dead!" as the body convulsed in a death rattle. Horror-stricken, Snyder pushed the dead boy's body between two beds. "My wife had started to come out of the cellar and she fell in a faint so I grabbed her, then I went and got some water that my wife had been preparing to wash the dishes in and tried to wash the blood off of Frank's face but the firing came so heavy I had to stop." For reasons that were never clear, Snyder then ran to an adjoining tent, where Ed Tonner's wife and children were hiding. He told her his son had been killed and urged her to keep her own children quiet and low to the ground, out of the bullets' paths. "If your children won't lay down . . . make them lay down," he said, then spread his arms wide. "They were full of blood."[91] The pace of the gunfire picked up, and Snyder returned to his own tent. "I got back home and I got down on the floor and took both of Frank's hands—he was just drawing up—and laid them across his chest and then went into the hole with my wife and other children."

By 7:00 P.M., a half hour before sunset, the militia had managed to push the strikers to the north of the colony, and eastward, where they made for the low rise known as the Black Hills. Despite the daylong gun battle, trains—both passenger and freight—continued to churn through Ludlow. A few minutes after 7:00 P.M., a southbound thirty-six-car C&S freight train rounded a curve a mile and a half north of Ludlow, and John F. Harriman, the conductor, saw fire in the distance. "I was up in the cupola of the caboose when I first noticed it," Harriman said. "I thought at first that it was the depot."[92]

The train was under orders to pull off on a siding at Ludlow to let a passenger train pass. It stopped adjacent to the tent colony to make the switch, forming a steel wall between the tents and about fifteen militia-men—probably Carson and his men—who had taken up positions along a thousand-foot stretch of the western side of the track from the pump house north of the colony south to the rail switch. Several of the men jumped onto the engine and, pointing guns in the engineer's face, ordered him "to move on and be damn quick about it or they would shoot him." Harriman, meanwhile, had climbed out of the caboose for a closer look at the burning tents. "The bullets weren't in my range, but just as I started to get back in a bullet sung by me through the air."[93] At the front of the train, brakeman A. J. Riley and the train's engineer and fireman were hastily obeying the soldier's order to move on. Riley looked out onto the tent colony, his eye drawn by two burning tents in the southwest corner. "Then I saw a man in a military uniform touch a blaze to the third tent."[94] Harriman, reacting to the close hits of bullets, doused the lantern over his desk as the train began moving again. Out the right side, the crouching militia-men's gun barrels flashed in the dusk. Out the left side, a panicky exodus of women and children was under way from the water well to the arroyo, and then on to Bayes's ranch. "They seemed to be . . . taking the advantage of the train while we were between them and the soldiers, and they were crying," Harriman recalled.

Seven-year-old Helen Korich and her mother and siblings were still in the well when the train pulled up, and an "Irish woman . . . who lived near the depot [and] was sympathetic to us" slipped into the well and urged the refugees to use the trains as a shield and run. "My mother didn't want to go. She thought we were safer in the tank. But the Irish woman said we'd all get drowned if the soldiers got in there to us." The women and children clambered up the rickety ladders and scooted to the arroyo, then began moving toward Bayes's ranch. "It was late afternoon and they were still shooting at us from all over. We didn't know where the union men were, because they'd scattered all about." They encountered two strikers in the arroyo as they fled, and one of them was hit as the women scampered by. "I stepped on him. I could see he was still alive. I was so scared that I ran through barbed wire, and it ripped my Easter dress, but I just kept running, dragging that barbed wire with me. It seemed like I was running for miles and miles with that wire dragging behind me."[95]

A few men were still left in the tent colony—including Tikas, Fyler, Costa, John Bartolotti, and the grief-stricken Snyder—but no one was armed or engaged in the fighting. And there were still dozens of women and children hiding in tents and in the pits under floorboards. Around the time the fire started, a group of militiamen who had progressed from Water Tank Hill under Linderfelt swept into the camp, a swirling, screaming mass meant to intimidate and scare anyone lagging behind.[96] It worked. Women and children "screamed and wailed" ahead of Linderfelt's thundering troops. "It was probably the most unearthly noise I ever heard in my life," Linderfelt said. The militia men swept through the unguarded camp in a looting frenzy, stealing with abandon as they rousted the stragglers ahead of the flames. Most were from the new Troop A and were strangers to the commanding officers, who were helpless—if they even tried—to stop the rampage, which drew harsh condemnation later by military investigators. "By this time, the time of the burning of the tents, the . . . men had passed out of their officer's control and had ceased to be an army, and had become a mob. . . . This too was accompanied by the usual loot. Men and soldiers seized and took from the tents whatever appealed to their fancy of the moment. In this way, clothes, bedding, articles of jewelry, bicycles, tools and utensils were taken from the tents and conveyed away. So deliberate was this burning and looting that we find that cans of oil found in the tents were poured upon them and the tents lit with matches."[97]

Mary Petrucci and her three children (Joe, four, Lucy, three, and six-month-old Frank) were hiding in the pit below their tent—Tent No. 1, anchoring the colony's southwest corner—when it caught on fire, the first to go up.[98] Yellow flickering light from the flames danced above the floorboards, and in a panic Petrucci grabbed her children and barreled from the burning tent into the sight of the militiamen arrayed on the far side of the railroad tracks. "I was running out and hollering with my three children, and they hollered at me to get out of the way and they were shooting at me."[99] She veered around her burning home, circumventing the flames, and ran into Tent No. 58, which covered the subterranean maternity chamber. The family quickly descended the earthen steps into the narrow darkness, which was already crowded with the pregnant Fedelina Costa, twenty-seven, and her two children, Onafrio, six, and Lucy, four; Patria Valdez, thirty-seven, and her four children, Rudolph, nine, Eulala, eight, Mary, seven, and three-month-old Elvira; and Alcarita Pedregone and her two children, Rodgerlo, six, and Cloriva, four.[100] All together four women and eleven children cowered in fear as the soldiers rampaged outside the low, narrow cave. After a few minutes the flames spread to the tent above, and smoke began drifting down the stairs.

"They're burning the tent and we'd better get out," Petrucci said, but Costa warned her to stay where she was. "It is safer in here," she said, because the flames would burn the tent over them but not reach the hiding spot below ground. But she was "not realizing about the smoke," which was already seeping down the earthen steps and making the women and children cough.[101] "The tent over us caught fire and blazed up big and the smoke commenced to come down on top of us," Pedregone said. The women started praying; "then the bigger children tried to climb up out of the cellar, and they took hold of the burning floor, and their little fingers were burned and they fell back on top of us."[102] Even more insidious than the smoke was the fire's ravenous appetite for oxygen, which it sucked from the below-ground chamber, robbing the women and children of air to breathe. One by one they slipped into unconsciousness.

The flames spread, but not without help. Tonner, the Snyders' neighbor, was still hiding in her tent when soldiers carrying a burning broom ran by, igniting the canvas sides. She and a friend, Gusta Retlich, scrambled out and into another tent, where Tikas stopped by moments later. "He helped me down into a hole and threw water in my face as I was fainting."[103] A baby began screaming somewhere else, but before Tikas raced off he urged Tonner, Retlich, and the others to "hit it" for the Bayes ranch. Some of the solders, including, apparently, Linderfelt, passed up the looting and also were urging women and children to flee the burning colony.[104] The military report to the governor argued that this was the first time that the militia learned about the below-floor pits, a conclusion that strains credulity given the presumed presence of spies in the tent colony and the previous sweeps the militia had made looking for weapons. The soldiers found that the women and children preferred gambling with fire to cooperating with the few soldiers trying to help them. "[W]omen refused to accompany the soldiers and even fought against being taken away. They said afterwards they believed the soldiers would kill them. They had to be dragged to places of safety." Lieutenant Benedict and other militiamen testified later that some women ran from the flames screaming, "Dynamite!" and that several explosions rocked the camp. "I saw one of the tents lifted into the air twenty or thirty feet before it took fire. . . . Whenever an explosion occurred, it would throw burning embers into the air."[105] Curiously, none of the strikers mentioned explosions, nor did noncombatants like Bayes, which raises suspicions that the explosions were invented by the militiamen—who denied spreading the fire—to account for how tents erected wide distances apart could have caught fire on a night with little wind.

With the soldiers overrunning the colony, Tikas fled north and slipped into the bullet-scarred pump house, joining Fyler, who had hidden there earlier.[106] As the colony burned, militiamen continued moving northward on the west side of the railroad cut until they reached a steel bridge over the Del Agua Arroyo, which had earlier given protection to Thomas and other women and their children, and which had been used by armed strikers during the battle. From the bridge, the soldiers had a commanding view of the cut and routed the last of the strikers, ending the battle. Some of the militiamen found Tikas and Fyler, and rushed Tikas, a trophy, down the rail track to the crossroads at the southwest corner of the burning tent colony, shouting, "We got Louis the Greek!" They drew a crowd that quickly swelled to more than fifty men. Jeers and curses rang in the night and some began yelling for a rope to hang Tikas as the other militiamen arrived with Fyler, and yet another small group walked up with a third unidentified prisoner.[107]

Linderfelt joined the throng and took over. "I thought you were going to stop this?" Linderfelt sneered at Tikas.[108] The two men argued over who was responsible for the day's violence. Tikas, at five-foot-seven and 150 pounds, was much smaller than Linderfelt, a bulldog of a man two inches taller and some sixty pounds heavier. As the argument escalated, Linderfelt grabbed his rifle by the barrel and swung it hard at Tikas, striking him in the head and breaking the gunstock. Tikas fell face first in the street, blood gushing from a one-and-a-half-inch bone-exposing gash on the right side of his head.[109] Linderfelt ordered an underling, Sergeant Cullen, to watch over Tikas and the other prisoners and then left, his broken rifle slung over his shoulder. Near the depot, he met up with Hamrock, R. J. McDonald, who was a military stenographer, and another man, They had heard the shouts from Tikas's captors and the cries to hang him. Linder-felt assured them the men wouldn't lynch Tikas, "but I broke or spoiled an awful good rifle."[110]

Moments later, a few members of the mob leveled their guns at the defenseless captives and opened fire.[111] Tikas, still on the ground, was shot three times in the back. Fyler was hit on the wrist, but another bullet hit to the right of his nose, slicing through the brain then blowing out the back of his skull. All three lay crumpled within a few yards of each other, the life draining out of them into the dirt in the flickering glow of the burning tents.

NINE

Insurrection

The land in the southwest corner of Frank Bayes's small ranch climbed a slight rise before dropping away to Dotson's property south of Del Agua Creek, where the strikers had built their Ludlow tent colony. Bayes could only see the tent tops from his yard, but if he climbed up his windmill, which he had done Monday night, the entire colony came into view. He watched uniformed men moving quickly among the tents, illuminated in the dusk by the glow of burning canvas. "It looked as though they would start one tent and then run."[1] His ranch and house had become a refugee camp, overflowing with exhausted children and fearful mothers unnerved by the daylong battle and anxiety over the fates of their husbands.

Bayes barely slept that night. Tuesday morning, just after sunrise, he ascended the wood-and-metal windmill again for a fresh look. About three-quarters of the tent colony lay in smoldering ruins, a blackened mess where a day earlier dusty white tents had stood in neat rows. The hubbub of the strikers' daily lives had been supplanted by the idleness of soldiers in control. Uniformed men milled around, some standing a laconic watch, others poking into the debris, still others firing occasional shots toward Bayes's ranch and eastward toward the Black Hills, where union men were firing their own infrequent and ineffective shots back at the camp. But in the northeast corner of the colony, closest to Bayes's ranch, a few of the soldiers were engaged in a purposeful duty—putting the torch to tents that had not yet burned.

Beneath the ashes in the southwest corner, Mary Petrucci awoke about 5:30 A.M. into a shocked consciousness. The poison of the smoke still crowding her lungs and bloodstream, Petrucci tried to rouse her children, but none would stir. She crawled, delirious, from the maternity chamber and looked for water. "I was so suffocated, and then I looked back and saw five or six tents that were not burned," Petrucci said. She stumbled out of the camp, confused and scared of the guards—"I was looking back for fear they would shoot me"—and staggered "like a drunken person" south to the Ludlow station, entering a scene of muted chaos still controlled by the troops but filled with refugees from the tent colony.[2]

Susan Hallearine, the Ludlow postmistress, had grown up with Petrucci in the mine camps. She was taken aback at the sight of the disoriented apparition covered in black soot. "I asked her where her children were . . . and she said she didn't know, she left them in a hole and she expected they were dead." Hallearine pressed Petrucci, and the mother told her she had left the children in the "second row in the back." Hallearine asked a couple of militiamen to go look, but they refused and sent her to Linderfelt at the depot. "He was lying on the floor sleeping, so they wakened him up and he told two or three men to go down there with me." But the men refused, saying it wasn't safe. "So I got a white handkerchief and went down." She walked among the debris to the second row from the back and peered into several pits but didn't find anyone.[3]

It wasn't until midmorning that someone looked down the earthen steps into the maternity chamber and saw the jumble of charred clothing and the bodies of two mothers and eleven children—in the second row from the road at the front of the colony, not the back.[4] Within the hour dispatches reached Trinidad, and then the outside world, and the story of the Ludlow Massacre spread fast and wide, usually in exaggerated detail. The mad rush to safety from the tent colony had led to the sudden separation of families—husbands from wives and mothers from children. This fueled rumors that scores more women and children were missing and presumed burned and that the National Guardsmen had buried the evidence of their crimes—the dead bodies—in secret mass graves.[5] Enraged strikers merged into a mob outside the union offices in Trinidad. Telegrams crisscrossed the nation, propelling a tide of outrage that swamped reports of the militia's military victory over the strikers. Runners from Ludlow and Trinidad brought the news to the unionists who had retreated to the Black Hills, and men who had moments before struggled against exhaustion and grief over the deaths of their comrades surged with rage, and the thirst for revenge.

In the coming weeks, a special military commission chaired by Major

The Ludlow tent colony after the massacre and fire. The nearest soldier stands in the wreckage of one of the strikers' tents, amid the family's burned belongings. *Credit: Courtesy Colorado Historical Society, ID No. 10034013. All rights reserved.*

Boughton would blame the fire on an accident of fate—an overturned stove or an exploding bullet—and the spreading of the flames on the winds and the passions of the out-of-control militia mob on Monday night. That version—that the fires were an accident the mob helped spread—has been etched into the historical perception of what happened, but it doesn't pass the smell test. The militia claimed all the tents burned Monday night, yet several witnesses echoed Bayes's report of seeing men with torches igniting tents Tuesday morning. Hallearine, for example, testified that she stood in the street in front of the Ludlow depot Tuesday morning and saw the ashy remnants and a small cluster of undamaged tents (as did the addled Petrucci). When Hallearine went looking for Petrucci's children a short time later, the remaining tents were on fire.[6]

The militia's explanation of an accidental start doesn't ring true. It stretches credulity to believe that the heavy, free-standing iron stoves used in the tents could be knocked over by a bullet, or that in a daylong gun battle a bullet or spark would just happen to ignite a tent the moment the militia began sweeping through the colony. It is equally hard to believe that the soldiers would start spreading flames unbidden by superiors. Unexplored in the later investigations is why the militia overran the camp in the first place. The striking miners had already moved off to the east, and the gunfire had died away. There was no military need to enter the colony, and no believable witness reported tent-to-tent combat as the soldiers moved through, leaving an intentional rampage of looting and arson as the only clear explanation. And for Boughton's commission to acknowledge that some of the tents were burned Tuesday morning would be to admit that the fires were part of a plan, not a spontaneous event. Bayes, though he suffered at the hands of the militia, had no reason to lie about the timing of what he saw. In fact, had he chosen to lie, he could have presented much more damning testimony on behalf of the strikers. There can be little serious doubt that the Colorado National Guard started the fire and spread the flames on Monday night, finishing the job Tuesday morning.

The agony of the events at Ludlow extended widely. "Women crazed by fear and the loss of their children wandered about the hills all night, not knowing where to turn, and frantic with anxiety over the fate of their husbands and children. Others huddled in ditches, gulches and similar shelters, listening to the screams of bullets overhead."[7] For two days women and children trickled into Aguilar, Walsenburg, and Trinidad after spending fearful nights in the cold with minimal clothing or protection, and no food. One woman gave birth alone among the prickly pear and prairie grasses. She staggered into Aguilar an hour or so after delivering her baby, "practically naked herself, and the little child completely naked. . . . My wife, myself and some of the church ladies had to go around and get clothes and boots for these people."[8]

Bowers had already wired his first report from Denver to Twenty-six Broadway, apparently before the bodies of the women and children were discovered: "Following withdrawal of troops by order of Governor an unprovoked attack upon small force of militia yesterday by two hundred strikers forced fight resulting in probably loss of ten or fifteen strikers, only one militiaman killed."[9] He reported the Ludlow tent colony "totally destroyed by burning two hundred tents, generally followed by explosions showing ammunition and dynamite stored in them." Bowers said he expected more fighting to come; with an eye toward spinning public opinion, he suggested "your giving this information to friendly papers." Rockefeller wired back: "Telegram received. New York papers have published full details. Today's news is appearing on ticker. We profoundly regret this further outbreak of lawlessness with accompanying loss of life."[10]

At Ludlow, the militia maintained tight control of the roads and, fearing a new attack by the strikers, shot at anything that moved. A detail of body wagons tried to get through Tuesday evening but was repelled by bullets thudding into the roadway.[11] The bodies were not ignored, however. Several soldiers approached the fallen men and in a macabre joke took up Tikas's lifeless hand and shook it, "wishing him well in the next world."[12] Throughout the day, militiamen in and around the tent colony fired sporadically at Bayes's ranch. A half-dozen bullets pierced the walls, one whizzing over a bed Bayes's two young sons shared.[13] One of Bayes's mules was struck in the hip.[14] By evening, Bayes, his family, and the colony refugees had fled, some to another ranch farther from the ashes of the tent colony, others to join the strikers amassing in the Black Hills. When Bayes returned to his ranch Wednesday morning, it had been ransacked and vandalized. "There was seventy-two barrels of water standing in the tank, and they drained it, took the plug out underneath. . . They went into the house and destroyed the furniture. They even stole a violin, and there was a bucket of eggs that had been gathered on the table, 125 eggs, and they were taken, and the preserves were scattered all over."[15] The marauders made off with canceled and blank checks and $19.50 in sales receipts for the oil company for which Bayes drove. They left behind a scrawled warning: "This is to be your pay for harboring the Union. Cut it, or we will call again." It was signed "B.F. and C.N.G.," which Bayes took to stand for Baldwin-Felts and Colorado National Guard. He also found a soldier's belt, button, and cartridge amid the rubble.

In Washington, D.C., sporadic reports began reaching Governor Ammons late Monday. Some came in angry missives from coal operators and officials in Colorado. But most of Ammons's information came from reporters traveling with him. He spent a sleepless Monday night monitoring details as they trickled in, then kept his appointments Tuesday. Late in the day he learned of the discovery of the women's and children's bodies, bringing Monday's death total to twenty-two. Ammons canceled the rest of his trip and boarded a westbound train, hopping off at stations to send and receive telegrams as he lobbied friendly government officials to support what he knew would be an eventual call for help to President Wilson.[16]

In the strike district, confusion and grief reigned. Union men converged on the Black Hills, where John Lawson was setting up a de facto headquarters to replace Ludlow, "their ranks . . . swelled by grim-faced men who tramped overland in the dark, carrying guns and ammunition from neighboring union camps."[17] Ed Durant watched a lumber wagon filled with fourteen silent men approach from the direction of Trinidad and pass his ranch, southwest of the Black Hills, in Wednesday's predawn light. They were grim and armed with rifles. Others passed later in the day, walking in smaller groups or riding two or three to a buggy or wagon, "people . . . that said they were going to fight."[18] Some of the gathering army carried bullet-stuffed bandoliers; others made do with what they could find, throwing ammunition into flour sacks and flinging them over their shoulders as they made their way to the growing encampments.[19]

Chase, in Denver, told reporters that he believed that the violence was over and that the militia would not make any further sorties against the strikers. Large numbers of miners, he said, had left Ludlow and moved on to Trinidad, which he saw as defusing the confrontation—not recognizing the flow of miners as the mustering of a guerrilla army.

Brake, the state's deputy labor commissioner, decided to head south from Denver to investigate firsthand. He took a midday train and encountered a uniformed militiaman aboard, who was also a detective for the Burlew agency. The militiaman told Brake that Chase had ordered him to Ludlow with seventy-five hundred rounds of ammunition "for the coal companies, not the militia." Brake tried to leave the train in Ludlow, but armed militiamen forced him and other passengers to stay aboard as the ammunition was unloaded. Brake opened a window and listened in on some of the two dozen militiamen guarding the idling train. "Their entire conversation was boasting of having killed so many people, boasted of killing Louis Tikas, and regretted their inability to kill . . . John Lawson." The soldiers bragged of killing "sixteen in one pile," an apparent reference to the thirteen dead in the pit and the nearby killings of Tikas and the other two union men.[20]

The Rev. James McDonald, a Methodist minister and occasional boiler mechanic, heard in Aguilar Monday evening that the "tent colony was being burned up, that the people were being slaughtered down there." No specific details reached him before he retired for the night, but when he walked down to Aguilar's Main Street on Tuesday morning the town was in an uproar. Some two dozen Greek miners with rifles roamed the street. "I found that these were the men who had been fighting over there in the Ludlow district with the militia." McDonald encountered the mayor, and the two men went to the train depot to wire President Wilson "telling him of the conditions and that the town was entirely out of the control of the town authorities." More strikers were clearly visible on the hillsides above Aguilar, moving southwest toward Hastings. McDonald saw a pit boss he knew, who gave him the latest rumor that the militia "are going to come in here with dynamite and . . . guns on the hill, and they are going to clean us up tonight." The attack never materialized.[21]

In Denver, state union leaders gathered at noon Tuesday to plan a mass protest for the following Sunday. One of the leaders invited Senator Patterson to the meeting. "I found in the outer rooms several hundred men, frenzied, and in the interior room forty or fifty representatives of different Denver trades-unions." Man after man stood up and railed against the atrocities at Ludlow, and against the mine owners, the militia, the Baldwin-Felts detectives, and anyone else who came to mind, in a visceral outpouring of anger, grief, and hatred—"perhaps the most inflammatory speeches I ever listened to." Patterson tried to talk the union men out of holding the protest rally, fearing that the lack of accurate details of what had happened at Ludlow could propel already inflamed passions to deadly consequences. "I begged them to delay because the object of everybody should be to preserve peace, and not to add to the excitement . . . but I might as well have talked to the wind." The next day, Wednesday, Patterson joined a chamber of commerce meeting in Denver, where "the minds of the sedate members of that body were in an equally inflamed state. It was one of the clearest evidences of class consciousness that I ever saw." Patterson helped defuse a "series of speeches that were quite incendiary in their character," and persuaded the chamber to postpone any policy resolutions until it could appoint an investigatory committee to determine what had occurred. The committee "never investigated and never reported, but it was appointed and it allayed the trouble there."[22]

But trouble in the strike district had already boiled over.

To wage a war, you need an army. On Wednesday, the unions issued a "Call to Arms" to build theirs, a national mustering of union fighters signed by Lawson and other UMWA officials as well state labor leaders outside the mine workers' union. The missive, reprinted in newspapers, urged union locals around the country to "organize the men in your community in companies of volunteers to protect the workers of Colorado." Claiming that the mustering was for "defensive measures," they asked union locals to draft lists of volunteer companies and wire the names of the leaders and number of men available to W. T. Hickey, secretary of the state Federation of Labor. "The state is furnishing us no protection and we must protect ourselves, our wives and children from these murderous assassins." The usually unflappable Lawson explained the call-up to reporters in emotional terms: "It has now become a war of extermination." He cited Rockefeller's earlier public comments that he would risk his fortune to defeat union organizers. The union men could be just as intractable, Lawson said, describing the killings at Ludlow as "a harvest of death [that] has cinched the determination to fight to the finish."[23]

Over the next few days scores of telegrams poured into the UMWA and state Federation of Labor offices pledging help and financial support. Frank Mancini, editor of the Italian-language newspaper *Il Risveglio* in Denver, wired fellow Italian Americans in Cambria, Wyoming, with an ethnic appeal: "More than one-half of the men, women and children slaughtered in southern Colorado are Italians. Organize your men. Arm them. Hold them ready for call. . . . We will wire when we need you."[24] Several hundred Greek miners in Wyoming walked out of the mines and headed south. Wyoming governor Joseph M. Carey, a Democrat, pledged to stop the men at the state line, an act that threatened to expand the war.[25] Other telegrams flooded the White House—already busy dealing with the growing crisis in Mexico, where a U.S. attack on Veracruz was imminent—with pleas for help, many tinged with desperation. John White, the UMWA president, wired President Wilson the day after the initial battle and included a plea from Doyle: "For God's sake urge the Chief Executive of this nation to use his power to protect helpless men, women and children from being slaughtered."[26] White followed up with his own appeal, invoking the five hundred thousand organized miners nationwide who belonged to the union, and asked for "prompt action in order that lives of innocent men, women and children will not continue to be ruthlessly sacrificed on the altar of greed."

Waging war costs money, and the striking coal miners suddenly found checkbooks open to them. Doyle's union financial records show that about $8,700 in outside donations, separate from the hundreds of thousands of dollars the UMWA had been paying in strike benefits, came in between the start of the strike and April 20. In the three weeks after the Ludlow Massacre, more than $80,000 arrived in contributions ranging from a $4,000 check written by a union local to individual gifts of only a few dollars.

At Ludlow, the militia maintained tight control. The bodies of Tikas and the other two union men were left where they fell, drawing complaints from the C&S rail line whose passengers were aghast as they looked out the windows of passing trains. Soldiers made play of shooting the camp dogs, which roamed free and confused. Autos traveling north-south on the dirt road were fired upon without warning.[27] On Wednesday morning, undertakers accompanied by McLennan and Brake were given permission to collect the bodies of the sixteen dead. They traveled in a caravan of two cars and two horse-drawn wagons; Brake rode one of the wagons, which fell behind the faster cars. As the wagons neared Ludlow, a man who lived along the road hailed them and warned that if they continued they likely would be shot. "While we were talking to this man, an auto appeared along the top of the hill and started toward Trinidad, immediately the machine guns were turned on this machine."[28] E. A. Evans, a reporter for the *Denver Express,* was among the soldiers in the camp when one of them lifted his field glasses for a closer look at the car and reported that he could see a white flag. "That doesn't make a bit of difference," said another. The soldiers opened fire, "and suddenly we heard a machine gun sing out."[29] The driver sped up as bullets slammed into the body of the car, shattering glass and kicking up dirt from the roadway until the driver cleared a low rise and escaped the line of fire, slamming on the brakes near where Brake and the others were watching. "When the machine came up to where I [Brake] was, the windshield was shot off and many holes were in the top and body of the machine."[30] No one inside—driver J. E. Levers, his daughter Wava Levers, and his son and daughter-in-law Mr. and Mrs. Roland Levers, en route from Rocky Ford, Colorado, to Roswell, New Mexico—was seriously injured.

The militia might have had Ludlow firmly under its thumb, but that would soon be the only stretch of the strike district they could claim. Even before the "Call to Arms" was issued, union men were swiftly taking control of the countryside. In predawn darkness Wednesday, miners began moving along the plains, up the canyons, and over hillsides. One estimate put the number at more than fifteen hundred armed men,[31] and they struck with a vengeance.

By late morning on Wednesday, April 22, several hundred strikers and supporters had amassed at the Aguilar tent colony, many filtering in from Del Agua Canyon, where three mine guards—Fred Daugherty, twenty-six, Dave Donovan, fifty-five, and Karl Johnson—already lay dead, a day after another mine guard, Karl Persson, twenty-seven, had been gunned down there. At Tabasco, in nearby Berwind Canyon, CF&I employee Benjamin Phillips, pressed into service as a mine guard, had also been mortally wounded.[32] Clyde M. Lane, a former militiaman, was offered twenty-five dollars a day to help organize and lead a detachment of strikers and was dispatched in a wagon to the nearby mine settlement of Augusta, a few miles southeast of Aguilar, to pick up supplies.[33] He returned with four boxes of guns that he unloaded in the union hall basement.

McDonald, the Aguilar minister, watched about seventy-five men walk past his parsonage Wednesday morning. An hour later, the sound of gunfire drew McDonald to his door, where he saw more men moving up the foothills toward the Southwestern Mine Co.'s Empire mine and could hear the distant crack of rifles and the steadier roar of what he thought was a Gatling gun.[34] The strikers quickly overwhelmed the small detachment of mine guards, and mortally wounded Superintendent William Waddell. The guards, mine managers, scabs, and their families—about thirty-five people altogether—retreated to the mine for protection, only six of them armed. The strikers set up a siege at the mine mouth, and the guards tried to keep them at bay with shots from inside the mine. "We was shooting whenever a man came in sight," said strikebreaker H. C. Cossum, one of the armed men in the mine.[35] They managed to kill two strikers—Ben Vigil, eighteen, and J. P. Gomez—about 6:00 p.m. before strikers finally took control of the mouth of the mine by laying down a steady stream of rifle fire. As Cossum and the others ducked for cover deep in the mine mouth, the miners began placing boxes of dynamite around the entrance and down a ventilation shaft.

In Aguilar, H. D. King—part-owner of the Southwestern Mine Co., whose brother-in-law and fellow owner John Siple was inside Empire with Cossum and the others—went to McDonald's house to ask the minister to intervene.[36] Together they found the mayor, and after a brief talk the mayor and McDonald went in search of the strike leaders. About an hour after Vigil and Gomez were killed, they found an organizer named Gorman on the streets of Aguilar. McDonald pressed the union man to find ways to end the shooting. As they spoke, blasts boomed through the canyon: The miners had set off the dynamite at Empire. Not all of it had detonated, and the mine entrance was only partially collapsed, but McDonald didn't know that and feared the miners were engaged in wholesale slaughter—which, in fact, was their intent. He urged Gorman to gather up miners from the different ethnic groups to meet with him. "Let me appeal to them," McDonald said. King pressed the case on his own, urging strikers to let him arrange a rescue party, but was told "to remember how the women died in the pits at Ludlow. He says they have told him they will shoot down any person who goes to the rescue."[37]

After sunset, McDonald and the mayor moved among the strikers gathered on Aguilar's Main Street, where word had spread that the mine had not been completely sealed. The two men beseeched the strikers to send messengers to Empire to stop the miners from finishing the job. "They did that and we kept talking to them until well in the morning." McDonald tried to get the men to discuss how to get the trapped people out of the mine. "They were not at all unanimous in their desire to get them out." Several of the miners had family members killed at Ludlow, and as a group the men were "insane in their grief." Their resolve seemed to strengthen as wounded strikers were ferried back down the hill into Aguilar by wagon, and in one case carried on a striker's back.[38]

By nightfall Wednesday, eight mines were in flames or already reduced to ashes; the guards and strikebreakers and their families in many cases sought refuge in the mines themselves. Newspapers filled their afternoon front pages Wednesday and Thursday with stories of the battles. The papers declared thirty-five people in the Empire mine to have been "given up for dead" and said that another twenty-five strikebreakers, mine officials, and family members were similarly under siege at the Southwestern mine.[39] Many of the details, in the end, were wrong, and worth little in determining what actually happened. The tone of their coverage, though, is evidence of the broad sense of shock and fear—and did much to fan both—as guerrilla warfare spread. In Denver, "the whole working population . . . was terribly excited; they were in a frame of mind that bordered on desperation."[40]

From Aguilar, King wired U.S. Rep. Edward Taylor and Governor Ammons at 5:37 P.M. with a desperate plea for intervention: "Empire mine burned strikers now attacking Green Canon [sic] three miles south of Primrose and moving north we beg that you rush troops to Rugby Colo. Should be there in eight hours or great loss of life will occur."[41] Grisham, the Las Animas County sheriff, followed up a half hour later with his own wire from Trinidad to Ammons and Taylor, admitting defeat and suggesting federal troops be summoned. "Strike situation absolutely beyond control. Life and property in jeopardy, Sheriff's office and local police entirely helpless." Trinidad mayor W. P. Dunleavy and the city council described the situation as "critical" and bordering on open insurrection.[42] Trinidad livestock man Jose Urbano Vigil wired his congressman, Representative Keating, twice that afternoon and Ammons once. "The insurrection in this county is becoming worse every minute. The slaughtering and destruction of property has assumed such proportions in my opinion requires federal intervention." Fighting raged at Hastings and while Vigil thought the militia could handle the outbreak, it would come at the "cost of many lives. . . . [A] troop of United States soldiers will do more good than all the bullets the militia can fire into the strikers." After the deaths at Ludlow, the strikers were highly agitated and "have no respect for or confidence in the state militia or mine guards. Such being my opinion, immediate action by the Federal Government is important to stop the butchering."[43] The CF&I's Welborn warned in a 1:07 A.M. Thursday telegram to Ammons, "Care Penna Train No. 55, Pittsburgh," that unless help was sent immediately, the onslaught would likely force the shutdown of the coal fields and the steel works. Any delay in sending in the troops "cannot be regarded as anything short of criminal."[44]

Ammons was hearing nothing different from Denver. General Chase joined with Lt. Gov. Stephen Fitzgarrald—acting governor—in wiring Ammons in Washington that "affairs in coal field getting worse every hour." They ran through overly high estimates of the dead and those still threatened and warned that "reports seemingly reliable show that additional miners in great numbers are going to the help of the strikers from all directions. Telephones and telegrams reaching your office every minute demanding help. The coal camp country is helpless." Chase said he could send six hundred militiamen, "but men will not move without some assurance of pay." They urged Ammons to call a special session of the state legislature. Ammons agreed the state soldiers were needed again. "I will make all arrangement necessary to pay troops. Send them at once. . . . Ask clearing house to provide temporary funds until provision can be made." But he balked at calling the special session, vaguely saying that "I prefer to consult about contents of call if extra session be required."[45]

Calling the Guard back out proved to be difficult. Chase declared late Wednesday, around midnight, that he would lead six hundred men south to seize control of the strike district, but more than a third of the men failed to respond or openly defied orders to go. Several of the units were wracked by desertions and, in the case of Company C, mutiny. That unit had returned from the field the previous week and the soldiers had been living "at the Broadway armory in a cold, dirty, foul room."[46] None had been paid in months, and the men refused to return to duty until they received their back pay—a personally embarrassing development for General Chase: Two of his sons and three other relatives were members of Company C, which was known as the "Chase troop." But the response was lethargic across the units. Of the thirty-five men who belonged to a Greeley-based unit, only ten answered the call. Several Denver companies reported in with only half their men, the rest in hiding or simply refusing to respond. Some fifty officers reportedly submitted resignations rather than go; the letters were refused.

Chase had planned for the troop train to depart about 10:00 A.M. Thursday with six hundred men. The first six engine crews refused to move the train; a crew was finally found that agreed to take the train as far as the strike zone, where a National Guard officer was delegated to take over. As the soldiers boarded, they were jeered by some members of a small crowd that had gathered, while others—relatives of the militiamen—watched with teary-eyed anxiety. When the train finally pulled out at 12:25 P.M., nearly two and a half hours after its scheduled departure time, only 242 soldiers were aboard the twenty-three-car train led by two engines protected by a squadron of sharpshooters. Field artillery guns were strapped down atop two flatcars, and three baggage cars carried guns and ammunition.[47] A second train holding another one hundred men and equipment pulled out about twelve hours later. Doyle, in Denver, cabled UMWA officials in Trinidad, Walsenburg, and Florence after the first train left to warn that the troops were on their way and hinted that the union men should try to stop the train. "Denver report says flat car with Gatling gun will be placed in front of engine; also that men will detrain before reaching center conflict. In order that these militiamen with their two additional machine guns may not repeat the horrible Ludlow massacre of women and children, we urge you to watch for their approach."[48]

Despite the dire warnings and frenzied reportage, all those who had run to the mine shafts for safety survived. The camps themselves, though, were mostly burned to ashes, and in the process at least twelve men were killed and uncounted others wounded.[49] In addition to the three mine guards killed at Delagua and the two strikers at Aguilar, mine guard Benjamin Phillips, twenty-seven, died in fighting at Tabasco, and John Church, a mine employee, died at Delagua, though the circumstances of those deaths remain unclear. The dead also included Waddell, superintendent of the Empire mine, who died of wounds he suffered near the beginning of the attack, before he and the others could retreat into the mine shaft.

Trinidad teemed with angry miners, who controlled the streets. Several militiamen were rumored to have tickets for the 8:00 P.M. Wednesday Santa Fe train, and as the train loaded, eight armed union men arrived and "took up a position on the lawn" of the depot, guns trained at the passenger cars.[50] The train's departure was delayed while cooler union heads were summoned, and the showdown was defused. At the nearby Cardenas Hotel, where months earlier Linderfelt had stood in the shadows and watched the supplicants approach the visiting Governor Ammons, militia captain Randolph "was spirited away" before he could finish his dinner—and before the union men could spot him.

Wednesday evening, rain and hail drenched southern Colorado. Foul weather and high winds continued Thursday, with spring snow falling sporadically.[51] Skirmishes broke out up and down the district but the full assaults on the mines ebbed, dampened no doubt by the bad weather. Lieutenant Governor Fitzgarrald, while Ammons was still traveling back to Denver, tried to negotiate a peace with the strikers through Horace Hawkins, the UMWA's lawyer in Denver. On Thursday, McLennan was aboard a train from Walsenburg to Trinidad when militiamen boarded it during its Ludlow stop and arrested him.[52] They took him before Linderfelt, who searched him and his valise and confiscated his papers. He was held overnight at the depot, then taken to the militia encampment the next morning and held in the cookhouse while the gunmen threatened him repeatedly in "very vile, very foul language." One of the gunmen, weapon in hand, told McLennan, "I would like to take a shot at you right now."

Hawkins made McLennan part of the truce negotiations—the union would agree to a cease-fire if McLennan was freed and the militia did not move beyond their established encampments. Fitzgarrald agreed, and the tentative truce went into effect on Friday. Within an hour the gunfire stopped up and down the district, which now covered some 175 miles. Though the union men observed the truce, reinforcements continued to flow into the district, and Hawkins's own unionists denounced him for agreeing to a cease-fire.[53]

As Chase's troop train made its way south, strike leaders in Aguilar rang a large bell at union headquarters, a summons for men who were then ordered to the town of Lynn, on the C&S rail line a few miles away. Miners filed through the union hall gathering ammunition and bandoliers and moved out around 10:30 P.M. in a large group to take up their positions; stragglers trailed behind for an hour or more.[54] Chase's troop train had passed Pueblo about 8:00 P.M. and continued its slow run south. About 1:30 A.M. on Friday, the train pulled into the Walsenburg station, where soldiers unloaded horses under the watchful eyes of union spotters. The train stopped several more times as it journeyed south from Walsenburg, letting off a few men at a time to protect stations along the route. Campfires twinkled on the ridges as miners watched the train progress, but except for occasional potshots no effort was made to stop it despite Doyle's plea. By daylight the troops had arrived in Ludlow, three days after Mary Petrucci had emerged alive but shattered from the death pit.

The militia now controlled the area around Ludlow and north along the rail line to Walsenburg, but the strikers held the countryside, surrounding the troops. They also controlled portions of Walsenburg and all of Trinidad, where they erected their own military camp on the grounds of the San Rafael Hospital that had been Mother Jones's jail and where the militia had earlier had their camp. The strikers called the new settlement Camp Beshoar after the Trinidad doctor who had tended to their medical needs since the strike began.[55]

Governor Ammons's train was due to arrive in Denver around eight o'clock Friday night, and thick crowds converged on the depot in anticipation. Scores of city police and undercover men surrounded the depot as rumors swirled of an assassination attempt. But the train stopped before it reached the depot, and Ammons stepped off into a waiting car, which whisked him to his office suite. After briefing Ammons, Fitzgarrald emerged to tell reporters that he blamed the union leaders for the campaign of violence in the southern district, citing the speed with which the cease-fire went into effect—less than an hour after he and Hawkins had agreed to it. Such a quick response, he said, could not have happened were the marauding strikers not organized and under the union leaders' control.[56]

Ammons awoke Saturday, April 25, his first full day back in Denver, to a United Press report out of Washington that the "strike with its civil war conditions and a death list that eclipsed the Veracruz battle occupied much of the attention of today's [Friday's] cabinet meeting."[57] The wire report said that the president and his cabinet discussed the strike, its causes, and possible solutions to the violence but concluded that without an appeal from Ammons, the federal government had no authority to intercede. Ammons immediately wired Tumulty, the president's secretary. "Conflicting reports as to action of Cabinet meeting yesterday morning have been received here. What I would be greatly obliged to know is if we cannot control situation in southern field can we have federal troops." Despite the speculative tone of Ammons's questions, he was already preparing his telegram formally seeking federal help. He detailed a systemic breakdown of authority that began with the September 23, 1913, walkout and the violence that led to the calling out of the National Guard, the Guard's removal, and the subsequent clashes at Ludlow and elsewhere within what he described as a zone "eighty miles in length." Despite the return of the militia to the field, Ammons wrote, bedlam reigned. "Armed men in open defiance of law are congregating from various portions of the state in the affected district. There are probably three thousand armed men in open insurrection" facing a state militia with fewer than 650 men (he did not mention the mass refusals of soldiers to serve).

Wilson, despite the international crisis in Mexico that dominated his time, responded himself by telegram. The cabinet discussion, he said, was "merely for the sake of information. I cannot conceive of the authority of the State of Colorado being ineffective and earnestly suggest that renewed effort be made to prevent hostile action on either side or any action that might provoke hostility." What the president and his advisors failed to recognize was that the state of Colorado had been "ineffective" for months in the southern district, where years of coal company domination had sowed the seeds of class revolution.

The fragile truce was holding—in part because the union men were busy burying their dead. Fyler, Larese, and Rubino were laid to rest on Friday, and the next morning some fifteen hundred miners and their families, wearing dark wool jackets and dresses, gathered outside Holy Trinity Church across from Northcutt's *Trinidad Chronicle-News* building.[58] Standing in silence beneath leafless trees, they watched as two large horse-drawn wagons from the Hall-McMahon funeral home pulled up with fourteen coffins, three dark wood ones holding one of the dead men and the two dead mothers, and eleven smaller white coffins holding the children.[59] After the service, the bodies were taken in a near-silent parade to the Catholic Cemetery on East Main Street. That afternoon, the Snyder boy was buried. On Monday morning the funerals for Tikas and two other Greeks—Nick Loupikas and Nick Tomich, killed near Aguilar—were also held at Hall-McMahon. After a Greek Orthodox funeral mass, described by Northcutt's xenophobic *Chronicle-News* as a "strange ceremony" that used both incense and "a weird chant,"[60] the funeral procession began. A horse-drawn hearse moved through city streets, trailed by a solemn line of dark-dressed miners walking two abreast, to the Knights of Pythias cemetery. Pictures show men trailing far back out of camera range. The route took them near their new Camp Rafael military headquarters, and as the procession passed, about twenty strikers—some of the few who did not attend the funeral—stood in silence, hats in their hands.

After the burials, a handful of union men attacked the Trinidad city jail,

The funeral procession through Trinidad for Louis Tikas, a Greek union organizer and one of the leaders of the Ludlow tent colony. He and two other men
were captured as the tents burned, and apparently executed by National Guard
troops. *Credit: Courtesy Colorado Historical Society, ID No. 10029246. All rights
reserved.*

firing off several rounds in an otherwise unremarkable confrontation. But
a more serious breach of the truce had already occurred as miners in
Cañon City in Fremont County—between Ludlow and Denver—launched
a daybreak attack on Victor-American's Chandler mine, killing a mine
guard, sending families and strikebreakers fleeing, and then methodically
burning the tipple and the mine works to the ground. On Sunday they
moved on to the nearby Royal Gorge mine as residents in Cañon City held
a mass meeting to draft contingency plans in case the miners attacked the
town itself.

Ammons, reacting to the violence, declared the fragile truce broken by
the strikers and all but called the union leaders liars for insisting they
couldn't get word through to the men in Fremont County to lay down their
arms. "Gen. Chase has been ordered to push, aggressively, his campaign

against disorder in the strike zone, irrespective of future promises from the strikers."[61] But few expected the militia would be able to end the bloodshed. Coal operator E. G. Bettis, who owned the small Royal Gorge Coal and Fire Clay Co. in Cañon City, sent his dire appeal directly to the White House, describing a "reign of anarchy" in Fremont County's coal district. "The hills surrounding the mines are covered with armed striking miners. Lives have been lost. More in danger. Local and state authorities unable to cope."[62] What was needed, he said, joining a growing chorus of voices, was federal troops.

Ammons's papers include a couple of intriguing letters from a man identified only as "Cimic," apparently an informant high up in the UMWA, reporting on April 25 and again on April 29 that the union "agreed to the truce for the express purpose of giving them more time to secure arms and ammunition and muster up as big a body of men as possible, and so give them a better chance to whip the militia. . . . They intend to carry this fight through to a finish in order to gain recognition, or else destroy every mining property." Wobblies were showing up, too, including an organizer named Monovich, brought in "for the express purpose of stirring up trouble and helping along with the dirty work." Cimic reported that the union men had used five cars to move six hundred guns from Littleton, just southwest of Denver, skirting established towns, and were doling them out to striking miners and fresh reinforcements, though he didn't say where. "Under the circumstances, and judging by the talk around headquarters, the worst is yet to come in the southern field" under a broad plan to establish a semipermanent civil revolt until the union won recognition.[63]

The White House was still trying to draw the Rockefellers directly into the crisis, hoping to defuse Colorado from afar. It didn't work. Wilson wired Rockefeller on Saturday that Representative Foster, who as chair of the Mines and Mining subcommittee had held hearings in the strike district earlier in the year, planned a quick return to Colorado.[64] Wilson asked Rockefeller whether Foster could meet with him in New York before heading west. The magnate wired back that he was retired from the business but "shall be happy" to arrange a meeting between Foster and his son. It was held at Twenty-six Broadway on Monday, April 27, with JDR Jr. flanked by Starr Murphy, the ever-present legal counsel, and an unidentified CF&I director. Foster came with a specific message from Wilson to the Rockefellers: that if the president sent in the troops, he would also shut down the coal mines until the strike was settled. Foster urged JDR Jr. to agree to arbitration to end the impasse but failed to sway him. Afterward, Foster wired the White House that he "delivered your message" to Twenty-six Broadway and that JDR Jr. "thinks it a threat to him." But JDR Jr. called the president's bluff. "Mr. Rockafella [sic] will not listen to any proposal to arbitrate claiming nothing to settle but recognize the Union, which he will not do."

JDR Jr. wired his own account of the session to the White House on Monday, affirming an earlier telegram in which he warned that any further delay in sending out the federal troops would mean "enormous loss of property and many lives." And he pointedly rebuffed Wilson's strong-arm threat to close the mines. "[S]uch a policy, if adopted by you, would give great encouragement to those who are now engaged in making war upon the State of Colorado and thereby make it all the more difficult for the Federal troops to put down the insurrection." Shutting the mines, JDR Jr. said, would put thousands of people out of work and paralyze the region's economy. He suggested Wilson send the troops with a public statement that they would be used to enforce the law and protect strikebreakers and strikers alike—in essence, to fulfill the role the militia fumbled so badly.

Pressure built on the White House from all corners. In Congress, U.S. Rep. J. F. Bryan, a Progressive from Washington state, introduced a bill setting aside $10 million to nationalize the Colorado mines.[65] Representative Keating led a delegation that was waiting at the White House after Wilson attended Sunday morning church services. Ammons was sending regular updates to federal elected officials, seeking to enlist their help in lobbying the White House. About 6:00 P.M. Sunday, Ammons wired U.S. Sen. Charles Thomas, one of Colorado's two senators, that while the strikers were observing the truce they were also continuing to ship in men, guns, and ammunition from out of state. "Leaders insist that they are trying to control their men while people through the strike zone insist just as strenuously that strikers are taking advantage of truce to strengthen themselves." He asked Thomas to share the telegram with the rest of the Colorado delegation.[66]

In fact, miners had been flowing into the district in a steady stream, and those already there joined larger bands in Aguilar, Walsenburg, the Black Hills, and Trinidad. Forty-seven miners armed with rifles and wearing belts of ammunition gathered near the La Veta union hall around midday Monday then left as a unit for Walsenburg.[67] Neelley, the co-owner of the Walsenburg hardware store who had been working with Germer earlier in the strike to bring in guns, tried to drive in a carload of rifles from Pueblo, but his car skidded off the road. He transferred the guns to another car only to have it run out of gas. The guns finally arrived the next morning, and Neelley replenished the makeshift arsenal in a stone house near the Jackson mine, at Toltec just north of Walsenburg, where strikers had begun showing up Saturday to claim rifles.[68] In Walsenburg itself, word went out to the striking miners to pick up fresh guns at the union headquarters in the Oxford Hotel, where plans were laid for a final assault on the mines and the militia. The goal: to burn the McNally and Walsen mines, then dynamite Farr's stronghold, the Huerfano County Courthouse.[69]

On Tuesday, April 28, a week after the bodies were found beneath the burned tent, President Wilson and his cabinet held a long meeting to discuss Colorado and the proper federal role. Wilson, despite his earlier threat to close the mines until the strike ended, was adamant that the troops should not be used to settle the strike but only to preserve peace. Late in the day he wired Ammons that the troops were on their way. "My duty, as I now see it, is to confine myself to maintaining a status of good order until the state can reassert its authority." His proclamation ordered the troops "to cause all those who have been indulging in domestic violence, or whose acts are likely to give rise to disorder, to disperse and retire peaceably to their respective abodes." And he insisted that Ammons withdraw the state militia as soon as the federal troops arrived, to avoid the "manifest disadvantages of having two military forces under separate control, operating within the same localities."

Ammons quickly wired back his thanks—and an ominous update. "The trouble has spread today into Boulder County, within thirty miles of the city of Denver and also into the Walsenburg district, and our need is therefore all the greater."

TEN

Final Engagements

The coal war was now being waged along a 225-mile front, from the striking miners' occupation of Trinidad, near the New Mexico border, northward along the front range to the coal mines near Louisville, north of Denver, where a ten-hour gunfight broke out the same day President Wilson authorized the use of federal troops. No one was killed outright, though several men were critically wounded and two strikebreakers—Peter Stamoff, shot through the head, and Nicholas Papas, with a shattered jaw—were not expected to live.[1] Other attacks occurred in Crested Butte, Oak Creek, and Cañon City, where mine guard William King was shot dead April 27.[2] Louisville's Hecla mine was under siege and Boulder County undersheriff R. L. Euler was "unable to communicate with [the] sheriff," who was inside the camp "and unable to control the situation."[3]

The militia read the scope of the attacks as a concerted effort by the union forces to spread the National Guard too thinly to be effective, and to seize control of the district.[4] But there seemed to be no rhyme or reason to where the attacks occurred. Wherever there was a mass of angry and idle striking miners, violence followed, a regional outpouring of rage and revenge for the deaths at Ludlow. Yet each of the attacks was well organized, and all seemed to have the same goal: to destroy the operators' mine works, regardless of whether that meant killing guards, scabs, and soldiers in the process.

The Forbes attack began early on April 29, a Wednesday morning. Led by UMWA organizer John W. Brown, some 110 men filed out of Camp Beshoar hours before sunrise and headed into the hills, picking up a few

Armed strikers and their supporters at Camp Beshoar on the grounds of the San Rafael Hospital outside Trinidad during the guerrilla war that erupted in the aftermath of the Ludlow Massacre. *Credit: Denver Public Library, Western History Collection, Call No. X-60418.*

more gunmen along the way.[5] The union men later claimed they were merely scouting for militia troop movements when someone from the mine fired on them; the mine officials said the men marched to the canyon intent on laying waste to the mine camp. Given the actions up and down the strike district, the union's story is transparently false. The squadron of men plainly intended to destroy the mine works.

The mine camp knew they were coming. The night before, the brother of a camp bartender called to warn him to leave town, and word traveled quickly through the camp.[6] Nichols, the mine superintendent, called Hamrock at Ludlow, who refused to help because he didn't want to extend his thinly spread troops any further. George T. Peart, general superintendent for Rocky Mountain Fuel Co., which owned Forbes, called Nichols and ordered the camp's women and children to be hidden in the mine. Nichols had his men working into the night building a low wall of rock at the entrance, hoping it would be enough to keep the miners at bay. Near the mine office, T. W. Harris, Joe Watson, and two other mine guards manned the camp searchlight and machine gun, watching into the darkness for signs of attack.

As dawn lightened the sky, Harris spotted "a bunch of men coming over the hill"—Brown and his miners—forming a "skirmish line."[7] The guards rushed to ready the machine gun; Watson fired off two shots with his rifle, a prearranged signal that trouble was brewing. Colorado Supply Co. store manager K. E. Cowdery was in Nichols's house, where the superintendent was still on the telephone trying to arrange for help. They didn't hear the rifle shots, but several men ran in to tell Nichols the signal had been fired. Cowdery hurried out and was within fifty yards of his home "when the fire started like hail and the hail got uncomfortably close."[8] He ran inside and moved his wife and children to the kitchen and "barricaded them the best I could with mattresses." The miners laid down a continuous half-hour torrent of bullets, answered by the mine guards' rifles and the sporadic fusillade of the machine gun. Three bullets zipped through Cowdery's house, though no one was injured. Cowdery took to his back porch, partially shielded by the wooden supports, and fired off shots toward where he heard the miners' guns up the canyon wall to the east. The attackers were close enough for Cowdery to hear one of them shouting. "I took him to be Greek, giving orders."[9]

Gus Whitney was in the mule barn when the warning shots drew him out into the dirt street, where he joined Jack Smith and a few other men from the camp. Smith asked where they could find cover. "I says the best place I know of to get out of it is under that old rock house, across the arroyo."[10] The men ran, bullets whizzing past, some finding their mark. Smith and Edward "Abe" Kessler, a carpenter, fell to the dirt mortally wounded as the others dove into the stone house. The pace of the gunfire increased, and the men fled again. Whitney headed for the arroyo, but a striker spotted him and fired, clipping him in the arm. Whitney spun to fire back, but a second shot ripped into his abdomen and on out his back. He eventually crawled to safety near the entrance to Mine No. 7 (he survived his wounds).

The mine guards and strikebreakers, including a number of Japanese, kept the attackers at bay for a time, primarily because of Harris and the other men laying down rifle and machine-gun fire from their elevated position above Nichols's office. But after forty-five minutes they ran out of ammunition, so "we beat it over to the Majestic and stayed there" until the battle was over.[11] Without the machine gun to hold them back, the miners quickly gained the upper hand. Nichols was still on the phone trying to summon help when the line went dead about 6:45 A.M., and he and two other men fled the camp for a hillside. Another half-dozen strikebreakers and guards also snuck out of the camp, hoping to outflank the attacking miners. They were caught, but the miners released them unharmed up in the hills, an action indicating that while they had no apparent qualms about shooting to kill, their prime goal was destruction, not death.

The battle raged with a desperate ferocity, and deadly consequences. Three miners suddenly began running down a hillside for the camp, and the mine guards took aim. All three fell. Two managed to recover their footing and flee back up the hillside, but the third, Steve Dtoraka, lay unconscious and bleeding to death against a tree. In another part of the camp, guard S. A. Newman was moving along a tramway line near the tipple when a bullet struck him in the head, killing him instantly.

Cowdery, from his back porch, saw the buildings up the hillside above his home burning and went to his yard for a hose in case his house caught fire, too. A miner on the opposite side of the canyon squeezed off two quick shots, both missing Cowdery. One blasted through the windowsill and carried into the kitchen, lodging in the linoleum-covered floor near where his family was hiding behind the mattresses. Feeling increasingly endangered, Cowdery weighed the risk of running the fifty exposed yards between his house and the camp's refrigerating building, which offered more protection. "The fire was so heavy it would be almost suicide to jump out," but he decided that to stay would be certain death, so they ran. They drew fire, but luck was with them and no one was struck.[12]

As the mine guards moved out, the striking miners moved in until they had the run of the camp. George Francis Albert, a teamster, hid in the tipple at the start of the attack, joined by a couple of other men from the camp. Just after the battle started, one of the men took a shot at the miners on the hillside, drawing a fusillade in return. "We never got our heads up again." The other men slipped away, but Albert, unarmed, stayed put. He heard the gunfire tail off, then voices on the tram. "The first thing I knew there was three of them on the tipple and had three guns on me." The Italian miners, including one who acted as interpreter, rifled his pockets, then escorted him to his house, where his wife and baby were hiding. They passed Newman's body along the tram tracks—"I could see his toes sticking up on the track." The miners ordered Albert's wife, still in her bedclothes, to throw on an overcoat, and while they were all still in the house one of the

A body lies on rail tracks at Forbes after armed miners swept through and burned a portion of the mine camp to the ground. The man with the crutch is waving a white flag, and he and the person in the foreground are probably local journalists inspecting the battle scene. *Credit: Courtesy Colorado Historical Society, ID No. 10025643. All rights reserved.*

miners went into a back room and set a fire. As they left, smoke billowing out of the house, one of the miners grabbed an overcoat from the nearby barn to wrap the baby in the buggy; then the gunmen surrounded Albert, poking their guns into his ribs. "I think if it hadn't been for my wife they would have killed me," but after a few minutes they let the family go. It was too muddy for the baby buggy, so Albert scooped the child up, and they began walking down the canyon. "We got about ten feet further, they told us to stop again, and we looked around and this interpreter told us, 'Remember Ludlow.'"[13]

The marauding miners focused on the wooden mine works, sweeping through buildings with oil and torches. Joe Bonata, a mine clerk, was hiding in the mine office, which included the post office, when a handful of men stormed the building, breaking out windows and firing rifles through the rooms as they entered. Bonata lay motionless under a bed in a back room while the men trashed the offices. When they left, Bonata wiggled out and looked into the post office, already in flames. He stayed for a few minutes, uncertain whether to face flame or gunfire, before climbing out a window and hiding in a nearby shed.[14]

By 10:00 A.M., the mine office, the tipple, the boiler house, a boarding-house, and a mule stable—and the animals in it—had been leveled by fire. The only buildings that weren't burned lay in the direct line of fire of the mine guards barricaded with the women and children inside the mine—a stand of buildings that included Cowdery's house.[15] At least eleven men lay dead.[16] Dtoraka was the only striker fatality. Ten mine guards and strikebreakers died, including four Japanese men, who, in an apparent reflection of the biases of the era, were barely mentioned by name in the news coverage. They were Kenneth Ito, Telsugi Hino, Geohei Murakawi, and Mosuchi Niwa.[17] Ito died of a gunshot wound to the back, and Murakawi apparently bled to death from a shot to the right shoulder. Niwa's death also was attributed to a gunshot wound, but with no other details. Two of those men were sleeping when the battle broke out, and they were shot as they fled their boardinghouse in their underwear.[18] Hino, wounded, holed up in one of the mine buildings torched by the miners, and it is unclear whether he died of the gunshot or the fire.

Estimates from inside the Forbes camp were that anywhere from one hundred to three hundred men mounted the attack. But Fred J. Radford, who owned the Trinidad Foundry and Machine shop near Camp Beshoar, had to stop to wait for the returning army to pass. He counted 147 men, most of them marching two abreast. By noon, they were back in Trinidad.[19]

While the assault on Forbes was quick, violent, and efficient, the battle in Walsenburg dragged out as a siege, climaxing the same day as the Forbes attack. It began Monday with the union men taking control of a ridge, called the Hogback, that rises about two hundred feet and stretches west-ward from the northern edge of downtown. Covered with scrub brush, the ridge offered high-ground protection for attacking the massive Walsen mine and the smaller McNally mine to the south. In one of the many in-triguing side stories, the miners were operating under the leadership of Don MacGregor, the *Denver Express* reporter who had ridden into the strike district aboard General Chase's first troop train. After the deaths at Ludlow, MacGregor traded his pen for a gun and joined the miners who had regrouped in the Black Hills.[20] His trail disappears after the strike, and he was reported to have died in Mexico after joining Pancho Villa's marauders, though that remains unverified.

The miners swept through camps around Toltec and Pictou, north of the Hogback, on Monday and Tuesday, rousting the few remaining scabs and cementing their control of the territory. They mounted a roadblock outside the Toltec union hall, their de facto headquarters, and stopped "every rig that went through there as far as we could see and holding them up and searching them. Some they had turned back."[21] C. C. Packard ran a garage and livery service in Walsenburg and made several trips back and forth. "Every time we came through with a load they would stop me and search all the men that were in the car, and then I would go on."[22]

J. S. Cross, a meat cutter at the Colorado Supply Co. store at Pictou, watched on Monday as a squad of armed men carrying bedrolls walked southward toward the Hogback, as though marching to the front. Around 2:00 P.M. the Walsen mine whistle blew in the distance, and the striking miners still milling around Pictou and nearby Toltec jumped into action, running and riding horses for the ridge as though the whistle were a signal. A few of the mounted men spun their rides at the edge of town and galloped back to the Colorado Supply store. Like characters in a Wild West movie, "they rode their horses right up to the platform of the store, jumped off and came in." They demanded all the store's .45–70 ammunition. The manager said he didn't have any, but the miners—rightly—didn't believe him. As one leveled a rifle the others jumped the counter and pawed through the ammunition boxes "and got what they wanted," then remounted and galloped off to the Hogback. The store closed early as word spread that even more miners were on their way, and the manager ordered it to remain closed the next day. Cross stayed home the first part of Tuesday morning, then went to feed some mules. He was intercepted by a handful of armed miners who forced him to unlock the store then stripped it of all the remaining ammunition. For the next two days Cross manned the store under the threat that if he didn't the miners would break in and loot it. Even with Cross present, the miners treated it like their own quartermaster supply house.

Other miners went door to door seizing guns wherever they found them. Striking miner Enoch Muir and a dozen other men showed up at Frank Campbell's house near Pictou early Monday morning while his son Charles was still in bed and asked Campbell for whatever guns he might have.[23] Campbell turned over his only weapon, a Colt .45 six-shooter. "The old man says, 'I have no other choice,'" Charles said later. Manuel Martinez, a striker who tried to stay out of the fighting, was surprised to see his own rifle in a stack of guns at the Toltec union office. He had left it home in Talpa when he was summoned to take part in what he was told was a union delegate meeting; when he arrived, union officials were mustering an army, and Martinez refused to join. But after he left the house, miners his wife didn't recognize had come through and confiscated his rifle. Martinez told the Toltec union officials he wanted his gun back. "They said . . . that all the weapons that belonged to the union people had to stay there, and then they told me that if I didn't want to stay there that that gun was going to stay there."[24]

Some of the miners got creative in the rush for weapons. John Strauss, who was a machinist and boiler man, George Conder, and a third man built a small cannon from scratch in the Toltec mine machine shop. Strauss packed one pipe inside another and capped the end, and unidentified miners hauled it up to the Hogback, but the device blew apart the first time the men tried to fire it.[25]

The army continued to grow. A "large body" of miners walked past the Campbell house in the dark of Monday morning. It is telling that in hundreds of pages of testimony, most of the witnesses had trouble identifying strikers by name; some they recognized by sight, but many said the men they encountered were strangers, and new to the district. Some of the witnesses likely were lying to avoid implicating friends and colleagues, or out of fear of reprisals, but it is clear that the fighting involved many men who answered the "Call to Arms." With that many strangers in the field, the miners decided to use swatches of white cloth or white ribbons on their arms to identify themselves, replacing the red kerchiefs they had worn in the early days of the strike.

The Walsenburg battle began in earnest on Tuesday, with the miners attacking the McNally mine between the Hogback and the miners' main target, the Walsen mine. Blas Mimovitch, a strikebreaker at McNally who had been off work while a broken leg mended, stumbled into his basement when the gun battle began. He hid for a half hour or so before the strikers overran the camp and one of the miners sweeping through the houses found him. As McNally was being burned to the ground, Mimovitch was taken back over the Hogback to the Toltec union hall, where he was beaten into unconsciousness. An hour later, after he stirred, a friend among the strikers, Steve Cockalaiche, persuaded the others to let him drive Mimovitch to Maitland, where he was kept under guard.[26]

The fighting was intense both between the Hogback and Walsen mine and along West Seventh Street, the artery between the mine and the heart of Walsenburg. Michael Lenzini, seventeen, was in the family's grocery store on West Seventh Street as the fighting moved from building to building. The store was struck by several bullets, and one pierced a vinegar barrel.[27] Lenzini had pulled out a pocketknife and a piece of wood to whittle a stopper when a bullet struck him in the stomach. He died two days later at a Pueblo hospital. A few doors away, striking miner George Bock, forty-one, was also found shot. A bullet passed through a wall or some other barrier, caught Bock just below the tear duct of his right eye, and ricocheted upward, tearing off a piece of skull behind his eyebrow.[28] Married with five children, Bock had a loaded but unfired .38-caliber handgun and a handful of bullets in his pockets—along with a UMWA union card signed by Germer and a WFM card issued several years earlier. Clearly he was a union man, but with the gun unfired it is unclear whether he was part of the battle.

Out near the McNally mine, already in flames, striker Frank Angelo, thirty-nine, raced down the hill into one of the burning houses, looking for loot. He found a coat that fit better than the one he was wearing, so he exchanged them and then ran back out of the house. In his haste, and with the bullets flying, he had not transferred the white ribbon identifying him as a striker from the old coat to the new. As he ran "somebody on the Hogback shot him." Angelo crumpled to the ground and slowly, over the next several hours, bled to death from a chest wound as the battle raged around him.[29]

The fighting terrorized Walsenburg. Families hid in basements. Farr, his kingdom overrun, once again barricaded himself in the granite county building and ringed it with guards. But not everyone was cowed. Dora Andes Lowry and her family moved from their home on West Seventh Street into the Morris Hotel in downtown Walsenburg to get away from the gunfire.[30] A family friend and local blacksmith, Henry Lloyd, stopped by around 5:00 P.M. on his motorbike and took Lowry's younger brother and sister, then her mother, for a short ride around nearby streets. He asked Andes if she wanted a ride, too, and she asked him where they'd go. "Just up the hill, to see where all that shooting is coming from." Lowry climbed on the back of the motorbike and off they went along the Pueblo Road. They cleared the eastern end of the Hogback and continued on about six miles "out past Sample's ranch and turned around and came back. The roads were rough, all rain and wet." They rode for a couple of miles, then heard a gunshot close to them, fired by one of two men sitting on the rail line heading to nearby Pictou. A bullet hit the ground. "Dora, duck," Lloyd called out as the young woman "kind of scrooched down in the seat." Lloyd asked Lowry if she wanted to stop. "I told him if he thought best, so he stopped the motorcycle. When he stopped they hit him." The motorcycle tipped over on top of them both. "I shook him and talked to him but he wouldn't say anything, he couldn't speak." The bullet, fired from a distance, struck Lloyd in the left jaw, then severed the spinal column at the base of the brain, killing him instantly.[31] As Lowry struggled to free herself from beneath the overturned motorbike and Lloyd's body, the two armed miners approached and told her they fired because they thought the motorbike was carrying two men. They asked Lowry if the dead man was "union," and whether her father was. She told the men Lloyd wasn't a miner but was pro-union. The motorbike was too damaged to start back up, and Lowry, shaken, walked to a nearby ranch house, where she spent the night after telephoning her mother and deciding it was too dangerous to try to get back to town.

Chase had already ordered Colonel Verdeckberg, in command of the troops at Ludlow since Sunday night, to deploy sixty men to Walsenburg.[32] With the gunfight raging Tuesday, Chase sent more men and Verdeckberg himself, who had first commanded the troops there until they had been withdrawn April 11 under Ammons's demobilization order. Leading 132 men, Verdeckberg arrived about 7:30 A.M. Wednesday, April 29, at Farr's fortress in the heart of downtown. He immediately wired Chase that "a battle between mine guards and strikers was then going on at the Walsen mine, that the buildings on the McNally Mine property were on fire and that before we left Ludlow we could hear firing at Forbes" but could not move to defend Forbes because of the orders to proceed to Walsenburg.[33] It is unclear whether Verdeckberg and his men could have stopped the slaughter underway, given how quickly the miners struck.

In Walsenburg, Verdeckberg's orders were to have his men "clear the hills of all strikers at once," which turned out to be more optimistic than realistic. Verdeckberg went to the Walsen mine, where a pitched battle with the strikers secreted along the Hogback was going on, and sent six men on a reconnaissance mission back toward Walsenburg to try to get a sense of how those miners were arrayed along the Hogback. He decided to establish his command post back toward town two hundred yards behind a ridge near Walsenburg's Water Tank Hill, where a detachment of mine guards had been holed up for some forty-eight hours. A squad of strikers had mounted the hill a couple of days earlier but then fell back after the commander, Bob Roll, lost his nerve for the fight.[34] Like the Water Tank Hill south of Ludlow, Walsenburg's Water Tank Hill offered a commanding advantage for whoever held it. The ridge was south and slightly east of the Hogback. In the hands of the strikers, it would have provided two angles from which to fire on the mine guards at the Walsen mine, as well as controlling access to the Hogback from the town itself. In the hands of the militia, it offered a high-ground vantage point for both watching the miners on the Hogback and keeping them from swooping down the open slope and overrunning the mine. Verdeckberg and his men relieved the mine guards and took command. "This placed men along the entire ridge to the right [east] of Water Tank Hill." As they dug in, Lieutenant Morrison, in charge of a small detail, sent word that they were pinned down, but before Verdeckberg could respond the detail showed up at Water Tank Hill, with one wounded.

Around 10:00 A.M., Verdeckberg decided the best way to clear the Hogback was to take it. He ordered a detachment of men under Lieutenant Scott to spread out and begin to push the strikers from the Hogback by first controlling an area called Capitol Hill, a rise of land in the northwest corner of town. It was slow going, as the strikers set up a steady stream of gunfire from the ridge, and the mine guards and militiamen returned fire from Walsen to the south and from Water Tank Hill to the east. About 12:30 P.M., Lieutenant Scott sent a messenger to Verdeckberg with word that they had "reached the top of Capitol Hill and advancing on strikers who have been firing on us from Hogback since 10:15. Send re-inforcements. I will take up a position about four hundred yards to the right of the Hogback."

Lieutenant Scott and his men had run into a battle line of about thirty strikers hiding behind rocks and trees. Striking miner Tom Matsumoto watched from behind a thick pine as a half-dozen soldiers sprinted along a ditch, then around a short rail bridge at the bottom of the Hogback. As the soldiers reached open ground, "some one opened fire to attack against the soldiers, and all opened, started to fire, and then these six soldiers retreated back to this railroad track."[35] Captain Charles G. Swope was part of Lieutenant Scott's contingent "moving up from cover to cover, going to the railroad cut."[36] Swope saw Scott get hit, a bloody but not serious wound in the neck. Major Pliny Lester, a Walsenburg physician and longtime Guard member, moved up from the rear of the line and asked Scott to let him dress the wound. As he worked, Lester, wearing a red cross on his arm, straightened up slightly, offering one of the miners a tempting target about twenty-five feet from Swope. "I turned and saw him throw his hands up . . . and he says, 'They got me!' and one of the men hollered out, 'Major is shot!'" Swope moved to Lester and saw that he had been hit in the right side of the chest. "He died very soon." Two other soldiers were also wounded, a Private Wilmouth of Boulder, with a bullet in the leg, and a Private Miller of Longmont, with a gunshot wound to the mouth.

After a couple of hours of occasional gunfire, and a snow squall, the soldiers stopped firing and retreated, leaving Lester dead in the swale. Matsumoto said that one of the strikers made his way down to the rail track, found the soldiers gone and returned with evidence of a casualty—cotton and a spool of bandage, a soldier's cap, and a water bag. Other strikers went for a look and returned with a notebook and some letters, a medical bag, a knife, and a watch. Matsumoto did not say so, but the strikers had apparently found Lester's body.[37]

With the strikers comfortable atop their natural fortress, the militia failed to gain much ground anywhere. The battle at that point had raged for more than two days, with wavering degrees of intensity. In Denver, Hawkins, the union lawyer, was busy on the telephone with state officials, including Chase. They agreed on a cease-fire until the federal troops, which were nearing the strike district, could arrive and take control. Verdeckberg had received a telephone call from Chase a few minutes before 1:00 P.M. ordering him to stay near his own phone and await confirmation that a truce was in place. The call came fifteen minutes later from a Major Cohen, who said that the militia should withdraw from the battle. "I asked him what the strikers were going to do and he said they would cease firing, that there would not be another shot fired in Huerfano County, but they would not lay down their arms."

Hawkins also called Verdeckberg and told him he had spoken with MacGregor, who was moving back and forth between the miners' firing lines on the Hogback and the phone at the Toltec union office.[38] The former journalist promised to get the men to stop shooting. Verdeckberg had already rearranged his men, stationing his troops at the east and west ends of the Hogback and letting the mine guards fill in the middle. At 1:45 P.M. Chase called Verdeckberg and said "that all firing was to cease for one hour, and to meet and arrange with Don MacGregor, the leader of the strikers, the laying down of all arms in the possession of the strikers, and report."

Verdeckberg issued his cease-fire order at 2:00 P.M. and told MacGregor that if the miners had not stopped and withdrawn by 3:00 P.M., the militia would resume its attack. But MacGregor could not control his men, and the shooting continued. Just before 2:30 P.M., Verdeckberg received word from Lieutenant Scott that his men were in trouble. "Heavy firing on us two hundred yards up Hogback. Major Lester killed. I am wounded, not seriously. Myself and fifteen men have become separated from Capt. Swope—have been obliged to fall back one hundred yards to stronger position. Will remain here. Send re-inforcements."

There weren't many soldiers left to send. Verdeckberg had already deployed Capt. W. B. Lightbourn to a position to the west of the Hogback, "which was the Elk's Country Club with a very large lake, to inform me of the situation at that point."[39] Lightbourn reported back that the Hogback was unoccupied at that end, below the high point called Walsen Crag. Verdeckberg sent Capt. Robert B. Baird, two officers, and thirty-one men to meet up with Lightbourn and move to the peak. But by the time the additional men arrived, the strikers had already spread west and taken the position. Baird and his men were pinned down. Captain Long had gone out to check on a wounded man in Baird's company and reported back that their hopes of flanking the strikers on the ridge top had failed. "Baird cannot retire until dark without loss of life. Firing is heavy."

Word from the eastern end was no better. Captain Swope sent word to Verdeckberg about 3:35 P.M. that with Major Lester dead and Lieutenant Scott suffering a head wound, the "men [were] badly shaken. Have fallen back to east of Walsenburg (Pueblo Road) guarding out. Enemy in rifle pits along the ridge west of wagon road out on Walsenburg–Pueblo Road. Need reinforcements. Ought to have artillery."

The militia was spread out over three miles, a thin line of 175 soldiers and uncounted mine guards and scabs. The battle kept up until after sundown. MacGregor was supposed to have met Verdeckberg at a bridge between the Hogback and Walsenburg, but gunfire pinned him on the ridge until nightfall. He finally met with Verdeckberg and Major Cohen in Cohen's office about 8:00 P.M. MacGregor arrived with three other men and told the militia officers that initially he had been unable to communicate the cease-fire to all the men along the battle line but that with sunset the message had reached all the men. He said he had added an ultimatum: He would have a squadron of strikers fire on anyone from the union side who broke the cease-fire.

With the guns silenced, the two sides agreed to meet again at 10:00 A.M. Thursday. Verdeckberg asked MacGregor to delegate a striker to accompany the soldiers to bring in Major Lester's body. MacGregor agreed, in return for protection for strikers to collect Angelo's body from near the McNally mine. In the dark, Captain Swope climbed the Hogback with several men and retrieved Major Lester's body.[40] They loaded it onto a wagon and ferried it to a Walsenburg undertaker, who determined that Lester had been shot twice after he was already dead—both bullets passing through near his heart. His pockets had been rifled and turned inside out, a military emblem had been ripped from his arm, and his wristwatch, money, and papers had been taken.[41]

MacGregor and Verdeckberg, with the other militia officers, were to meet at 10:00 A.M. the next day. MacGregor was an hour late. Verdeckberg angrily asked him about the condition of Lester's body and about the missing items. MacGregor said he had retrieved the items from his men the night before and had burned the letters, which he said were personal, but would turn over the rest of Lester's possessions.

Verdeckberg pressed MacGregor on when his men would turn over their arms, which is what Chase had told him was one of the terms of the cease-fire. MacGregor demurred and suggested they just let things rest until the U.S. Army arrived—at that point scheduled for 3:00 P.M. Verdeckberg agreed.

With the fight gone out of both sides, MacGregor trudged back up to his men on the ridge while Verdeckberg awaited his replacements. The troop train finally arrived about 4:15 P.M., bearing U.S. Army captain Smith and seventy soldiers from Fort Leavenworth. The miners faded from the Hogback. Before midnight Verdeckberg and his men had packed up their gear and boarded a train for Ludlow. Two days later, the federal army firmly in control, the National Guard left the district entirely, and the violence in the southern Colorado coalfield left with them.

In ten days, no fewer than fifty-four men, women, and children had been killed.

Epilogue

LUDLOW, COLORADO, MAY 30, 1918. The people began arriving well before the ceremony was scheduled to begin, some riding up in wagons and cars, others walking and alighting from trains at the Ludlow station. They gathered at the barren, wind-swept spot just east of the C&S railroad tracks, some three thousand people in all, talking and catching up in front of the large flag-draped obelisk under the warm late spring sun. Most were dressed in mine camp finery—ironed dresses and worn but clean dark jackets. A few wore the suits and ties of success, union officials looking like bankers. When the program finally began, it was in a mix of languages, mostly English but also Italian, the "Slavonic languages" and, of course, Greek.[1] One by one the speakers sang the praises of the assembled throng and recalled their sacrifices during the strike. Together they remembered the dead as they congratulated themselves for their more recent generosity— a subscription of donations, from people who could not afford it, that had raised $12,000 to build the monument they were about to see.

At the appointed time, Mary Petrucci, whose three children had died near that very spot four years earlier, stepped up to a thick string and gave it a tug, collapsing the large silken American flag and unveiling the result of the miners' fund-raising: a twenty-foot granite spire anchored by life-sized statues of a miner, a miner's wife, and a miner's child, symbolizing the lives that had been lost in a battle for dignity and freedom that, with an unimaginably deadly war raging in Europe, was already fading from public consciousness.

At some point near the start of the day's program, a hired car pulled up along the dirt road and parked. A messenger stepped out and, as surreptitiously as he could, made his way to the side of the monument. He spoke quietly with the ceremony organizers and handed them a printed card with a single name on it: John D. Rockefeller Jr. The man himself, with his wife, Abby, his adviser W. L. McKenzie King, and Mrs. King, stepped out of the car and moved close enough to hear the speeches but remained far enough from the crowd that few noticed him, and fewer still recognized him. As the ceremony came to a close, JDR Jr., the man many considered responsible for the deaths of Mary Petrucci's three children, and more than seventy-five other people, slipped unobtrusively back into his hired car and was driven away.

JDR Jr. had been in the southern coalfields with King, one of his family's advisers for the past four years, inspecting the CF&I properties. He wasn't invited to the monument's unveiling—it isn't clear, in fact, when he learned of it and why he decided to attend. But in some ways, his surprise presence at the site of the former tent colony brought the strike, and the class war that it unleashed, full circle. The aftermath of the violence could be the subject of a book in and of itself, and has been.[2] Since this work focuses on the historical record of the strike and war, the story has a natural end with the arrival of the federal troops. But the ensuing controversy over the "disruption" in Colorado, as JDR Jr. had taken to calling it, bears some note. Although the violence stopped with the army's arrival, the strike sputtered on until the UMWA finally called it off in December 1914, after spending more than $2 million.[3] By then, though, the call to end the strike was a formality. The strikers had been replaced, the mines were back on normal footing, and the UMWA had failed in reaching its only real goal: recognition by the coal operators and contracts for its members.

The operators to the end refused to meet with the union men, who they steadfastly insisted fronted a lawless organization committed to violence. The accusation "would have greater force if it came from men who themselves have been conservators of the peace, but these companies have not been," Secretary Wilson wrote to his boss, the president, on May 11, 1914. "They have maintained for years an armed guard ostensibly to protect their property, but which has been used to intimidate the workmen and others. I have in mind a number of instances where organizers of the mine workers have been waylaid on the highway or attacked while sitting peacefully in their seats on passenger trains and hammered into insensibility by those guards with guns in their hands."[4]

The UMWA monument in August 2006 at the site of the Ludlow tent colony.
Credit: Margaret Mercier-Martelle.

Stewart, Secretary Wilson's mediator, had earlier summed up the show-down as "a strike of the twentieth century against the tenth century mental attitude, and the presence of the company gunmen was 'the real splinter under the skin.'" He saw the strike as a human struggle against shackles. "The companies created a condition which they considered satisfactory to themselves, and ought to be to the workmen, and jammed the workmen into it, and thought they were philanthropists. That men have rebelled grows out of the fact that they are men, and can only be satisfied with con-ditions that they create, or in the creation of which they have a voice and a share."[5]

With scores of bodies buried across the coal district, the Rockefellers' public reputation, long controversial to begin with, had taken a beating. In June 1914, JDR Jr. stepped away from his father's long-held practice of not engaging his detractors and hired Ivy Ledbetter Lee, a former newsman turned publicity agent, and McKenzie King, former Canadian deputy minister of labor and future prime minister, for overlapping jobs. Lee was tasked with presenting "the truth" about the strike and the events at Lud-low to political and business leaders and the general public. King was charged, through the Rockefeller Foundation, with exploring the conflict between labor and management and methods for defusing future prob-lems. Lee's legacy: He devised what seems to be the first major public rela-tions spin campaign, releasing a series of documents (in many cases with erroneous details) about the strike, helping to cement his standing as the founder of modern corporate public relations. King's legacy: He helped JDR Jr. devise his Colorado Industrial Plan, a blueprint for company unions, the internal management-drafted labor committees that theoreti-cally removed the need for outside unions. That model became the in-dustrial rage until the 1935 Wagner Act established the National Labor Relations Board, which granted workers the right to join independent unions without reprisals from their bosses and banned company unions.

Bowers, not surprisingly, opposed even company unions, but by the time they came into play he had already been forcibly retired by JDR Jr., who, listening to his new advisors, was persuaded that the Rockefellers' management style of empowering people they trusted left too much dis-tance between them and the work that was done in their name. "It was clear to [King] that Rockefeller had erred seriously at the very onset of the strike by failing to inform himself of the actual state of affairs. His rigid ad-herence to the conventions of delegated authority had led him astray—to the point of abdicating his responsibility."[6] With King whispering in JDR

Jr.'s ear, Bowers was "bumped upstairs"—pulled from Denver to play an ill-defined role as advisor to the Rockefellers. In an exchange with JDR Jr., Bowers was confused and suspicious, unable to contain his sense of being betrayed by the father and son he had served so faithfully for so long. "That there is some underlying reason for this move in asking my retirement from every position in that company, after so many years of activity, is hardly to be doubted." Word in Denver was that Bowers "had been put into 'cold storage' by the influence of your advisors, for the purpose of doing away with my opposition to their scheme of playing 'the soft pedal' to suit the labor organizations and win their goodwill."[7] Labor-management relations were moving forward, and Bowers had been left behind. He returned to Binghamton, where he pursued his investments in real estate and the stock market and tended to his anchor firm, which boomed in the World War I military economy. He died in 1941, never having seemed to reconcile himself with his role in the bloodletting in Colorado and as the Rockefellers' scapegoat.

Bowers was the only person to be held even remotely accountable for the violence. In the weeks after the National Guard was replaced by the federal troops, several courts martial looked at the men involved in the Ludlow massacre. All were exonerated in hasty proceedings that included few, if any, strikers as witnesses and that seemed designed to keep the soldiers from being prosecuted by state authorities. The only militiaman to be found at fault was Linderfelt, and that for abusing a prisoner—Tikas—by breaking his rifle over the organizer's head. Linderfelt was demoted but went on to serve in the U.S. Army in World War I, though the records are unclear on whether he ever left the country. By 1926 he was living in Oklahoma, where he applied for a military pension. In the 1930 Census he is listed as a miner in Santa Rosa Pueblo in Arizona's Pima County, after which he made his way west to Los Angeles, where he died in 1958 and is buried in the National Cemetery, a final resting place for veterans and, ironically, heroes.

It should not be surprising that the strikers bore the brunt of the post-strike legal problems. In a series of indictments, some four hundred men were accused of a wide range of crimes, including murder. Few ever went to trial, and the only two apparent convictions were of Zancanelli, for the murder of George Belcher, and Lawson, for the murder of militiaman John Nimmo. Both convictions were later overturned.

The strike exacerbated preexisting tensions within the UMWA, and in February 1917, shortly after Lawson's conviction was thrown out, the UMWA executive board suspended the District 15 charter and abolished all the leadership positions, throwing out Lawson, Doyle, and others. The two friends later tried to form their own union, but it sputtered, then died. Lawson hired on as a labor agent for Osgood's Victor-American Fuel Co. In 1927 he became a vice president for the Rocky Mountain Fuel Co., after owner John Roche died and his progressive-reformer daughter Josephine Roche took over. One of Lawson's first duties: negotiate a contract with the UMWA.

The biggest change was political. In the November 1916 elections, Governor Ammons and Frederick Farrar, the attorney general who sought the indictments against the strikers, were swept out of office by a state electorate deeply dissatisfied with the way the strike had been handled. Farrar had no trouble finding work—CF&I hired him as its chief legal counsel. There were profound changes in Huerfano County, too. In the 1914 sheriff's election, Farr faced a tough challenge by Neelley, the hardware store co-owner and gunrunner for the striking miners. Neelley was also part-owner of the *Independent,* a newspaper in competition with Farr's *World.* The *Independent's* business manager, Robert Mitchell, author of articles savaging the Farr machine, was shot dead in an ambush after turning over evidence of election fraud to the U.S. attorney for Colorado. The killing was generally believed to have been political, though Farr made a show of having a bloodhound follow a trail to a nearby mine and ascribed the killing to burglary even though nothing was missing.

The sheriff's campaign was close. Neelley won in every Huerfano County precinct except seven: Cameron Precinct No. 27, Rouse Precinct No. 22, Pryor Precinct No. 21, Oakview Precinct No. 20, Walsen Mines Precinct No. 18, Ravenwood Precinct No. 15, and the unfortunately named Niggerhead Precinct No. 14. Each of those precincts was contained within a closed mine camp, each poll judge was a mine employee, and, to no one's surprise, Farr's margin of victory was high enough in those precincts to overcome by 329 votes his losses elsewhere. Neelley challenged the results in court, and in June 1916 the Colorado Supreme Court, in a withering decision that served as an unofficial indictment of Huerfano County's political system, awarded the race to him. Farr was ordered to step down as sheriff, a forced abdication in the Kingdom of Farr.

But in the end, little changed in the way the mine camps were run, and in the lives of the miners. On April 27, 1917, three years and a week after the carnage at Ludlow, an open safety lamp deep within the Victor-American Co.'s Hastings mine, near the former Ludlow tent colony, ignited a pocket of coal gas and dust and exploded in a massive blast and then fire. The concussion collapsed the main tunnel, trapping and killing all 121 men in the mine at the time, some perishing instantly and others lingering in the dark and foul air as scores of miners desperately tried to dig them free. As the debris was cleared away and the bodies discovered—many charred beyond recognition—the rescue teams became corpse carriers. Singly and in groups the bodies of coal miners, union men and scabs alike, were hauled from the darkness. Among the men who assumed that final grim task was John Lawson.[8]

Appendix A:
Key Figures

Ammons, Elias   Elected governor of Colorado in November 1912. Sought to mediate an end to the strike and ultimately ordered in the Colorado National Guard.

Belcher, George; Belk, Walter   Baldwin-Felts detectives who killed UMWA organizer Gerald Lippiatt in a brief shootout five weeks before the strike began. Belcher was later killed, likely by striking miner Louis Zancanelli.

Bell, Sherman   Led the Colorado National Guard during the 1903 strike.

Bowers, Lamont Montgomery   The Rockefellers' representative in Colorado and a key executive for the Colorado Fuel & Iron Co.

Brake, Edwin   Colorado deputy labor commissioner, sympathetic to the strikers.

Brown, David W.   Head of the Rocky Mountain Fuel Co., one of the "big three."

Chase, Gen. John   Led the Colorado National Guard during the occupation of the strike district. Also a key militia leader in the 1903 strike, he saw his role as outside of constitutional restraints.

Doyle, Edward   Union miner. Secretary-treasurer of UMWA District 15 (covering Colorado and several other states) during the strike, handling most organizational details.

Farr, Jefferson B.   Corrupt sheriff of Huerfano County and business associate of CF&I middle managers.

Felts, A. C.   Brother of the co-founder of the Baldwin-Felts Detective Agency. Ran the agency's strike operations in Colorado; built the notorious Death Special armored car.

Gaddis, Eugene   Former head of the CF&I's Sociological Department overseeing medical and social programs for workers. Later testified for the miners at congressional hearings about the inhumane conditions in the mines and mine camps.

Gates, Frederick T.   Close adviser to the Rockefellers. Bowers's uncle.

Appendix A

Germer, Adolph   Socialist and UMWA organizer, directed strike operations in Walsenburg, including procuring arms.

Grisham, James   Sheriff of Las Animas County. Not as corrupt as Farr in Huerfano County but a key ally of the coal operators. Deputized several hundred mine guards.

Hawkins, Horace   UMWA lawyer in Denver who brokered cease-fires.

Hayes, Frank   UMWA vice president based in Indianapolis, in charge of early strike strategies; by fall he had turned control over to John Lawson.

Hendrick, John J.   District attorney for Las Animas and Huerfano counties. Used CF&I lawyer Jesse Northcutt as unofficial assistant and investigator into allegations of illegal activity by union members and supporters, confirming the strikers' belief that the local power structure was aligned with the coal operators.

Jones, Mary Harris "Mother"   Legendary labor organizer who galvanized Colorado miners. Was deported from the strike district and illegally detained when she returned.

Lawson, John R.   Coal miner, Colorado union official, and leader of the strike efforts. Was later convicted of murder on perjured testimony, but the verdict was thrown out on appeal after some of the witnesses recanted.

Linderfelt, Karl E.   National Guardsman in charge of detachments in and around Ludlow; a particularly brutal military leader who exacerbated tensions and played a key role in the battles surrounding the Ludlow Massacre.

Lippiatt, Gerald   UMWA organizer killed by Walter Belk and George Belcher, Baldwin-Felts detectives, in a brief shootout in downtown Trinidad five weeks before the strike began.

MacGregor, Don   Journalist for the union-friendly *Denver Express*. In the last days of the coal war, he was leading union men in a siege of Walsenburg.

McLennan, John   UMWA District 15 president at the start of the strike.

Murphy, Starr J.   The Rockefellers' lead legal counsel at Twenty-six Broadway.

Neelley, E. L.   Co-owner of a Walsenburg hardware store who helped the strikers obtain weapons. Later ousted Farr as Las Animas County sheriff.

Northcutt, Jesse G.   Publisher of the *Trinidad Chronicle-News* and lawyer for the coal operators. Helped import weapons, hired gunmen for the mines, and assisted in prosecutions of striking miners.

Osgood, John C.   Co-founder of CF&I ousted by the Rockefellers. He then formed the Victor-American Fuel Co., one of the "big three."

Patterson, Thomas   Former U.S. senator and publisher of the *Rocky Mountain News;* sought with Governor Ammons to mediate an end to the strike.

Peabody, James H.   Governor of Colorado during the 1903 strike; used extra-legal tactics to bust union organizing drives.

Pearce, James B.   Colorado secretary of state and ex officio state labor commissioner during the strike.

Rockefeller, John D., Jr.   Son of the oil baron, he was running the family businesses during the strike.

Rockefeller, John D., Sr.   Oil baron whose investments in CF&I (the biggest of the "big three") made him a key publicity target of pro-union activists.

Stewart, Ethelbert   Federal labor mediator assigned to the coal strike.

Thomas, Mary O'Neal   Striking miner's wife and strike activist who wrote a memoir of her experiences.

Tikas, Louis   Union organizer and leader of the Greek community of strikers with the Ludlow tent colony.

Van Cise, Philip S.   Denver lawyer and National Guard captain.

Verdeckberg, Edward   Colonel in the National Guard who led the troops deployed at Walsenburg.

Welborn, Jesse   CF&I president whose authority was overshadowed by the presence of Bowers, the Rockefellers' appointed man in the field.

White, John   UMWA president, based in Indianapolis.

Wilson, William B.   Former UMWA official and congressman; first secretary of the federal Department of Labor.

Wilson, Woodrow   President during the strike; his attention was focused more on military engagements in Mexico.

Appendix B:
The Dead

At least seventy-five people were killed during the 1913–1914 coal strike. The following list is drawn from the Las Animas County coroner's records and the funeral registers held at the Trinidad Carnegie Library; the work of Clare V. McKanna for the Historical Violence Database (data available at http://cjrc.osu.edu/hvd.html); and verifiable contemporary news accounts. Confusion over some names conspires against a clear count. It is also likely that several more people were killed beyond Las Animas and Huerfano counties, deaths that were not readily discernible in a review of the records. This list is broken down by affiliation, in chronological order, with identifying details where known.

UNINVOLVED VICTIMS

Sept. 26, 1913: Mike Driscoll, 50, ran a boardinghouse used by strikebreakers, found dead in an arroyo near Aguilar (likely beaten).

Oct. 9, 1913: Mack Powell, 35, striking miner working as a ranch hand, shot while riding horse near Ludlow during battle.

April 20, 1914: Primo Larese, struck by stray bullet while watching the Ludlow battle from the roadside.

April 28, 1914: Michael Lenzini, 17, shot in family store during Walsenburg battle.

April 29, 1914: Henry Lloyd, shot by strikers as he rode motorcycle north of Walsenburg.

STRIKING MINERS AND SUPPORTERS

Aug. 16, 1913: Gerald Lippiatt, 38, UMWA organizer, Trinidad.

Oct. 17, 1913: Luka Vahernik, 50, shot at Forbes tent colony.

The Dead

Oct. 24, 1913: Kris Kokich, Andy Auvinen, and Cristo Croci, shot during confrontation with guards on Walsenburg's West Seventh Street.

Jan. 5, 1914: Gus Marcus, died after incarceration in harsh circumstances at Huerfano County jail in Walsenburg.

March 16, 1914: Jack Gill and Johann Demosa, killed in confrontation at Oak Creek in Routt County.

April 20, 1914: John Bartolotti, Charles Costa, James Fyler, Frank Rubino, Frank Snyder, and Louis Tikas, shot dead during the battle surrounding the Ludlow Massacre.

April 20, 1914: Miners' wives and children: Fedelina Costa, 27, and her children, Onafrio, 6, and Lucy, 4; Rodgerio Pedregone, 9, and Cloriva Pedregone, 4; Frank Petrucci, 6 months, Lucy Petrucci, 3, and Joe Petrucci, 4; Patria Valdez, 37, and her children Rudolph, 9, Eulala, 8, Mary, 7, and Elvira, 3 months. All found suffocated in a pit dug beneath tent in the Ludlow colony, which was burned to the ground by the Colorado National Guard, mine guards and strikebreakers.

April 20, 1914: Nick Tomich, 30, shot in confrontation at Southwestern mine.

April 22, 1914: Ben Vigil, 18, and J. P. Gomes, strikers, shot outside Empire mine near Aguilar.

April 28, 1914: George Bock, 41, shot inside house during Walsenburg battle. Frank Angelo, striker, shot near Walsenburg hogback by fellow strikers; mistaken identity.

April 29, 1914: Steve Dtoraka, 33, shot at Forbes mine.

STRIKEBREAKERS, MINE GUARDS, AND COLORADO NATIONAL GUARDSMEN

Sept. 24, 1913: Robert E. Lee, 48, mine guard, shot at Segundo.

Oct. 25, 1913: John Nimmo, 38, mine guard, shot at Ludlow.

Oct. 26, 1913: Thomas Whitney, about 50, mine guard, shot at Berwind.

Oct. 28, 1913: Angus Alexander, 25, mine guard, shot at Hastings.

Nov. 8, 1913: Harry Bryan, mine guard captain, and fellow guards Walter Whitten, Luke Terry, and R. G. Adams, shot in ambush at La Veta.

Nov. 8, 1913: Pedro Armijo, 60, strikebreaker, shot at Aguilar.

Nov. 20, 1913: George W. Belcher, 26, Baldwin-Felts detective, assassinated at Trinidad.

Dec. 2, 1913: Robert McMillen, 42, mine guard, shot at Delagua.

March 8, 1914: Neil Smith, strikebreaker, 45, found dead at a rail siding at the Suffield mine, likely beaten to death.

April 20, 1914: Librado Moro, shot and killed between Walsenburg and the Pryor mine camp.

April 20, 1914: Alfred Martin, 30, National Guardsman shot in Ludlow battle.

April 21, 1914: Karl Persson, 27, mine guard, shot at Delagua.

Appendix B

April 22, 1914: William Waddell, mine supervisor, shot at Empire mine near Aguilar.

April 22, 1914: John Church, shot at Empire mine near Aguilar.

April 22, 1914: Karl Johnson, mine guard, shot at Delagua.

April 22, 1914: Fred Daugherty, 26, mine guard, shot at Delagua.

April 22, 1914: Dave Donovan, 55, mine guard, shot at Delagua.

April 22, 1914: Jose Chavez, 28, mine guard, shot at Delagua.

April 22, 1914: Benjamin Phillips, 27, CF&I employee, shot at Tabasco.

April 23, 1914: Carl Hockensmith, 22, strikebreaker, shot at Green Canyon.

April 23, 1914: Nick Loupikas, 25, strikebreaker, shot at Southwestern mine.

April 27, 1914: William King, mine guard, shot at Cañon City mine.

April 29, 1914: Jacob Smith, strikebreaker; K. Jones, mine guard; Edward Kessler, carpenter; S. A. Newman, mine guard; George Hall, strikebreaker; K. Stow; Joseph Upson, oiler; Kenneth Ito, strikebreaker; Telsugi Hino, strikebreaker; Geohei Murakawi, strikebreaker; and Mosuchi Niwa, strikebreaker, all shot at Forbes mine.

April 29, 1914: Maj. Pliny Lester, National Guard officer and medic, shot in battle at Walsenburg.

Notes

Investigation, Made Under House Resolution 387," Document No. 1630, 63rd Congress, 3rd session.

NA   National Archives
NYT   *New York Times*
RAC   Rockefeller Archive Center
RMN   *Rocky Mountain News*
TCN   *Trinidad Chronicle-News*

INTRODUCTION

1. A reliable tally of the dead has never been established, and estimates have run as high as one hundred. This total is based on coroner's records, uncontradicted contemporary newspaper accounts, and congressional testimony. It is likely that several more people died.

2. Daniel O'Regan, "The Colorado Militia and the Strike," 46, CIR/NA, Reel 4.

3. Doyle's notes from union meetings, Edward Lawrence Doyle Papers, DPL/WHC, Box 1, FF54. The notes do not say whether the union spent the money. Fink's book (Denver: Williamson-Haffner, printers, c. 1914) came out after the massacre and offered an inflammatory, pro-union version of those events.

4. Records and contemporary accounts offer inconsistent name spellings. I have sought to check names against U.S. Census and other records and to use spellings that seem most accurate.

5. Official history of the U.S. Department of Labor, http://www.dol.gov/oasam/programs/history/dolchp01.htm.

6. Ramón Eduardo Ruiz, *Triumphs and Tragedy: A History of the Mexican People* (New York: Norton, 1992), 326.

7. "The Ludlow Camp Horror," *NYT,* April 23, 1914.

8. Dean Saitta, interview with the author.

PROLOGUE

1. "Labor Delegates Prepare for Most Critical Meeting State Has Seen," *DE,* Aug. 16, 1914.

2. Edwin V. Brake, *Twelfth Biennial Report of the Bureau of Labor Statistics of the State of Colorado, 1909–10* (Denver: Smith-Brooks Printing, 1911), 231.

3. Diary of Edward L. Doyle, Doyle Papers, Box 1, FF37. The charge is not specified.

4. "Lippiatt Known in Weld County," *TCN,* Aug. 18, 1913.

5. Records of local union meetings, Doyle Papers, DPL/WHC, Box 1, FF55.

6. Zeese Papanikolas, *Buried Unsung: Louis Tikas and the Ludlow Massacre,* rev. ed. (1982; repr. Bison Books, 1991). 49.

7. "Minutes," p. 3, Doyle Papers, DPL/WHC, Box 1, FF53.

8. Barron B. Beshoar, *Out of the Depths: The Story of John R. Lawson, a Labor*

Leader (1942; Denver: Colorado Labor Historical Committee of the Denver Trades and Labor Assembly, 1957), 53. The quote is also included in Winnifred Banner's unfinished *Struggle Without End,* June 16, 1938, in John R. Lawson Papers, DPL/ WHC, Box 3, FF14.

9. "Rugby Girl Weeps over Lippiatt's Bier," *CSG,* Aug. 22, 1913.

10. O'Regan, "The Colorado Militia and the Strike," CIR/NA, Reel 4.

11. Baldwin-Felts detectives also were involved in the violence fictionalized in John Sayles's 1987 movie, *Matewan,* about the 1920 shootout in Matewan, West Virginia, in which A. C. Felts and nine other men were killed in a showdown with local police chief Sid Hatfield, who was assassinated a year later by Baldwin-Felts men.

12. O'Regan, "The Colorado Militia and the Strike," CIR/NA, Reel 4.

13. A. C. Felts testimony, MMH, 341.

14. From multiple contemporary news accounts and testimony at the Las Animas County coroner's inquest and the CIR.

15. "Lippiatt Killing Justifiable Is Verdict," *TCN,* Aug. 19, 1913.

16. LACC.

17. "Labor Delegates in Mourning for Slain U.M.W. Organizer," *DE,* Aug. 18, 1913.

18. LACC.

19. "Union Recognition or Strike, Is Mine Workers' Ultimatum," *RMN,* Aug. 19, 1913.

20. Patterson testimony, CIR/*FR,* 6479.

21. Doyle testimony, CIR/*FR,* 6934.

ONE. MONEY IN THE GROUND

1. Anthracite was in demand for industrial use, particularly for coking steel plants, while bituminous had more general uses, including heating homes and firing industrial boilers and gas production.

2. M. McCusker, "Report on the Colorado Situation," 2, CIR/NA, Reel 4.

3. Ibid.

4. Greg Lewicki and Associates, "Raton Basin Coal Mine Feature Inventory," Colorado Oil and Gas Conservation Commission, July 2001.

5. MMR, 4.

6. Priscilla Long, *Where the Sun Never Shines: A History of America's Bloody Coal Industry* (New York: Paragon House, 1989), 220.

7. Dalrymple testimony, CIR/*FR,* 6463–6469, 6469 quoted.

8. George S. McGovern, "The Colorado Coal Strike, 1913–14" (Ph.D. diss., Northwestern University, 1953), 49–50.

9. Dalrymple testimony, CIR/*FR,* 6469.

10. Compiled by the U.S. Mine Rescue Association from the Annual Reports of the State Inspector of Coal Mines, Dept. of Natural Resources, State of Colorado, 1884–1962.

11. William M. Boal, "The Effect of Unionism on Accidents in Coal Mining, 1897–1929," 36. Available at http://www.drake.edu/cbpa/econ/boal/acc.pdf.

12. Ibid., 18.

13. MMR, 5.

14. Anthony DeStefanis, "Guarding Capital: Soldier Strikebreakers on the Long Road to the Ludlow Massacre" (Ph.D. diss., College of William and Mary, 2004), 4–5.

15. J. Anthony Lukas, *Big Trouble: A Murder in a Small Western Town Sets Off a Struggle for the Soul of America* (New York: Simon & Schuster, 1997), 101–104.

16. For a fuller exploration of the WFM, see Lukas, *Big Trouble.*

17. George G. Suggs Jr., *Colorado's War on Militant Unionism: James H. Peabody and the Western Federation of Miners* (rpt. Norman: University of Oklahoma Press, 1991), 17.

18. Ibid., 20.

19. See *Congressional Record* for Saturday, June 13, 1914, "The Colorado Coal Strike—Enforce the Law, Extension of Remarks," by U.S. Rep. George J. Kindel of Colorado.

20. Copy in Lawson Papers, DPL/WHC, Box 1, FF2.

21. Long, *Where the Sun Never Shines,* 220.

22. For a detailed discussion, see Suggs, *Colorado's War on Militant Unionism,* 84–117.

23. Ibid., 81.

24. Ibid., 95.

25. Ibid., 96.

26. Chase eventually was relieved of command on October 3, 1904, during a scandal over padded payrolls, though he survived the inquest.

27. "Dynamiters Try to Blow Up Mine," *Durango Democrat,* Nov. 22, 1903, and John H. Nankivell, *History of the Military Organizations of the State of Colorado, 1860–1935* (Denver: W. H. Kistler Stationery Co., 1935), 164.

28. Nankivell, *History of the Military Organizations of the State of Colorado, 1860–1935,* 173.

29. "Dogs in Hunt for Dynamiter," *NYT,* June 7, 1904.

30. "Reign of Terror in Cripple Creek," *Durango Democrat,* June 7, 1904.

31. "Shots Fired from Windows," *NYT,* June 7, 1904.

32. Ibid.; Suggs, *Colorado's War on Militant Unionism,* 111. A military report included in Nankivell, *History of the Military Organizations of the State of Colorado, 1860–1935,* identifies the striking miner as Alf Miller (174).

33. "Reign of Terror in Cripple Creek," *Durango Democrat,* June 7, 1904; Nankivell, *History of the Military Organizations of the State of Colorado, 1860–1935,* 175.

34. "Conditions Still Volcanic," AP, *LAT,* June 8, 1904.

35. "Last Batch of Miners Exiled," *NYT,* June 15, 1904.

36. The notorious Harry Orchard confessed to the bombing, both in court cases and in interviews with journalists and at least one biographer. However,

no court ever ruled on his guilt, and no corroborating evidence was recorded. He died in an Idaho prison in 1954 for his role in the assassination of Idaho governor Frank Steunenberg.

37. Long, *Where the Sun Never Shines,* 238.

38. H. Lee Scamehorn, *Mill and Mine: The CF&I in the Twentieth Century* (Lincoln: University of Nebraska Press, 1992), 34–35.

39. Brake to Louis Freeland Post, assistant secretary of labor, Nov. 21, 1913, BLS/ES, Folder 41–10.

40. Brake, *Twelfth Biennial Report,* 22.

41. Russell D. George testimony, MMH, 8–10.

42. Testimony of James H. Blood, a lawyer and director of the Northern Coal and Coke Co., CIR/*FR,* 7220.

43. McCusker, "Report on the Colorado Situation," 3, CIR/NA, Reel 4.

44. Ibid., 4.

45. Gross report in Brake, *Twelfth Biennial Report,* 35–36.

46. Oral history interview, April 30, 1971, COPH-F.

47. Oral history interview, May 3–4, 1971, COPH-F.

48. Miners' affidavit, letter dated Aug. 3, 1908, MMH, 2566.

49. Inis Weed, "The Colorado Strike," CIR/NA, HF.I4463, Important Strikes, C7: Colorado, p. 21. Judge Patterson testimony CIR/*FR,* 6786.

50. See Brake's summary report in *Twelfth Biennial Report,* 19–22, 27.

51. George S. McGovern and Leonard F. Guttridge, *The Great Coalfield War* (Niwot: University Press of Colorado, 1996), 81, and contemporary news accounts.

52. Colorado attorney general Fred Farrar testimony, CIR/*FR,* 7179; Bowers testimony, CIR/*FR,* 8739.

53. McQuarrie testimony, MMH, 2381.

54. "Huerfano's Notorious Sheriff," *Walsenburg Independent* via *Bayfield Blade,* Aug. 1, 1913. Also see McQuarrie testimony, MMH, 2375–2387.

55. Irma Menghini oral history, Spanish Peaks Library District, Walsenburg, available at http://www.spld.org/docs/text/Menghini_I.txt.

56. Judge Patterson testimony, CIR/*FR,* 6790.

57. U.S. Census, 1900 and 1910.

58. McGovern, "Colorado Coal Strike," 68, citing his interview with Dr. Ben Beshoar, who later provided medical attention to the 1913–1914 strikers and whose son wrote the history of the coal war *Out of the Depths* on behalf of Colorado unions. The son described Farr's "thumb" directions differently, writing unattributed that Farr would indicate the vote from the edge of the jury box. The McGovern version seems more plausible.

59. "The Kingdom of Jeff Farr," *LAT,* March 4, 1914.

60. Scamehorn, *Mill and Mine,* 36.

61. McQuarrie testimony, MMH, 2378, 2385, 2383.

62. Mike Livoda oral history interview by H. Black, CHS.

63. Lawson testimony, CIR/*FR,* 8039.

64. Colorado Supreme Court decision included in Krist S. Lovdjieff, "Memories of a Massacre," manuscript, CHS.

65. Record of Inheritance Proceedings, Sept. 15, 1930, CSA.

66. Stewart to Post, Nov. 21, 1913, BLS/ES, Folder 41–10.

TWO. COMPANY MEN AND UNION LEADERS

1. "The Newest Figure in Finance," *NYT*, Sept. 7, 1902.

2. Scamehorn, *Mill and Mine*, 9–10.

3. Sylvia Ruland, *The Lion of Redstone* (Boulder, Colo.: Johnson Publishing, 1981), 15.

4. "The Newest Figure in Finance," *NYT*, Sept. 7, 1902.

5. Scamehorn, *Mill and Mine*, 83–84.

6. Beshoar, *Out of the Depths*, 2; Rick J. Clyne, *Coal People: Life in Southern Colorado's Company Towns, 1890–1930* (Denver: Colorado Historical Society, 1999), 19; and others.

7. Gaddis testimony, CIR/FR, 8492.

8. "To Oust J. C. Osgood," *NYT*, June 28, 1902.

9. Scamehorn, *Mill and Mine*, 18.

10. Ron Chernow, *Titan: The Life of John D. Rockefeller, Sr.* (New York: Random House, 1998), 392–393.

11. Ibid., 373.

12. "Gould Heirs Liable for $50,000,000 Loss in Father's Estate," *NYT*, Nov. 12, 1925.

13. To avoid confusion, I refer on second reference to the elder as Rockefeller and to the son as JDR Jr.

14. Scamehorn, *Mill and Mine*, 18–19; Chernow, *Titan*, 571. The two authors disagree on the total investment. Scamehorn, relying on CF&I records, puts it at $3 million; Chernow, using the Rockefeller archives, puts it at $6 million, which seems the more accurate figure.

15. MMR, 4.

16. Chernow, *Titan*, 571.

17. Scamehorn, *Mill and Mine*, 24–25, 29.

18. Lamont Montgomery Bowers Papers, Binghamton University, State University of New York, Glenn G. Bartle Library, Box 27.

19. Chernow, *Titan*, 386, 364.

20. Allan Nevins, *Study in Power: John D. Rockefeller, Industrialist and Philanthropist*, 2 vols. (New York: Charles Scribner's Sons, 1953), 2:383.

21. Bowers memoir, manuscript in Bowers Papers.

22. Bowers to Charles M. Cabot of Boston, April 8, 1912, Bowers Papers, Box 28.

23. Diary of Clement G. Bowers, Bowers's son, Local History and Genealogy Center, Broome County Public Library, Binghamton, N.Y.

24. Bowers memoir, 64.

25. Ibid.

26. Ibid., 65.

27. Ibid., 67.

28. Ibid., 68.

29. Chernow, *Titan*, 386.

30. "Rockefeller to Boss," *NYT*, Oct. 20, 1908.

31. Scamehorn, *Mill and Mine*, 85.

32. Gaddis testimony, CIR/*FR*, 8486.

33. Bowers to JDR Jr. assistant Charles Heydt, May 13, 1913, Bowers Papers, Box 28.

34. Bowers to JDR Jr., May 13, 1913, CIR/*FR*, 8411–8412.

35. Bowers to JDR Jr., April 12, 1909, Bowers Papers, Box 81.

36. Bowers to Gates, Oct. 10, 1910, Bowers Papers, Box 28.

37. Bowers to Gates, Feb. 1, 1910, RAC, Box 20, Folder 182.

38. Bowers to JDR Jr., Feb. 23, 1912, Bowers Papers, Box 28.

39. Beshoar oral history, COPH-F.

40. U.S. Census, 1870. The following biographical details, corroborated when possible with public sources, are drawn from Banner's *Struggle Without End*, Lawson Papers, Box 3, FF14.

41. Banner described John Hood as a "landscape architect," though census records suggest he worked in mining in some capacity.

42. U.S. Census, 1900.

43. Banner, *Struggle Without End*, 4.

44. Reported with no small amount of glee in "A Lively Fracas," *Aspen Weekly Times*, Sept. 24, 1892.

45. Lawson testimony, CIR/*FR*, 8020–8021.

46. Banner, *Struggle Without End*, 7–8.

47. Lawson testimony, CIR/*FR*, 8035.

48. Ibid., 8034.

49. McQuarrie testimony, CIR/*FR*, 6780–6783.

THREE. TROUBLE IN THE FIELDS

1. "The Coal Mining Industry in 1910," *Telluride Daily Journal*, Jan. 9, 1911.

2. A. C. Felts testimony, MMR, 328.

3. Blood testimony, CIR/*FR*, 7220.

4. Ibid., 7223.

5. Pearce's report is included in Brake, *Twelfth Biennial Report*, 10.

6. Doyle testimony, CIR/*FR*, 6932.

7. The biographical details are from notes in the Lawson Papers, Box 3, FF22. They appear to be notes from an interview by Barron Beshoar but are unsigned.

8. Doyle Papers, Box 1, FF37.

9. Testimony before the U.S. Senate Committee on Education and Labor, 1921, available at http://www.as.wvu.edu/WVHistory/documents/076.pdf.

10. "Mongo Witness Arouses M'Kellar," *NYT*, July 21, 1921. The details of the murder case were not spelled out, nor was his undercover identity.

11. Those events were dramatized, with some license, in John Sayles's 1987 movie, *Matewan.*

12. Testimony before the U.S. Senate Committee on Education and Labor, Hearings on Conditions in West Virginia Coalfields, 67th Congress, 1st session, in David Alan Corbin, ed., *The West Virginia Mine Wars: An Anthology* (Charleston, W. Va.: Appalachian Editions, 1990), 86–93.

13. Lawson Papers, Box 3, FF22.

14. Doyle Papers, Box 1, FF1.

15. Most of the spy-related files are in Doyle Papers, Box 1, FF1.

16. Doyle to White, March 11, 1913, Doyle Papers, Box 1, FF20. Includes several letters involving different spies in the district.

17. Belk testified before a special board of inquiry in August 1915, appointed by Colorado governor George A. Carlson. Transcript in DPL/WHC. Elliott's fake name was stricken from the transcript.

18. The exchange of letters is reprinted in Brake, *Twelfth Biennial Report,* 257–265.

19. McLennan testimony, CIR/*FR,* 6520.

20. Bowers to Murphy. Sept. 24, 1912, Bowers Papers.

21. Livoda oral history, CHS. His ethnicity has been ascribed to various Balkan states, but he appears to have been Croatian.

22. McQuarrie testimony, CIR/*FR,* 6783.

23. Bowers to JDR Jr., Sept. 30, 1912, RAC, Box 20, Folder 182.

24. Ammons testimony, CIR/*FR,* 6407.

25. Hayes to Germer, Oct. 30, 1912, Adolph Germer Papers, microform (Frederick, Md.: University Publications of America, 1987), Reel 1.

26. U.S. Census, 1900.

27. Germer to White, Feb. 6, 1913, Germer Papers, Reel 1.

28. Germer to John W. Walker of Springfield, Ill., Feb. 7, 1913, Germer Papers, Reel 1.

29. CIR/*FR,* 7296–7311.

30. Farr testimony, CIR/*FR,* 6791. Farr said in response to a question about whether he vetted the appointees' background: "I made no examination of any of them."

31. Osgood testimony, CIR/*FR,* 6428–6430.

32. Beshoar, *Out of the Depths,* 46.

33. See Welborn's and Osgood's testimony, CIR/*FR,* 6433, 6550, and elsewhere.

34. Bowers to Gates, cited in McGovern and Guttridge, *The Great Coalfield War,* 82.

35. Germer to John P. White, April 21, 1913, Germer Papers, Reel 1.

36. McGovern and Guttridge, *The Great Coalfield War*, 89.

37. Beshoar, *Out of the Depths*, 50–51.

38. Brake testimony, CIR/*FR*, 7235.

39. Beshoar, *Out of the Depths*, 48.

40. Bazanelli oral history, COPH-F.

41. Brake testimony, CIR/*FR*, 7234.

42. McQuarrie testimony, CIR/*FR*, 6782.

43. Mary T. O'Neal, *Those Damn Foreigners* (Hollywood, Calif.: Minerva, 1971), 86–87. Her last name at the time was Thomas, which is how she is referred to here.

44. Edwin V. Brake, *Thirteenth Biennial Report: Colorado Bureau of Labor Statistics, 1912–13* (microform, Library of Congress), 165.

45. Brake testimony, CIR/*FR*, 7235.

46. Ammons to Hatfield, Aug. 22, 1913, Papers of Elias Milton Ammons, CSA, Box 26751, FF1.

47. Germer to White, Sept. 2, 1913, Germer Papers, Reel 1.

48. McLennan testimony, CIR/*FR*, 6515; a copy of the letter is in MMH, 2539.

49. Minutes, Doyle Papers, Box 1, FF53.

50. Germer to White, Sept. 2, 1913, Germer Papers, Reel 1.

51. Bowers to JDR, Sept. 4, 1913, Bowers Papers, Box 28.

52. Details on Dotson were gleaned from Las Animas County assessor records, land maps, and Polk directories of the Trinidad area.

53. See James Chace, *1912: Wilson, Roosevelt, Taft, and Debs—The Election that Changed the Country* (New York: Simon & Schuster, 2004), 34, 94.

54. Nevins, *Study in Power* 2:419.

55. Murphy to Bowers, Sept. 16, 1913, CIR/*FR*, 8413–8414.

56. "To Decide on Strike at the Convention Monday," *TCN*, Sept. 12, 1913.

57. Undated copy of letter to individual operators signed by Hayes, Lawson, McLennan, and Doyle, MMH, 2538–2539.

58. Holmes testimony, MMH, 322–323.

59. Welborn testimony, CIR/*FR*, 6612.

60. "Seven Demands Formulated by Convention; Declaration Made That Fight to Control Colorado Is to Be Made to Finish," *RMN*, Sept. 17, 1913

61. O'Neal, *Those Damn Foreigners*, 88–89.

62. "Hayes Predicts Strike Victory," *RMN*, Sept. 15, 1913.

63. O'Neal, *Those Damn Foreigners*, 88.

64. Pells Brewing and Ice Co. existed from 1910 to 1915 on Arapahoe Street in Trinidad.

65. Description based on contemporary newspaper accounts and "Proceedings of the Special Convention of District Fifteen, United Mine Workers of America, Held in Trinidad, Colorado, September 16th, 1913," Doyle Papers, Box 1, FF52.

66. Osgood testimony, CIR/*FR*, 6426.

67. "U.S. Fears Strike, Sends Agent to Denver, Federal Arbitration Trial, Eleventh Hour; Both Sides Firm, Face Gigantic Struggle," *RMN*, Sept. 21, 1913.

68. Welborn to McClement, Sept. 6, 1913, RAC, Box 23, Folder 211, rpt. in CIR/*FR*, 7116.

69. "U.S. Fears Strike, Sends Agent to Denver," *RMN*, Sept. 21, 1913.

70. Lawson testimony, MMH, 213–214.

71. "'Fight to Finish' Says Welborn of C.F.&I. Company," *TCN*, Sept. 17, 1913.

FOUR. THE STRIKE BEGINS

1. "U.S. Fears Strike, Sends Agent to Denver Federal Arbitration Trial, Eleventh Hour; Both Sides Firm, Face Gigantic Struggle," *RMN*, Sept. 21, 1913.

2. These numbers are contained in handwritten tables in BLS/ES.

3. Welborn to J. H. McClement, Nov. 11, 1913, CIR/*FR*, 7116–7117.

4. Lawson testimony, MMH, 213.

5. "Rain and Snow Add to Misery of Striking Miners as They Wend Their Weary Way over Steep Muddy Roads from Mining Camps," *DE*, Sept. 24, 1913.

6. Ibid.

7. Details of Mary Thomas's [Mary Thomas O'Neal's] experiences are from O'Neal, *Those Damn Foreigners*, 96–107, and O'Neal testimony, CIR/*FR*, 6356–6360. For a detailed personal remembrance of the camp, see *Foreigners*, chaps. 8 and 9. That memoir differs radically from her testimony, raising questions about how much she embellished at which stages.

8. This list was provided by Lawson to the congressional committee; see MMH, 264–265.

9. There have been many estimates. This is drawn from Lawson's testimony, MMH, 216, which seems to be the closest to an official count available.

10. U.S. Census, 1910.

11. LACC.

12. Don MacGregor, "King Coal Has Set Up Kingdom All His Own in Colorado, When His Armed Thugs Deny Citizens Right to Enter Post Offices," *DE*, Sept. 27, 1913.

13. "Hack Held Up by Strikers; 3 Are Captured," *RMN*, Sept. 26, 1913.

14. "Shooting Precipitates Serious Crisis," *TCN*, Sept. 24, 1913.

15. "First Strike Death; C.F.I. Marshal Shot Posse Hunt Greeks," *RMN*, Sept. 25, 1913.

16. MacGregor, "King Coal," *Denver Express*, September 27, 1914.

17. Bowers to son, Sept. 14, 1913, Bowers Papers, Box 28.

18. "First Strike Death," *RMN*, Sept. 25, 1913.

19. "Coroner's Jury Finds Lee Death to Be Felonious," *TCN*, Sept. 26, 1913.

20. "Women, Children, Beat Injure Nonunion Men," *RMN*, Sept. 25, 1913.

21. Bowers to President Wilson, *The Papers of Woodrow Wilson* (Princeton, N.J.: Princeton University Press), 28:507–514.

22. Bowers to Frances Bowers, "Wednesday Night," Sept. 24, 1913, Bowers Papers, Box 2.

23. Stewart to Wilson, Sept. 26, 1913, BLS/ES.

24. Ad appeared in *TCN*, Oct. 20, 1913.

25. "Sheriff Farr Calls on Governor to Send Troops into Huerfano," *TCN*, Sept. 30, 1913.

26. Statement of the Oakdale Coal Co., *RMN*, Oct. 2, 1913.

27. "Bullets Sweep Mine as Men Start Work; Frameup Union's Story," *RMN*, Sept. 30, 1913.

28. Lawson testimony, MMH, 221.

29. Farr to Ammons, Sept. 29, 1913, Ammons Papers, CSA, Box 26751, FF1.

30. Lawson testimony, MMH, 277.

31. Beshoar, *Out of the Depths*, 43.

32. Bowers to JDR Jr., Nov. 18, 1913, RAC, Box 20, Folder 182.

33. Ammons testimony, CIR/*FR*, 6410–6411.

34. "Bomb Wrecks Mitchell Mine Bulgar Shack," *RMN*, Oct. 4, 1913.

35. Ibid.

36. JDR Jr. to Bowers, Oct. 6, 1913, CIR/*FR*, 8419–8420; Bowers to JDR Jr., Oct. 3, 1913, CIR/*FR*, 8419.

37. From Red Cross "Report on the Colorado Strike," NA, RG 200 825.00, Box 55, Folder 816.

38. Belk testimony, MMH, 2479–2480.

39. "'Vets of Balkans Battle in Strike," *RMN*, Oct. 9, 1913.

40. "Strikers and Guards, in a Pitched Battle, Fire 800 Shots at Ludlow Camp; Troop of Militia Called Out; Three Injured," *RMN*, Oct. 8, 1913.

41. Maggie Dominiski testimony, CIR/*FR*, 8188.

42. "One Dead, 3 Wounded Result of Battle between Guards and Strikers," *TCN*, Oct. 10, 1913. The details were repeated in multiple later testimonies.

43. "Strikers in Ambush Fire upon Guards; 1 Killed, 3 Wounded," *RMN*, Oct. 10, 1913.

44. "One Dead, 3 Wounded," *TCN*, Oct. 10, 1913.

45. "Saw Uhlich in Trinidad," AP, *LAT*, May 22, 1915.

46. The autopsy reported two bullet wounds, one through the left arm and one into the left side, but it seems more likely that the same bullet caused both wounds.

47. LACC.

48. Grisham to Ammons, Oct. 10, 1913, Ammons Papers, CSA, Box 26751, FF1.

FIVE. HARDENED LINES

1. Report from Stewart to Labor Secretary Wilson, Oct. 13, 1913, in *The Papers of Woodrow Wilson* 28:426.

2. Bowers to JDR Jr., Oct. 11, 1913, Bowers Papers, Box 28, rpt. in CIR/*FR*, 8420.

3. Bowers to Streeter, Oct. 10, 1913, Bowers Papers, Box 28.

4. Welborn testimony, CIR/*FR*, 6562–6564.

5. Northcutt testimony, CIR/*FR*, 7138–7139.

6. Ibid., 7136.

7. Brake, *Thirteenth Biennial Report*, pp. 171–172.

8. Hendricks testimony, CIR/*FR*, 6907.

9. "Miners Driven Away from Work by Strikers; Twenty-two Arrested for Picketing," *TCN*, Oct. 15, 1913.

10. "Machine Gun Halts Strike Rush on Jail," *RMN*, Oct. 17, 1913.

11. Felts testimony, MMH, 339, 369–370.

12. Ibid, 369–370.

13. "One Dead, Three Wounded, Toll of Forbes Battle," *TCN*, Oct. 18, 1913.

14. Based on multiple reports in *TCN* and *RMN*, Oct. 18–19, 1913, and Felts testimony, MMH, 340, 392.

15. O'Regan, "The Colorado Militia and the Strike," 7, CIR/NA, Reel 4.

16. Zamboni testimony, MMH, 792.

17. Felts testimony, MMH, 340.

18. Doyle testimony, CIR/*FR*, 6940.

19. Hayes to Secretary Wilson, Oct. 20, 1913, BLS/ES, Folder 10-a.

20. Ibid.

21. Brake to Thomas, BLS/ES, Folder 10-a.

22. Doyle testimony, MMH, 2215–2216. Also see undated notes of that meeting in Doyle Papers, Box 1, FF49.

23. Gene Fowler, *A Solo in Tom-Toms* (New York: Viking Press, 1946), 330–333.

24. O'Neal, *Those Damn Foreigners*, 111.

25. Ibid., 102.

26. Ibid., 112.

27. Bowers to JDR Jr., Oct. 21, 1913, CIR/*FR*, 8421.

28. Clement G. Bowers diary entry, Oct. 20, Local History and Genealogy Center, Broome County Public Library, Binghamton, N.Y.

29. Holmes testimony, MMH, 323.

30. Shy testimony, Las Animas County grand jury, Frederick Farrar Papers, DPL/WHC, Box 3, FF1.

31. Snyder testimony, Las Animas County grand jury, Farrar Papers, Box 3, FF 8.

32. Linderfelt testimony, CIR/*FR*, 6900–6901, 6870–6871.

33. Or New York. Census records vary.

34. Donald G. Davis Jr., ed., *Dictionary of American Library Biography* (Westport, Conn.: Greenwood Publishing, 1978), 316.

35. U.S. Census, 1880.

36. Linderfelt testimony, CIR/*FR*, 6866.

37. "He Left Town," AP, *LAT*, Dec. 27, 1894; "He Has Been Punished Enough," AP, *LAT*, July 14, 1892.

38. Author e-mail interview with Fred Burwell, Beloit College archivist, March 14, 2005.

39. Linderfelt testimony, "Minutes of the Court of Inquiry ordered by Gov. George A. Carlson, commencing August 26, 1915," 1105, Farrar Papers, Box 2, FF5.

40. *NYT,* April 24, 1898.

41. Linderfelt testimony, CIR/*FR*, 6866–6870.

42. This is according to testimony given by Linderfelt in February 1916, apparently in the poststrike criminal case against John Lawson. The unattributed transcript is in the Lawson Papers, Box 1, FF38.

43. Linderfelt testimony in Carlson inquiry, 1105, Farrar Papers, Box 2, FF5.

44. Linderfelt testimony, CIR/*FR*, 6900–6901.

45. MMH, 2626.

46. Linderfelt refers to this scene in his CIR testimony, but in their papers none of the other principals mention having met Linderfelt at this point, or knowing his identity.

47. "The Colorado Militia and the Strike," 4–5, CIR/NA, Reel 4.

48. Doyle testimony, MMH, 2215.

49. LACC.

50. "Aerolites a Menace; Two Rescuers Die in Helmets," *LAT,* Oct. 25, 1913.

51. "Mine Rescuers Perish," *NYT,* Oct. 25, 1913.

SIX. DEADLY ENCOUNTERS

1. M. Edmund Vallejo, "Recollections of the Colorado Coal Strike of 1913–14," CHS.

2. "2 Dead, 1 Dying, 3 Wounded Is Toll of Strike Battle on Street at Walsenburg," *RMN,* Oct. 25, 1913.

3. These first-person accounts, unless otherwise noted, are in CIR/*FR*, 7334–7343.

4. "Fortress Made of Courthouse," *RMN,* Oct. 26, 1913.

5. Vallejo, "Recollections of the Colorado Coal Strike," 10.

6. Thorne statement, Farrar Papers, Box 6, FF19.

7. "Two Dead and Four Wounded Toll of Last Battle," *TCN,* Oct. 25, 1913.

8. Germer testimony, MMH, 69.

9. "Two Dead and Four Wounded," *TCN,* Oct. 25, 1913.

10. "Urges Probe by Congress," *RMN,* Oct. 25, 1913.

11. "2 Dead, 1 Dying, 3 Wounded," *RMN,* Oct. 25, 1913.

12. Ibid.; Germer testimony, MMH.

13. Linderfelt testimony, CIR/*FR*, 6871.

14. Statements by Tafoya and another soldier named Charles, no last name, taken at Tabasco, April 13, 1915, part of poststrike criminal investigation, Farrar Papers, Box 6, FF16.

15. "Denver Man Shot to Death; Striker Wounded; 4-Hour Battle in Hills at Ludlow," *RMN,* Oct. 26, 1913. Nimmo was sworn in as a deputy Oct. 23, 1913, according to records reprinted in MMH, 2627.

16. Battle description drawn from Linderfelt testimony, CIR/*FR*, 6871–6878.

17. Tafoya/Charles statement, Farrar Papers, Box 6, FF 16.

18. "Battle at Mine Lasts 12 Hours," *RMN*, Oct. 27, 1913.

19. News accounts and 1910 U.S. Census forms.

20. Linderfelt testimony, CIR/*FR*, 6873–6876.

21. The following account of the battle, unless otherwise noted, is from Harvey Deuell, "State Militiamen Are Routed by Bullets from Strikers," *RMN*, Oct. 28, 1913.

22. Felts testimony, MMH, 392.

23. Ibid.

24. Linderfelt testimony, CIR/*FR*, 6878.

25. From Ellis Island database and U.S. Census, 1910.

26. "1,000 Troops Occupy Strike Zone at Daylight," *RMN*, Oct. 29, 1913.

27. Patterson testimony, CIR/*FR*, 6479.

28. Welborn testimony, CIR/*FR*, 6601.

29. Patterson testimony, CIR/*FR*, 6481; Welborn testimony, CIR/*FR*, 6601.

30. Patterson testimony, CIR/*FR*, 6481.

31. Ammons testimony, CIR/*FR*, 6412.

32. Ammons testimony, CIR/*FR*, 6415.

33. "No Pay for Militia! Kennehan Declares," *RMN*, Oct. 27, 1913.

34. Ammons testimony, CIR/*FR*, 6415.

SEVEN. ENTER THE MILITIA

1. "Strike Has Been Called for Sept. 23," *CSG*, Sept, 17, 1913.

2. Chase testimony, CIR/*FR*, 6826.

3. "1,000 Troops Occupy Strike Zone at Daylight," *RMN*, Oct. 28, 1913.

4. Nankivell, *History of the Military Organizations of the State of Colorado, 1860–1935*, 190.

5. Fowler, *A Solo in Tom-Toms*, 337.

6. Col. Edward Verdeckberg, "Report of the District Commander, Camp at Walsenburg, from October 28, 1913, to May 5, 1914," John Chase Papers, DPL/WHC, Box 1, FF1.

7. "Bridge Blown Up and Bomb Exploded in Camp," *Pueblo Chieftain*, Oct. 30, 1913. Despite the dire headline, the bomb did no damage and the bridge was repaired within a couple of hours, according to the story.

8. Verdeckberg, "Report of the District Commander," 5.

9. "Post Office and Tipple Burned Near Aguilar," *TCN*, Oct. 29, 1913.

10. George West, *Report on the Colorado Strike* (Washington: U.S. Commission on Industrial Relations, 1915), 108. West was one of several CIR investigators dispatched to the strike zone. West's report, drawn from his colleagues' reports, was published, unlike theirs.

11. Chase testimony, CIR/*FR*, 6827.

12. Van Cise testimony, CIR/FR, 6806.

13. Ibid.

14. "1,000 Troops Occupy Strike Zone at Daylight," *RMN*, Oct. 29, 1913.

15. Northcutt testimony, CIR/FR, 7143.

16. Ibid., 7143–7144.

17. Chase testimony, CIR/FR, 6827.

18. Verdeckberg, "Report of the District Commander," 7.

19. Van Cise testimony, CIR/FR, 6806–6807.

20. Linderfelt testimony, CIR/FR, 6878.

21. Ibid., 6879.

22. Van Cise testimony, CIR/FR, 6807.

23. "Strikers Defeat Soldiers 19 to 6," *TCN*, Nov. 3, 1913.

24. "General Chase Orders Military Occupation of Forbes Following Strikers Attack at Camp Early Today," *TCN*, Nov. 5, 1913.

25. Guerriero oral history, COPH-Fullerton.

26. Gamblin testimony, CIR/FR, 2655. The following descriptions, unless otherwise noted, are based on his testimony and that of R. G. Adams, 2653–2658. Gamblin's name is reported as W. H. Gambling in MMH, but at least two other spellings are found in contemporary news accounts. None of the spellings can be corroborated in contemporary directories. I opted to go with Gamblin.

27. "Four Shot Dead, 3 from Ambush, in Strike Riots," *RMN*, Nov. 9, 1913.

28. "Terror Rules Coal District After Shooting," *RMN*, Nov. 10, 1913.

29. Ibid.

30. "Situation Is Critical, Says General Chase," *RMN*, November 9, 1913.

31. Hendricks testimony, CIR/FR, 6904.

32. Ibid.

33. Order rpt. in MMH, 2585.

34. McGovern, "The Colorado Coal Strike, 1913–14," 241–242.

35. O'Regan, "The Colorado Militia and the Strike,"CIR/NA, Reel 4.

36. "Assault Cases Taken in Charge by Military, Films Confiscated," *TCN*, Nov. 17, 1913.

37. Hendricks testimony, CIR/FR, 6905.

38. Ibid.

39. Belk testimony, MMH, 2489. Details of the incident are drawn from multiple stories in *TCN*, Nov. 21–22, 1913, confirmed in later testimonies.

40. LACC.

41. Felts testimony, MMH, 334.

42. The George S. Minot Papers at DPL/WHC include a memoir in which Minot, assigned to guard Zancanelli, claims the union man confessed during their hours together, buttressing witness accounts and Zancanelli's on-the-scene arrest by the Trinidad policeman.

43. *The Papers of Woodrow Wilson* 28:475.

44. Ibid., 540.

45. Ibid., 547. The rest of Post's comments are taken from the same letter, 546–556.

46. Ibid., 563.

47. Bowers to Wilson, Nov. 25, 1913, in ibid., 589–560.

48. Bowers to JDR Jr., Nov. 18, 1913, RAC, Box 20, Folder 182.

49. JDR Jr. to Bowers, Nov. 24, 1913, CIR/*FR*, 8423.

50. Ammons to Wilson, Nov. 19, 1913, and the other telegrams in this exchange are in FMCS, Box 89, Folder 41–10A; Wilson to JDR Jr., Nov. 20, 1913, and JDR Jr. to Secretary Wilson, Nov. 21, 1913, RAC, Box 20, Folder 182.

51. It's telling that despite the overwhelming presence of Italian, Greek, and other ethnic miners among the strikers, the three men chosen by Ammons have Anglo names.

52. Welborn to McClement, Dec. 4, 1913, CIR/*FR*, 7117–7119.

53. Secretary Wilson to President Wilson, Dec. 10, 1913, *The Papers of Woodrow Wilson* 29:31–32.

54. Murphy to Bowers, Dec. 1, 1913, Bowers to Murphy, Dec. 6, 1913, and Murphy to Bowers, Dec. 9, 1913, RAC, Box 23, Folder 211.

55. JDR Jr. to Bowers, Dec. 8, 1913, ibid.

56. RAC, Box 49, Folder 358.

57. "Dist. Secy. Treas. Doyle on United Mine Workers Jailed; Believed to Know Whereabouts of M'Gary," *TCN*, Nov. 24, 1913.

58. "Uhlich 'Dangerous and Undesirable Alien' Finding of Military Commission," *TCN*, Dec. 3, 1913.

59. U.S. Census, 1920.

60. Germer testimony before the Lawson commission, p. 642, transcript in Farrar Papers, Box 1, FF2.

61. Mabel Germer testimony before the Lawson commission, pp. 618–610, ibid.

62. Colnar affidavit, CIR/*FR*, 7045–7046.

63. *Report on the Strike Investigation*, 13.

64. Details of the blizzard of 1913, unless otherwise noted, are from William E. Wilson's intriguing "Colorado Is Snowbound," from the Autumn 2003 issue of *Colorado Heritage*.

65. LACC.

66. Nogare oral history, Spanish Peaks Library District, Walsenburg, available at http://www.spld.org/docs/text/Nogare_B.txt.

67. Guerriero oral history, COPH-F.

EIGHT. THE BATTLE AT LUDLOW

1. Welborn testimony, CIR/*FR*, 6621.

2. Patterson testimony, CIR/*FR*, 6489–6490.

3. Welborn to McClement, Dec. 4, 1913, CIR/*FR*, 7117–7119.

4. Details come from Adams testimony, MMH, 115–122.

5. It's unclear whether this was an employment agency, a law firm, or a land grant office.

6. Ammons Papers, CSA, Box 26751, FF5.

7. Garwood testimony, CIR/FR, 6803–6805.

8. Kimsey testimony, MMH, 842.

9. Fowler, *A Solo in Tom-Toms*, 338.

10. Van Cise testimony, CIR/FR, 6810.

11. Linderfelt testimony, CIR/FR, 6881.

12. Van Cise, Exhibit No. 2, CIR/FR, 7327. Written in May 1914, the report adopts the militia's position that the miners started the violence but also evidences the deep rifts among the National Guard officers in startlingly frank terms.

13. Susan Hallearine testimony, MMH, 761.

14. Jury report, MMH, 2554.

15. "Indict Union Heads as a Labor Trust," AP, *NYT*, Dec. 2, 1913.

16. The jury report is in MMH, 2553–2556.

17. "I Am Not Worried," *LAT*, Dec. 2, 1913.

18. Newell testimony, MMH, 299.

19. White and Hayes to Secretary Wilson, Jan. 5, 1914, FMCS, Box 89, Folder 41–10.

20. Jones to Secretary Wilson, Jan. 11, 1913, and Wilson response, Jan. 12, 1913, FMCS, Box 89, Folder 41–10. Jones's version of these events in *The Autobiography of Mother Jones* (Chicago: Charles H. Kerr, 1925) says that she was already in D.C. when she read about Ammons's comments that she would not be allowed back and hopped a train that night to Denver. But the timing of these telegrams suggests that Jones never made it to D.C. and was in Denver.

21. Jones, *Autobiography*, 178–186. Jones's autobiography is filled with suspiciously detailed reconstructed conversations, which I avoid using as they are not verifiable elsewhere.

22. Chase testimony, CIR/FR, 6833.

23. White to President Wilson, Jan. 12, 1914, FMCS, Box 89, Folder 41–10.

24. McGovern, "The Colorado Coal Strike, 1913–14," 256.

25. Dozens are contained in Wilson's letters at the Library of Congress and in the Office of Mediation files at the National Archives.

26. "To Rescue Mother Jones," *NYT*, Jan. 17, 1914.

27. "Troops Charge Unionist Mob," AP, *LAT*, Jan. 23, 1914.

28. "Great Czar Fell! And in a Fury Told Troops to Trample Women!" *DE*, Jan. 23, 1914.

29. The list of wounds was compiled by the *Denver Express* reporter through interviews with the protesters. "Children Beaten, Women Sabred, Men Arrested in Name of State," *DE*, Jan. 23, 1914.

30. "Riot Follows Efforts of Mob to March on Hospital and Release 'Mother Jones,'" *TCN*, Jan. 22, 1914.

31. Report to Ammons from the panel, in Brake, *Thirteenth Biennial Report*, 178.

32. House Resolution 387, enacted Feb. 2, 1914.

33. MMR, 16.

34. Ibid., 17, 37.

35. Ibid., 42.

36. "Report of the Military Commission," May 2, 1914, CIR/FR, 7311.

37. "Body of Unidentified Man Found on Track—Murder Suspected," *TCN*, March 8, 1914; LACC. McGovern and Guttridge wrote that the train crew reported Smith stumbled drunkenly onto the tracks, but that they weren't called to testify before the coroner's jury: *The Great Coalfield War*, 187.

38. Ammons Papers, CSA, Box 26751, FF1.

39. Ammons testimony, CIR/FR, 6415, 6421.

40. Ibid., 6416.

41. Van Cise report, CIR/FR, 7327.

42. Ammons testimony, CIR/FR, 6416.

43. Bowers to JDR Jr., Bowers Papers, Box 28.

44. Huerfano County coroner's inquest, Farrar Papers, Box 6, FF9.

45. Linderfelt testimony, CIR/FR, 6888. Unless otherwise specified, this is the source for details on Linderfelt's actions.

46. Pearl Jolly testimony, coroner's inquest, WN.

47. Linderfelt said he received the letter, but other militia officers testified that the woman showed up at the Ludlow military camp with the letter the next morning.

48. Jolly testimony, coroner's inquest, WN.

49. Dominiski testimony, CIR/FR, 8189.

50. Dominiski affidavit, CIR/FR, 7379–7381. It's unclear who took the photos, or how they were developed so quickly. It's likely Dominiski was talking about pictures taken at the Roman Catholic Easter celebration the Sunday before, April 12.

51. William Snyder testimony, CIR/FR, 7371.

52. Dominiski testimony, CIR/FR, 8186.

53. Hamrock testimony, WN.

54. Linderfelt testimony, CIR/FR, 6888.

55. None of the records indicate how they came to be with Hamrock that morning.

56. Boughton testimony, CIR/FR, 6366.

57. Hamrock testimony, coroner's inquest, WN.

58. Hallearine testimony, coroner's inquest, WN.

59. This is according to testimony given by Hamrock in February 1916, apparently in the poststrike criminal case against John Lawson. The unattributed transcript is in the Lawson Papers, Box 1, FF38.

60. Lawson had ordered the first of the pits dug in October. Lawson testimony at court-martial of Capt. Edwin F. Carson, May 21, 1913, transcript in Farrar

Papers, Box 1, FF4. Carson was accused of being in charge of the troops that torched the tent colony but was acquitted by the military tribunal along with the rest of the National Guard.

61. Lamme testimony at Carson court-martial, Farrar Papers, Box 1, FF4.

62. Farber testimony, CIR/*FR*, 6862.

63. Boughton testimony, CIR/*FR*, 6367.

64. "Report of the Military Commission," May 2, 1914, CIR/*FR*, 7311–7312.

65. Bayes testimony, coroner's inquest, WN, and before the Las Animas County grand jury, Farrar Papers, Box 3, FF8. One wonders whether Bayes's wagon was one of the carts whose quick exit from the colony fed Benedict's conclusion that the strikers were about to attack.

66. Dominiski affidavit, CIR/*FR*, 7380.

67. O'Neal, *Those Damn Foreigners*, 133. She wrote that Tikas, using a loud-speaker, urged the strikers and their families to flee the colony—women and children to the arroyo for protection and the armed strikers to the hillsides. However, hers is the only version of events that day that includes that detail.

68. Dominiski affidavit, CIR/*FR*, 7380.

69. O'Neal, *Those Damn Foreigners*, 134.

70. Frank Didano affidavit, *Trinidad Free Press*, April 24, 1914.

71. Korich later married, and her oral history is under the name Helen Krmpotich in the Marat Moore Collection, East Tennessee State University, Accession 311, Box 2, Folder 11.

72. Ibid.

73. Boughton testimony, CIR/*FR*, 6366, and "Report of the Military Commission," May 2, 1914, CIR/*FR*, 7319. Boughton used this atrocity as an excuse for the militia's own ensuing carnage.

74. Aca Harvey testimony, coroner's inquest, WN.

75. Krmpotich oral history.

76. Dr. Perry Jaffa testimony, coroner's inquest, CIR/*FR*, 7365.

77. R. J. McDonald testimony, CIR/*FR*, 7368.

78. "Thirteen Killed in Battle at Ludlow; Strikers' Tent Colony Burned," *RMN*, April 21, 1914. The first crew was later fired.

79. R. J. Hall testimony, coroner's inquest, CIR/*FR*, 7374.

80. Hall testimony, CIR/*FR*, 7373.

81. McDonald testimony, CIR/*FR*, 7368.

82. The following details are from testimony by Aca Harvey and Frank Bayes at the coroner's inquest, WN.

83. Dominiski affidavit in Brake, *Thirteenth Biennial Report*, 194–195.

84. Lawson testimony at Carson court-martial, Farrar Papers, Box 1, FF4.

85. Hamrock testimony at Lawson trial, Feb. 1916, Lawson Papers, Box 1, FF38.

86. "Report of the Military Commission," May 2, 1914, CIR/*FR*, 7320.

87. Lieutenant Lamme testimony at Carson court-martial, Farrar Papers, Box 1, FF4.

88. Boughton testimony, CIR/*FR,* 6366.

89. Krmpotich oral history.

90. The following description is from William Snyder's testimony at the coroner's inquest, WN.

91. Tonner affidavit, CIR/*FR,* 7385.

92. John F. Harriman testimony, coroner's inquest, WN.

93. Ibid.

94. A. J. Riley testimony, coroner's inquest, CIR/*FR,* 7376.

95. Krmpotich oral history.

96. This is according to testimony given by Linderfelt February 21, 1916, apparently in the poststrike criminal case against John Lawson. The unattributed transcript is in the Lawson Papers, Box 1, FF38.

97. Report to the governor by the military commission led by Boughton, CIR/*FR,* 7321–7322.

98. Petrucci believed her tent was ignited from the outside, and it was the first to burn, though she did not see the start of the fire. Petrucci testimony, CIR/*FR,* 8195–8196. .

99. Ibid., 8193.

100. Spellings of the names of the people in the pit have vexed chroniclers since that very day, with conflicting accounts appearing sometimes in the same newspaper. These spellings are based on those included on a monument to the dead—as close to written in stone as can be found.

101. Petrucci testimony, CIR/*FR,* 8194.

102. "And Then We Had to See All the Children Die, One by One, in Death Hole," *DE,* April 23, 1914. The story quotes Pedregone as saying she and Petrucci escaped that night, which conflicts with Petrucci's account. Since Petrucci was seen by Hallearine the next morning, it seems likely Pedregone escaped Monday night but didn't know Petrucci had not followed her out.

103. Tonner affidavit, CIR/*FR,* 7385.

104. This scene is repeated in multiple places, including Linderfelt testimony at Lawson trial, Feb. 1916, Lawson Papers, Box 1, FF 38.

105. Benedict testimony at Hamrock court-martial, "Record of the General Court Martial," 63, in Farrar Papers, Box 1, FF3.

106. The following details are from "Report of the Military Commission," May 2, 1914, CIR/*FR,* 7322.

107. The identity of the third man has been elusive, but it was likely either Charles Costa, whose wife and child lay dead in the maternity cave, or John Bartolotti.

108. Linderfelt testimony, Lawson Papers, Box 1, FF 38.

109. Dr. E. J. Scannell testimony, coroner's inquest, WN.

110. McDonald testimony, coroner's inquest, CIR/*FR,* 7368.

111. The military commission concluded, based on soldiers' statements, that the three men were killed in a crossfire between the militia and the strikers, but by

then the battle had ended and the militia had control of the colony. Other militia reports claimed that the men were killed as they tried to escape. The only witnesses were the militiamen, and their stories conflict so drastically that none is to be believed. It seems most likely the union men were executed in cold blood. The wound details are from coroners' testimonies, CIR/FR, 7363–7465.

NINE. INSURRECTION

1. Bayes testimony, coroner's inquest, WN.
2. Petrucci testimony, CIR/FR, 8194.
3. Hallearine testimony, coroner's inquest, WN.
4. Ibid.
5. These details were reported in several newspapers, including *DE*, and Brake, *Thirteenth Biennial Report*, 174.
6. Susan Hallearine testimony, Las Animas County grand jury, Farrar Papers, Box 3, FF8.
7. O'Regan, "The Colorado Militia and the Strike," 47, CIR/NA, Reel 4, repeated in West, *Report on the Colorado Strike*, 132.
8. McDonald testimony, CIR/FR, 6775.
9. Bowers to JDR Jr., April 21, 1914, RAC, Box 23, Folder 211.
10. JDR Jr. to Bowers, April 21, 1914, RAC, Box 23, Folder 211.
11. "Search for Dead Bodies in Ruins of Ludlow Colony Halted by Battle Today," *TCN*, April 22, 1914.
12. McCusker, "Report on the Colorado Situation," CIR/NA, Reel 4.
13. Bayes testimony, coroner's inquest, WN.
14. O'Regan, "The Colorado Militia and the Strike," 46, CIR/NA, Reel 4.
15. Bayes testimony, coroner's inquest, WN.
16. Ammons testimony, CIR/FR, 6416.
17. "Mothers and Babies," *RMN*, April 22, 1914.
18. Durant testimony, Las Animas County grand jury, Farrar Papers, Box 3, FF8.
19. "Gov. Ammons Issues Call for Extra Session State Assembly to End Strike," *CSG*, April 26, 1914.
20. Brake, *Thirteenth Biennial Report*, 174.
21. McDonald testimony, CIR/FR, 6775.
22. Patterson testimony, CIR/FR, 6491.
23. CIR/FR, 7359
24. "Armed Miners Invading State," *RMN*, April 25, 1914.
25. Ibid.
26. *The Papers of Woodrow Wilson* 29:479.
27. The description in this paragraph is drawn from Brake, *Thirteenth Biennial Report*, 175, and "Express Reporter, Deported from Ludlow, Returns Undetected," *DE*, April 23, 1914.
28. Brake, *Thirteenth Biennial Report*, 175.

29. "Express Reporter, Deported from Ludlow, Returns Undetected," *DE,* April 23, 1914.

30. Brake, *Thirteenth Biennial Report,* 175.

31. "1,500 Armed Miners Rushing in to Exterminate Guardsmen," *RMN,* April 21, 1914.

32. The details of those attacks are lost to time, overwhelmed in contemporary accounts by the Ludlow killings and the violence that would soon follow the Delagua and Tabasco attacks. The May 2, 1914, *TCN* ("Tabasco Man Shot by Strikers Dies at Pueblo Hospital") said Phillips had been shot during a strikers' assault on the camp Monday, April 20, the day of the massacre, but the time reference is likely wrong since the attacks came the next day.

33. Lane statement, Sept. 1914, at Trinidad City Hall, in Farrar Papers, Box 6, FF20. Many of the statements contained in the Farrar files are suspect, but Lane's statement meshes with other events of that day, and he provides an interesting look at the color of the confusion, without apparent ax-grinding.

34. McDonald testimony, CIR/*FR,* 6775.

35. The following details from the scene at the mine are from H. C. Cossum testimony, Las Animas County grand jury, Farrar Papers, Box 3, FF8.

36. McDonald testimony, CIR/*FR,* 6775.

37. "1,000 Armed Miners Organize to Repel Troops from Denver; Women Trapped, Mines Afire," *RMN,* April 23, 1914. It is unclear how King, as a mine owner, went unmolested in Aguilar. He likely made his entreaties by phone.

38. Marie Whitner testimony, Las Animas County grand jury, Farrar Papers, Box 3, FF8.

39. "1,000 Armed Miners," *RMN,* April 23, 1914.

40. Patterson testimony, CIR/*FR,* 6491.

41. Ammons Papers, CSA, Box 26751, FF1.

42. Ibid.

43. Vigil to Ammons's Denver office, April 23, 1914, 5:50 P.M., Ammons Papers, CSA, Box 26751, FF1.

44. Welborn to Ammons, April 23, 1914, Ammons Papers, CSA, Box 26751, FF1.

45. The exchange is included in Ammons Papers, CSA, Box 26751, FF1.

46. "Guardsmen Won't Fight Until Salaries Are Paid," *RMN,* April 24, 1914.

47. "1,000 Miners Gather to Fire on Militia," *RMN,* April 24, 1914.

48. CIR/*FR,* 7359.

49. Based on coroner's records, McKenna's research, and verifiable newspaper reports.

50. "1,000 Armed Miners Organize," *RMN,* April 23, 1914.

51. Multiple stories in *TCN,* April 23, 1914, and *RMN,* April 24, 1914.

52. McLean testimony, CIR/*FR,* 6521.

53. West, *Report on the Colorado Strike,* 136.

54. "1,000 Miners Gather," *RMN,* April 24, 1914.

55. Dr. Beshoar was the father of Barron Beshoar, the journalist who wrote *Out of the Depths*, the union-sponsored book about the 1913–1914 strike.

56. Report by S. Poulter Morris, director of the Red Cross Mountain Division, p. 22, NA, RG 200, Box 55, Folder 816.

57. This and the following exchange can be found in *The Papers of Woodrow Wilson* 29:502–504.

58. "1,500 at Burial of Ludlow Dead," *RMN*, April 24, 1914, and photos of the scene.

59. Scene described from photographs held by DPL/WHC.

60. "Hundreds of Greeks Attend Funeral of Leader Louis Tikas," *TCN*, April 27, 1914.

61. "U.S. Troops for Colorado. Wilson Expected to Order Them out Today," AP, *LAT*, April 27, 1914.

62. Bettis to Wilson, April 26, 1914, Wilson correspondence, Library of Congress.

63. Cimic letters in Ammons Papers, CSA, Box 26751, FF5.

64. This and the following exchange can be found in *The Papers of Woodrow Wilson* 29:504–514.

65. "Wilson Sends Federal Troops to Colorado," *NYT*, April 29, 1914.

66. Ammons to Thomas, April 26, 1914, Wilson correspondence, Library of Congress.

67. Martin testimony, Huerfano County grand jury, Farrar Papers, Box 3, FF8.

68. Arthur Quinn testimony, Las Animas County grand jury, Farrar Papers, Box 3, FF8. Quinn was an active combatant for the strikers but cooperated afterward with the investigation. This scenario is repeated in other testimony, but the exact day it happened—Saturday or Sunday—remains unclear. Testimony of Ruben Kaster, a strikebreaker, and E. V. Martin, a meat cutter in a La Veta butcher shop, a striker, Huerfano County grand jury, Farrar Papers, Box 3, FF8. Given the repetition of such sightings, and the gun battles to follow, the testimony seems legitimate. And these may have been the guns that "Cimic" warned Ammons the strikers had slipped into the district.

69. Testimony of Alec Osvark, likely a misspelling of Alexander Osvirk, striking miner, Huerfano County grand jury, Farrar Papers, Box 3, FF8. The obvious organization of the miners on the Hogback lends credence to Osvirk's testimony.

TEN. FINAL ENGAGEMENTS

1. "Six Men Wounded in 10-Hour Fight," *RMN*, April 29, 1914. No death records for either man could be readily found, so they are not included in the overall death tally.

2. "Six Witnesses Heard in Cañon City Trial," *CSG*, Dec. 13, 1914. Other accounts list as many as four killed, but coverage of the ensuing trial indicates only

one man died; at least one of the others reported killed at the time of the attacks appeared as a witness.

3. Telegrams from Euler and Boulder mayor W. L. Armstrong, April 28, 1914, Ammons Papers, CSA, Box 26751, FF1.

4. Nankivell, *History of the Military Organizations of the State of Colorado, 1860–1935*, 196.

5. The following battle details are from multiple stories in both *RMN* and *TCN*, April 30, 1914, and later testimony by participants. For the sake of narrative flow I only provide notes for the details that seem to require them.

6. K. E. Cowdery testimony, Las Animas County grand jury, Farrar Papers, Box 2, FF6. Some of the testimony before the grand jury was later found to have been perjured, as Baldwin-Felts agents bought off witnesses to target specific union members, such as Lawson, for indictment (Lawson would later see a murder conviction overturned after the perjury came to light). With that in mind, I avoid citing grand jury testimony from anyone who seems to have been targeting specific individuals, and use only testimony that seems untainted and describes scenes rather than people engaged in criminal acts.

7. T. W. Harris testimony, Las Animas County grand jury, Farrar Papers, Box 2, FF6.

8. Cowdery testimony, Las Animas County grand jury, Farrar Papers, Box 2, FF6.

9. Most of the other people in Forbes that day said the attackers were speaking mostly Italian.

10. Whitney testimony, Las Animas County grand jury, Farrar Papers, Box 2, FF6.

11. Harris testimony, Las Animas County grand jury, Farrar Papers, Box 3, FF8.

12. Cowdery testimony, Las Animas County grand jury, Farrar Papers, Box 2, FF6.

13. Albert testimony, Las Animas County grand jury, Farrar Papers, Box 2, FF6.

14. Bonata testimony, Las Animas County grand jury, Farrar Papers, Box 2, FF6.

15. Cowdery testimony, Las Animas County grand jury, Farrar Papers, Box 2, FF6.

16. Contemporary accounts—and the ensuing works on the strike—list nine dead at Forbes, but a close review of the Las Animas County coroner's records shows a tally of at least eleven dead, and possibly twelve.

17. LACC. All four of the Japanese men were buried in Trinidad's Masonic Cemetery, not far from Tikas's grave, on May 2, for fifty dollars each, paid for by the Masons.

18. Cowdery testimony, Las Animas County grand jury, Farrar Papers, Box 2, FF6.

19. Radford testimony, Las Animas County grand jury, Farrar Papers, Box 2, FF6.

20. George Creel, *Rebel at Large: Recollections of Fifty Crowded Years* (New York: G. P. Putnam's Sons, 1947), 338.

21. This scene is drawn from J. S. Cross testimony, Huerfano County grand jury, Farrar Papers, Box 3, FF7.

22. Packard testimony, Huerfano County grand jury, Farrar Papers, WHC/DPL, WH 1071, Box 3, FF7.

23. Charles Campbell testimony, Huerfano County grand jury, Farrar Papers, Box 3, FF7. Campbell's timeline is muddled; he described this scene as Sunday morning but also said it was the morning the fighting began, which would have been Monday, when the miners took control of the Hogback.

24. Martinez testimony, Huerfano County grand jury, Farrar Papers, Box 3, FF8.

25. Strauss testimony, Huerfano County grand jury, Farrar Papers, Box 3, FF7. Conder in his testimony denied being involved; see Conder, ibid.

26. Mimovitch testimony, Huerfano County grand jury, Farrar Papers, Box 3, FF8.

27. Irma Menghini (his niece) oral history, Spanish Peaks Library District, Walsenburg, available at http://www.spld.org/docs/text/Menghini_I.txt.

28. Autopsy report by Dr. Baird, conducted 3:00 P.M. April 28, 1914, Farrar Papers, Box 6, FF10. Bock's name is also spelled Bak in some records.

29. Autopsy report by Dr. Baird, Farrar Papers, Box 6, FF15, and Quinn testimony, Huerfano County grand jury, Farrar Papers, Box 3, FF8.

30. Andes testimony, Huerfano County grand jury, transcript in Farrar Papers, Box 3, FF 7, and Huerfano County coroner's inquest, Farrar Papers, Box 6, FF10. The following description is drawn from her testimony; her maiden name appears in other records as Endees.

31. Autopsy report by Dr. Baird, Farrar Papers, Box 6, FF10.

32. Verdeckberg, "Report of District Commander," 44.

33. Ibid., 46. The following details of the militia's portion of the battle are drawn from 46–56.

34. Osvark testimony, Huerfano County grand jury, Farrar Papers, Box 3, FF7.

35. Matsumoto testimony, Huerfano County grand jury, Farrar Papers, Box 3, FF7.

36. Swope testimony, Huerfano County coroner's inquest, Farrar Papers, Box 6, FF11.

37. Matsumoto was already in custody on suspicion of murder, and his testimony before the grand jury had the tenor of someone who wanted to appear cooperative without incriminating himself or others.

38. Several witnesses appearing before the Huerfano County grand jury testified to the same thing. For one example, see E. V. Martin's testimony, Farrar Papers, Box 3, FF8.

39. This appears to be the current Lathrop State Park, about three miles west of downtown.

40. Some accounts say this occurred in the morning, but Swope testified at the coroner's inquest into Lester's death that they went that night, a timeline that gibes with Verdeckberg learning about the postmortem gunshots and missing papers discovered before meeting with MacGregor at 11:00 A.M.

41. Coroner's report, Farrar Papers, Box 6, FF11.

EPILOGUE

1. "Rockefeller, Jr., Attends Ludlow Shaft Unveiling," *RMN,* May 31, 1918.

2. See Howard Gitelman's *Legacy of the Ludlow Massacre: A Chapter in American Industrial Relations* (Philadelphia: University of Pennsylvania Press, 1988), a complete, compelling, and well-documented exploration of the strike's aftermath.

3. Doyle Papers, Box 1, FF21,

4. FMCS, Box 89, FF41–10A, Pt. 1.

5. Stewart to Post, Nov. 21, 1913, FMCS, Box 89, FF41–10.

6. Gitelman, *Legacy of the Ludlow Massacre,* 72.

7. Bowers to JDR Jr., Feb. 17, 1915, Bowers Papers, Box 28.

8. Beshoar, *Out of the Depths,* 357–359.

Selected Bibliography

ARCHIVES AND MANUSCRIPT COLLECTIONS

Binghamton University, State University of New York, Glenn G. Bartle Library
Lamont Montgomery Bowers Papers; includes "Biography: Lamont Montgomery Bowers, 1847–1941," by Jerry Pepper
Broome County Public Library, Local History and Genealogy Center, Binghamton, N.Y.
Clement Bowers Journals
Colorado Historical Society, Stephen H. Hart Library, Denver
Numerous local newspapers on microfilm, including *Trinidad Chronicle-News, Rocky Mountain News,* and *Denver Express*
"Recollections of the Colorado Coal Strike of 1913–14," M. Edmund Vallejo
Edward Verdeckberg Collection
Jesse Floyd Welborn Collection
Colorado State Archives, Denver
Papers of Elias Milton Ammons
Denver Public Library, Western History Collection
Elias Ammons Papers
John B. Chase Papers; box 1 includes "Report of the District Commander, Camp at Walsenburg, from October, 28, 1913, to May 5, 1914," by Col. Edward Verdeckberg
Colorado Office of the Adjutant General Papers and Reports
Edward Lawrence Doyle Papers
Frederick Farrar Papers
Hildreth Frost Papers
John R. Lawson Papers
George S. Minot Papers

Selected Bibliography

East Tennessee State University Archives of Appalachia
Marat Moore Collection: Helen Korish Krmpotich oral history, c. 1984
National Archives, College Park, Md.
American Red Cross Papers, RG 200
Unpublished Reports, U.S. Commission on Industrial Relations, RG 174.6.1
Federal Mediation and *Conciliation* Service Case Files, Dispute Case Files,
1913–1948, RG 280
Records of the Bureau of Labor Statistics, Office Files of Ethelbert Stewart,
1904–1931, RG 257.3
George West Notes, RG 174
New York Public Library, New York, N.Y.
Frank P. Walsh Papers
Rockefeller Archive Center, Sleepy Hollow, N.Y.
John D. Rockefeller Papers
John D. Rockefeller Jr. Papers
Trinidad (Colo.) Carnegie Public Library, History Collection
National Funeral Register, July 23, 1913, to June 19, 1915
Las Animas County Coroner's Reports

SECONDARY SOURCES

Adams, Graham, Jr. *Age of Industrial Violence, 1910–1915: The Activities and Findings of the United States Commission on Industrial Relations.* New York: Columbia University Press, 1966.

Baker, James H., ed. *History of Colorado.* Denver: Linderman, 1927.

Beshoar, Barron B. *Out of the Depths: The Story of John R. Lawson, a Labor Leader.* 1942; 3d ed., Denver: Colorado Labor Historical Committee of the Denver Trades and Labor Assembly, 1957.

Boyer, Richard O. *Labor's Untold Story.* New York: Cameron Associates, 1955.

Brake, Edwin V. *Twelfth Biennial Report of the Bureau of Labor Statistics of the State of Colorado, 1909–10.* Denver: Smith-Brooks Printing, 1911.

———, *Thirteenth Biennial Report: Colorado Bureau of Labor Statistics, 1912–13.* Microform, Library of Congress.

Chace, James. *1912: Wilson, Roosevelt, Taft, and Debs—The Election That Changed the Country.* New York: Simon & Schuster, 2004.

Chernow, Ron. *Titan: The Life of John D. Rockefeller, Sr.* New York: Random House, 1998.

Clyne, Rick J. *Coal People: Life in Southern Colorado's Company Towns, 1890–1930.* Denver: Colorado Historical Society, 1999.

Corbin, David Alan, ed. *The West Virginia Mine Wars: An Anthology.* Charleston, W. Va.: Appalachian Editions, 1990.

Creel, George. *Rebel at Large: Recollections of Fifty Crowded Years.* New York: G. P. Putnam's Sons, 1947.

Selected Bibliography

DeStefanis, Anthony. "Guarding Capital: Soldier Strikebreakers on the Long Road to the Ludlow Massacre." Ph.D. diss., College of William and Mary, 2004.

Drennan, Dorothy D., and Helen B. Broverman, eds. *Illinois Sesquicentennial Edition of Christian County History.* Jacksonville, Ill.: Printed by Production Press, 1968.

Eastman, Max. "The Nice People of Trinidad." *The Masses,* July 1914.

Foner, Philip S. *The AFL in the Progressive Era, 1910–1915,* vol. 5 of *History of the Labor Movement in the United States.* New York: International Publishers, 1980.

Gitelman, Howard M. *Legacy of the Ludlow Massacre: A Chapter in American Industrial Relations.* Philadelphia: University of Pennsylvania Press, 1988.

Hallahan, Kirk. "Ivy Lee and the Rockefellers' Response to the 1913–14 Colorado Coal Strike." *Journal of Public Relations Research* 14 (2002): 262–315.

———. "W. L. McKenzie King: Rockefeller's 'Other' Public Relations Counselor in Colorado." *Public Relations Review* 29 (2003): 404–414.

Haskins, Jim. *The Long Struggle: The Story of American Labor.* Philadelphia: Westminster Press, 1976.

Hiebert, Ray Eldon. *Courtier to the Crowd: The Story of Ivy Lee and the Development of Public Relations.* Ames: Iowa State University Press, 1966.

Jones, Mary Harris. *The Autobiography of Mother Jones.* Chicago: Charles H. Kerr & Company, 1925.

Kenny, Kevin. *Making Sense of the Molly Maguires.* New York: Oxford University Press, 1998.

Laslett, John H. M., ed. *The United Mine Workers of America: A Model of Industrial Solidarity?* University Park: Pennsylvania State University Press, 1996.

Lens, Sidney. *The Labor Wars: From the Molly Maguires to the Sitdowns.* Garden City, N.Y.: Doubleday/Anchor, 1974.

Link, Arthur S. *Wilson: The New Freedom.* Princeton, N.J.: Princeton University Press, 1956.

Long, Priscilla. *Where the Sun Never Shines: A History of America's Bloody Coal Industry.* New York: Paragon House, 1989.

Lukas, J. Anthony. *Big Trouble: A Murder in a Small Western Town Sets Off a Struggle for the Soul of America.* New York: Simon & Schuster, 1997.

McGovern, George S. "The Colorado Coal Strike, 1913–14." Ph.D. diss., Northwestern University, 1953.

McGovern, George S., and Leonard F. Guttridge. *The Great Coalfield War.* Niwot: University Press of Colorado, 1996.

McGuire, Randall. "Letter from Ludlow: Colorado Coal Field Massacre." *Archaeology,* November/December 2004, pp. 64–70.

Nankivell, John H. *History of the Military Organizations of the State of Colorado, 1860–1935.* Denver: W. H. Kistler Stationery Co., 1935.

Nevins, Allan. *Study in Power: John D. Rockefeller, Industrialist and Philanthropist.* 2 vols. New York: Charles Scribner's Sons, 1953.

Norwood, Stephen H. *Strikebreaking and Intimidation.* Chapel Hill: University of North Carolina Press, 2002.

Selected Bibliography

O'Neal, Mary T. *Those Damn Foreigners*. Hollywood, Calif.: Minerva, 1971.

Papanikolas, Zeese. *Buried Unsung: Louis Tikas and the Ludlow Massacre*. Lincoln: University of Nebraska Press, Bison edition, 1991.

Reed, John. *The Education of John Reed: Selected Writings*. International Publishers, 1955.

Rockefeller, John D., Jr. "The Colorado Industrial Plan." Pamphlet, 1916 (in author's possession).

Ruiz, Ramón Eduardo. *Triumphs and Tragedy: A History of the Mexican People*. New York: Norton, 1992.

Ruland, Sylvia, *The Lion of Redstone*. Boulder, Colo.: Johnson Publishing, 1981.

St. John, Vincent. *The I.W.W.: Its History, Structure, and Methods*, Chicago: I.W.W. Publishing Bureau, 1917.

Scamehorn, H. Lee. *Mill and Mine: The CF&I in the Twentieth Century*. Lincoln: University of Nebraska Press, 1992.

Smith, Page. *America Enters the World: A People's History of the Progressive Era and World War I*. New York: Penguin Books, 1991.

Smith, Robert Michael. *From Blackjacks to Briefcases: A History of Commercialized Strikebreaking and Unionbusting in the United States*. Athens: Ohio University Press, 2003.

U.S. Commission on Industrial Relations. *Final Report of the Commission on Industrial Relations*. Chicago: Barnard and Miller Printing, 1915.

U.S. House of Representatives. Subcommittee of the Committee on Mines and Mining. *Conditions in the Coal Mines of Colorado*. Transcripts of hearings, 3 vols. Washington: GPO, 1914–1915.

———. "Report on the Colorado Strike Investigation, Made Under House Resolution 387," Document No. 1630, 63rd Congress, 3rd session.

Warne, Colston E., and Merrill E. Gaddis. "Eleven Years of Compulsory Investigation of Industrial Disputes in Colorado." *Journal of Political Economy* 35 (October 1927): 657–683.

West, George. *Report on the Colorado Strike*. Washington: U.S. Commission on Industrial Relations, 1915.

Zinn, Howard. *A People's History of the United States, 1492–Present*. New York: HarperPerennial, 1995.

Zinn, Howard, Dana Frank, and Robin D. G. Kelley. *Three Strikes: Miners, Musicians, Salesgirls, and the Fighting Spirit of Labor's Last Century*. Boston: Beacon Press, 2001.

Index

Index

Index

Davis, Robert, 54
Davis, W. A., 123
Dawson, New Mexico, 108–109
deaths in mine camps, 28
"Death Special," 96–98, 97
Debs, Eugene, 70
Del Agua Arroyo, 69
Del Agua Canyon, 126, 169, 185
Delagua mine, 67, 80, 108, 148, 149, 189
demonstrations, 103
Demosa, Johann, death of, 223
Denver, 34, 51, 83, 84, 87, 88, 155, 182,
    188, 189, 208; chamber of commerce,
    investigatory committee, 183; confer-
    ences, 99, 108, 120, 137–140; depot,
    191; reaction of workers in, 187;
    union meeting, 183
Denver & Rio Grande Railroad
    (D&RG), 36, 132
Denver Trades and Labor Assembly, 4
DePaulo, Angela, death of, 28
deputies, 62, 94–98, 107, 112–113, 117–119,
    128; killed in strike battles, 119–120;
    new recruits, 97; vs. strikers, 112–114
deputy sheriffs. *See* deputies
Derr, Marian, 165–166
desertions, 188
detective agencies, 57. *See also* Baldwin-
    Felts Detective Agency; Burlew
    detective agency; Burns Detective
    Agency
detectives, 29, 182
Deuell, Harvey, 115, 238n21
deWeese, H. L., 133–134
Dick, James B., 31
Dominiski, Joe, 161, 170
Dominiski, Maggie, 166, 167
donations to strikers, 184
Donovan, Dave, death of, 185, 224
Dotson, John M., 69
Douglass, T. F., 13
Doyle, Edward, 54–55, 57, 58, 63, 68,
    98–99, 108, 109, 184, 189, 216, 219;
    arrested, 141
Drake, Captain, 142–143

Driscoll, Mike, death of, 80–81, 222
Dtoraka, Steve, death of, 200, 223
Duncan, Elias, death of, 28
Dunleavy, W. P., 187
Durango Field, 50
Durant, Ed, 182

election fraud, 32–33
Elliott, C. D., 58
Empire mine, 186–187
Estep, Charles, death of, 13
Euler, R. L., 197
Evans, E. A., 185
Evans, T. X., 138
Evans Coal and Fuel Co., 59
explosions, 19, 24, 28, 30, 45–46, 49, 87,
    108–109, 175, 217

Farr, Jefferson B., 30–33, 44, 62, 86, 112,
    113, 158, 205, 216, 219, 232n30
Farrar, Frederick, 216
federal: government, 155, 191; grand
    jury, 151; law, 158; troops, 194–196,
    210
Felts, A. C., 15, 52, 57, 62, 96, 117, 118, 219;
    death of, 56, 227n11
film, 133
Fink, Walter, *The Ludlow Massacre*, 3,
    226n3
firearms. *See* guns
fires, 46; at Forbes, 202; at Ludlow,
    177–180
Fitzgarrald, Stephen, 188, 190, 191
Fleming, J. W., 14
Florence, 24, 75
Florence & Cripple Creek Railroad Co.,
    24
Forbes mine, 64, 68, 96–98, 128, 129,
    157, 201; attack on, 197–202; militia
    at, 128; tent colony, 80, 96–98, 156,
    157, 163
Foster, Martin D., 155, 159, 194–195
Four Corners, 25
Fowler, Gene, 99–100, 124, 149
Fox, M. P., 59

Index

Index

About the
Author

Scott Martelle, a veteran journalist, is a staff writer for the *Los Angeles Times*. He also has worked at newspapers in western New York state and Detroit, where he was an active participant in the 1995 newspaper strike. A native of Maine and raised in rural New York, he lives in Irvine, California, with his wife, Margaret, and their sons, Michael and Andrew.